LAW & SOCIETY
IN CLASSICAL
ATHENS

LAW & SOCIETY IN CLASSICAL ATHENS

Richard Garner

ST. MARTIN'S PRESS
New York

First published in the United States of America in 1987

Printed in Great Britain

ISBN 0-312-00856-2

Library of Congress Cataloging-in-Publication Data

Garner, Richard, 1953–
   Law and society in classical Athens.

   Bibliography: p.
   Includes index.
   1. Law, Greek. I. Title.
LAW   340.5'3'8   87-4587
ISBN 0-312-00856-2

Contents

Foreword

This book is aimed at a varied audience. I have tried to keep it accessible to all educated readers including those with no Greek. I hope particularly that it will be of use to those interested in the history of ethics and the history of law. Still, it is meant to be used most by classicists, and for this reason I have tried to include all the references, both to primary and to secondary materials, that a specialist might want or need.

The result is inevitably a text in which any given reader is almost certain to find some sections which are either too general or too specialized. Nevertheless, I feel that the material deserves to be presented to both audiences.

David Grene, James Redfield, and Arthur Adkins encouraged my earliest efforts in this work. The manuscript would never have materialized without a luxurious Fellowship in the Society of Fellows at Harvard University. In this atmosphere I gained immensely from the company of Peter Galison, Donald Reid, Terry Castle, Alec Marantz, Nita Krevans, Susan Blaustein, and Denis Feeney. Lillian Doherty, Victor Bers, and Elizabeth Meyer all read the manuscript and provided valuable comments. From the beginning to the end my greatest debt is to Anne Burnett. Her detailed criticism and suggestions are responsible for countless improvements in the text. The Greeks, who were so interested in quantity and who used quantification so much, would not have been able to measure what she has done or what I owe her in return. But then, they would not have needed to: they could simply call it *charis*.

Abbreviations

Abbreviations in the Text and Notes

FGrH   *Fragmente der griechischen Historiker*, F. Jacoby. Berlin and Leiden, 1923–58.

FHG   *Fragmenta Historicorum Graecorum*, 5 vols., C. Müller. Paris, 1841–70.

GHI^2 *A Selection of Greek Historical Inscriptions*, 2nd edn, M.N. Tod. Oxford, 1946–48.

IG   *Inscriptiones Graecae*

LSJ   *A Greek English Lexicon*, 9th edn, Oxford, 1940.

N^2 *Tragicorum Graecorum Fragmenta^2*, ed. A. Nauck. Leipzig, 1889.

Σ   Scholiast

SIG   *Sylloge Inscriptionum Graecarum*, ed. W. Dittenberger. Leipzig, 1915–24.

Titles of Journals Abbreviated in the Notes

AJAH American Journal of Ancient History
AJP   American Journal of Philology
CJ   Classical Journal
CP   Classical Philology
CQ   Classical Quarterly
CR   Classical Review
GRBS Greek, Roman and Byzantine Studies
HSCP Harvard Studies in Classical Philology
JHS   Journal of Hellenic Studies
TAPA Transactions of the American Philological Association
ZPE   Zeitschrift für Papyrologie und Epigraphik

References to classical authors and works generally use the abbreviations of LSJ. However, where doubt might arise, fuller forms have been used.

1 Justice, Traditional Values and Law

1. Introduction

In recent years there has been a great deal of writing and almost as much disagreement about popular values and moral thought in ancient Greece. One of the better known and more controversial books in this area is devoted entirely to the topic of justice. The review of the book which the author most liked included one particular criticism which he found the most interesting: the book does not deal with law.[1] The decision not to treat the topic is understandable. In any society the relationship between law and morality — and in particular between law and justice — may be complex and difficult to characterize. For example, the legal and moral uses of our word *justice* overlap but are not identical. Thus when we use the word to refer to an abstract ideal we may mean something very different from what is designated by the same word in the phrase 'the administration of justice'.

The development of legal thought in classical Greece and its relationship to Greek values and society have remained relatively unexplored. The great work by Gernet, cited by the reviewer and author above, is discussed at some length below; but it has called forth little response since it appeared almost seventy years ago. In part, the splendor of the Roman legal system has long eclipsed the importance of Athenian law and contributed to its neglect. Even excellent handbooks of Greek law have tended to go out of print quickly. The business of Athenian courts has often been treated or regarded as a chaotic or relatively isolated part of the society. In his *Rhetoric* Aristotle tried, after his fashion, to separate and systematize forensic oratory and the matters appropriate to law: accusation and defense should properly be made about the just and the unjust with regard to the past. He opposed this to two other types of oratory: deliberative rhetoric, which dealt with exhortation to the expedient or dissuasion from the inexpedient with regard to the future; and epideictic, which, in a timeless way, praised the noble and blamed the base.

1

Yet Aristotle was well aware that this was merely an ideal division (*Rh.* 1.1.5–6). Most courts admitted presentation of all sorts of materials; and the topic of expediency was one of the most common in fourth-century court speeches — even Aristotle allows that it must sometimes be considered (1.15.25). He acknowledges that there are those who consider justice unimportant (1.7.37–8) and that those most likely to break the laws are the eloquent and wealthy who have legal experience and many friends, all of which advantages make acquittal more likely (1.12.1–3). And he notes that success at competition in the law courts provides great pleasure just as it does in sports and games (1.11.15–16). All these observations indicate that law as practiced was not neatly separated along abstract conceptual lines.

Now as will become clear in the course of this study, by Aristotle's time legality was far more autonomous and clearly defined than it had ever been in Athens before. Nevertheless, many peculiarities had been inherited from a system which had developed under much different circumstances. In order to understand the Athenian popular courts and the administration of justice in them it is necessary to go back to their genesis in the mid-fifth century and the forces which shaped their formation and growth.

For the same reason that a book on justice would profit from a consideration of law, a book on Athenian law must come to grips with the topic of justice. This first chapter outlines the nature of the concept so that the degree of its relevance to the courts can be made clearer. However, the remainder of the book examines the nature of Athenian law and its place in society by approaching the topic in other ways. The second chapter concentrates on historical factors in the development of the popular courts which affected their place in the city. The third chapter characterizes Athenian law by identifying some unusual formal patterns in legal procedure and substantive law. The fourth chapter examines literature as one way of tracing the development of attitudes toward law. And the final chapter describes fundamental changes which occurred in law and legal thought in the fourth century BC.

Aristocratic leaders struggling for honor brought endless woes to the Greeks. Thus begins the *Iliad*. The quarrel of Achilles and Agamemnon is not settled by the rule of law. Theirs is a society of traditions and customs which apply to narrowly defined categories of persons and relationships rather than to general classes. These customs, *nomoi*, regulate the competition for honor and aristocratic rank. There are behaviors characteristic of various types of men. These may be called *dikai*; and the *dike* of even the 'best' men, the people's leaders, is not impartial (*Od.* 4.687–92). By the mid-fifth century BC in Athens, disputes were settled in court by large democratic juries. Customs had been supplemented with written laws, but the traditional competitive aristocratic value system had not been replaced or systematically augmented by a new moral or legal order of values. The words *nomoi* and *dikai* were used but had not been clearly redefined in terms of democratic institutions.

In Athenian law, therefore, we confront a great paradox. On the one hand, we find a high degree of institutional autonomy in the form of courts which probably involved a greater portion of the citizen body in more hours of court adjudication than in any society before or since. On the other hand, this activity occurs in a society in which the concept of justice is far from clearly defined. Athenian law had almost no methodological autonomy; there was no legal reasoning or style distinct from moral or political discourse.[2] As a result, the language of the democratic courts was peculiarly tied to a traditional aristocratic value system which at times placed competitive ideals above justice. Another way of describing the situation would be to say that 'justice' in some senses was not in clear conflict with competition or aggression.

In addition, Athenian legal procedure was linked to aristocratic competition by a pervasive isomorphism in Athenian public activities. Athletic competition, assembly meetings, dramatic festivals, and court cases all involved large groups of citizens who were the audience for a very small number of individuals competing against each other. In some cases, the law courts served merely as a forum for the extension of political conflict and power struggles.

Yet even though the administration of justice in Athens was remarkably susceptible to traditional competitive values, and the courts resembled other competitive institutions, the legal order was structurally committed to a cooperative resolution of conflict and was more general and autonomous than custom. The Athenians were quite proud of their laws which guaranteed a degree of civic equality in court.[3] And since the courts played such a large role in Athenian life, the formal aspects of the legal order had an effect on popular values and ethics. The effects may have been magnified by a general crisis in values in the late fifth century. At any rate, the laws and courts influenced the moral climate of the city, and the moral climate in turn determined how the laws and courts were used in the society.

In order to see how the legal processes grew out of the value system we will turn first to the uses of the word *dike* and the question of the traditional notions of justice. This will lead to a brief consideration of some other aspects of popular morality and values in mid-fifth-century Athens which are relevant to social behavior. Finally, we will consider the word *nomos* and attitudes towards law and laws.

2. *Dike* and Justice

The recent volume of work and intensity of debate on the notion of justice in ancient Greece stems at least in part from apparently deep disagreements on the subject.[4] It is difficult to identify an aspect of the topic which is not bitterly disputed. Some studies have focused on the use of certain words — the so-called lexical approach; others claim that this is too limited to be a satisfactory method. Some have held that ideas of justice change radically between the time of Homer and the classical period; others defend basic continuity. And it is even maintained by some that *dike*, the word often translated as 'justice,' is not a moral term at all in early Greek. In fact there is much less distance separating the various positions than many of their defenders claim.

The contention that *dike* does not have a general moral sense in early Greek derives from a fact on which everyone agrees: at least some uses of *dike* are non-moral. Specifically, in the *Odyssey* and later Greek, *dike* is often the order of nature, the way some group or class of people or things normally behaves. Various patterns and properties of society and nature may provoke various responses: the Greeks considered the world far from perfect, and the structure of society was obviously more pleasant for some members than for others. But each element of the standing order, if it is a mark or a characteristic of a group, is unquestionably *dike*. The common man does not commend or take comfort in the fact that kings behave out of bounds and act on partialities. But this is nonetheless the *dike* or the way of kings (*Od.* 4.687–93). Similarly, no one would claim that it is 'good order' or 'justice' when men lose their flesh and bones at death and the soul flies away. It is simply the way things are (*Od.* 11.216–22).[5]

Another meaning of *dike*, found in both the *Iliad* and *Odyssey* and potentially more important for moral usage, is 'ruling' or 'settlement'. It can be the decision itself or the process of peacefully settling a dispute whether by arbitration or higher command. Of this usage there are many instances. There is more to be said about Homeric usage, but there is also a point of non-usage stressed by those who make the case for the absence of moral connotation in *dike*. That is that *whatever* the word *dike* means, it is not important in Homer.

No important character is called *dikaios*; no one ever appeals to *dike* when he has been wronged; no warnings or threats mention *dike*; and none of the major actions of the epics, such as the avenging of Paris' theft, or the punishment of the suitors, or of Aegisthus, is ever spoken of as *dike*.[6]

Such analysis has been criticized both for its characterization of Homeric usage and for limiting its approach to the occurrence of specific words. Indeed, even using this lexical approach one finds that elsewhere in early Greek poetry, specifically in the works of Hesiod, *dike* figures much more prominently. Here, as in Homer, *dike* may sometimes simply mean 'settlement' or 'legal process'. But other uses, as well as the general framework of Hesiod's narrative, indicate that *dike* may mean more than this. Even as legal process, it is clear that it is a highly valued process which should help peacefully to protect a man from having his rights transgressed by another.[7] Moreover, there are Homeric uses for which the translations 'legal process' and 'settlement' seem forced and artificially restrictive (*Il.* 16.387–8, *Od.* 14.81–4). In these and similar passages, *dike* words seem to have a moral force as terms for evaluating the appropriateness of various human behaviors. Such a finding should not be surprising: other Homeric words such as *themis* and *hybris* are also used to approve or disapprove of men's actions. And yet this in itself indicates very little. As Plato's Protagoras explains so eloquently, no human society is possible without some orderly restraints on behavior (*Prt.* 322–3). But it is crucial to establish *what* guidelines for action the society sets. It is true that *dike* entails respecting a set of traditional limitations and commends the due order of Homeric society, perhaps even in a fairly abstract way. But it must be remembered that this due order need not necessarily include a commitment to a legal or democratic order which would apply equally to the community members with respect to their actions toward each other. In fact, in the aristocratic world of the Homeric poems *dike* even as a moral term will mean very different things for different men since rights and appropriate behaviors vary greatly from individual to individual.

In part, then, the modern confusion and disagreement over the meaning of *dike* have stemmed from this original range of Homeric and early usage which includes both the moral and the non-moral. As we shall see, both these senses continue into the classical period and at times partially fuse. This creates special difficulties in the uses of *dike* in reference to the gods. That is, the topic of theodicy, which might be of particular interest in a legal system, actually involves a number of complicated ideas rather than one clear one.

In turning to fifth-century usage, we find that '*dike* is used in prose predominantly in the senses "lawsuit", "settlement", "satisfaction", "penalty", i.e. the readjustment of a contested balance of gain or loss'.[8] In fact, as has been recently re-emphasized, '*dike* in the sense of "justice" is not an Attic usage'.[9] Poetic usage in the period is far more complex. But before examining poetry in detail, it is worth noting that *dikaiosyne*, a word which in the fourth century becomes common and is then the regular word for 'justice', is found only once in extant Greek literature before Herodotus and less than a dozen times before the fourth century.[10] Of these, the five which occur in Herodotus generally concern great men upholding specific agreements, and the remaining instances are mainly from sophistic fragments. *Dikaiosyne* seems not to have been a popular word in any sense. In tragedy it is confined to one Euripidean fragment $(486N^2)$.[11] Finally, it is noticeable that no rhetor cared to use it in any of the extant court speeches from the fifth century.

If we turn to tragedy, we find that the usage of *dike* and its related adjectives shows a general continuity and conformance with Homeric usage. For example, the chorus in *Medea* uses *dike* at line 411 in its common Homeric sense of 'natural order' ('both *dike* and all things are turning back'). As Verall explains (*ad loc.*):

> To give *dika* here its later sense of *justice* is exactly contrary to the meaning, for the women are arguing that justice is about to be satisfied, and women to have their rights through a signal contradiction of common experience.

A similar use of the *dike* words relates statements, appearance or behavior to the facts of the situation. In such passages the English should usually contain a phrase such as 'in fact' or 'really.' So when Jocasta explains that Apollo's oracle can never be fulfilled *dikaios orthon*, it makes no sense to import any moral terms into the phrase. It simply means 'as stated' or 'corresponding to actual events' (Soph. *O.T.* 852ff., 1282; cf. *Trach.* 347). Similarly, *dike*, especially in the phrase *pros dikes*, often has nothing to do with approval or disapproval of action. Rather it is used to clarify the sole logical response in a given situation. In these passages, the English would run something like, 'Given these facts, there is no need to fear/sigh etc.'[12]

This non-moral equation or weighing of two quantities is also found with the adjective *dikaios*. The regular construction for this sense uses *dikaios* applied to a person coupled with an infinitive followed by a finite form of *einai* (Eur. *Supp.* 186, *Heracl.* 142, 775), something like Aeschylus' *kyrios eimi throein* (*Ag.* 104). Perhaps the best single word for this usage is 'competent'. This was noted by Paley, who was more anxious than most to find justice in his Greek.[13] The adjective *axios* is used in the same way to indicate the required equivalent in totally matter-of-fact situations (Eur. *Hipp.* 236).

All this calculated balancing is likely to make us think of equity and the scales of Justice. Moreover, such associations are encouraged by passages such as *Agamemnon* 250 — '*Dike* weighs out understanding to those who have suffered.' But it will be almost impossible to obtain Greek sense from the Greek by using modern ideas of justice and of what things may be appropriately weighed against each other in the scales. More helpful material for comparison may be found in Greek poetry where we find that Bacchylides, Pindar and Aeschylus obsessively match various actions and events as the required or fated equivalents of each other. In epinician poetry and the tragic choral ode responsion, the existence of metrically equivalent positions which can be used for echoes is particularly suited for juxtaposing and relating quantities we would have considered neither commensurate nor commensurable.[14]

Now Greek tends to label these correspondences *dike*, and we are apt to confuse ourselves if we call the acts of birds which require the sacrifice of a child *justice*. Nevertheless, when something is called forth by something else, it is *dike*; and as we noted at the beginning of this discussion, that is a natural or expected occurrence. As Kitto says,

> Neither there [Soph. *El*. 1417–21], nor in the *Trachiniae*, nor here in the *Ajax*, is emphasis laid on the moral 'justice' so earnestly desired by modern criticism; rather, upon 'justice' as *dike*, the way in which the universe works.[15]

Indeed, this type of *dike* is the stuff of tragedy, which is full of delayed and reciprocal actions. Therefore, if in these senses of *dike* and *diakaion* the element of calculation begins to suggest the image of the scales of Justice, then it is necessary at least to remember that the Greek scales and ours are balanced by very different sorts of weights and measures. That is, when considering either the moral usage of *dike* — as a term suggesting acceptable behavior — or its non-moral usage — as a term for the structure of the universe — we must further specify the content of the moral or cosmic order.

Sometimes in tragedy the punishment or penalty labeled *dike* is simply a human reaction to the behavior of other individuals.[16] Similarly, the adjectives *dikaios*, *adikos*, and *ekdikos* are used to describe an individual in terms of behavior which may entail some punishment or penalty. Most often these words praise the observance or blame the breach of limits of human actions which are already traditional in Homer. It is *dikaion* to respect and help guests, masters, suppliants, and friends.[17] The penalty threatened or dreaded in case of violations of these limits is divine punishment and/or public shame and dishonor. Obviously in these traditional categories of behavior, justice and the natural order of the world are seen as very closely connected.

One could imagine a culture in which the uses of *dike* words were limited to the above categories. In such a culture moral values would differ significantly from ours; nevertheless the value system would include a certain sense of justice. In fact Greek values are considerably more complex, for *dike* and *dikaion* may be used of any rules and related behaviors established by the community. Furthermore, Greeks recognized that order and obedience were necessary for the welfare of society (Soph. *Aj*. 1245, *Ant*. 660) and that one who pursued gain in contravention of these rules was liable to harm the state (Eur. *Heracl*. 1ff.). However, for a given individual, contravention of these less traditionally established community rules might make considerable gain possible. In fact, gain and *dike* are often explicitly opposed (Eur. *Heracl.* 1ff., *Supp.* 232ff.). Indeed, it was difficult to claim that *dike* brought or insured any sort of practical advantage. The statement that one *dikaios* man can prevail over many *ouk endikoi* (not just) men occurs in a play which proves just the opposite (Eur. *Palamedes* fr.584N[2]).

One of the most obvious ways in which justice may be made more stable in a culture is through association with the gods — that is, through an idea of theodicy. Although the passage from the *Palamedes* just cited separates *dike* and *to theion* (the divine), there were connections between *dike* and the gods.[18] *Dike* had an honored seat alongside the ancient *nomoi* of Zeus (Soph. *O.C.* 1380). But *dike* was at best only one among the many divine powers. For instance, Eros had an equally established seat from which he worked against *dikaion* (Soph. *Ant.* 781ff.). Since the interests of the various Greek gods and goddesses were often at odds, the inclusion of *Dike* among these powers created the possibility that one might not be able to honor both it and some other divinity or divinities at the same time. This is in fact one of Antigone's dilemmas. In fulfilling some of her religious duties, she has had to transgress *dike* (the cosmic order which includes the city's laws) and other divine claims (Soph. *Ant.* 853).[19] Moreover, *dike* retained all the meanings we have discussed previously even when it was applied in the sphere of the gods. So *dike* could also be either divine punishment or even merely the way a god acted; and either of these could involve ruin for the innocent as well as the offender (Eur. *Hipp.* 48ff., *El.* 1349).

This confusing state of affairs has been well described by Hugh Lloyd-Jones in *The Justice of Zeus*. The traditional world of Greek religion is hard and ruthless and presents divine *dike* which is often extremely difficult to comprehend. It can seem capricious especially when it comes very late and falls on men who were not themselves participants in the events which set the *dike* in motion.[20] This view is demonstrated not just by word usage but by the whole shape of the narratives of Herodotus and Thucydides and in the plays of Sophocles. And in the end one must say, as Lloyd-Jones does, that 'in a nutshell . . . in one sense Zeus was but in another sense he was not just'.[21] Such a theodicy is not reliable, coherent backing for community standards of behavior.

Thus, having examined the repeated workings of explicitly identified divine *dike* in Greek tragedy, one may understandably characterize it as opaque and incomprehensible, an irrational and brute force — and all this has gotten quite far from an abstract ideal of justice.[22] It is sometimes asserted that the gods honor *dikaia* (Eur. *Supp.* 377). But the Greeks could also accept without complaint that gods did not necessarily act in accord with the categories of *dikaion* which might apply to mortals. For example, while it is *dikaion*, the expected or natural behavior, for Apollo (just as for a mortal prophet) to tell the truth, he cannot be forced (Soph. *O.T.* 280). Even a very ardent supporter would not expect him to speak if the result would not be to divine advantage (Eur. *Ion* 370–3).

In sum, associations with the gods did not enhance *dike* and *dikaion*. *Dike* had no privileged place in the cosmos. The *dikai* of the gods did not translate into action any more regularly or comfortingly than did the *dikai* of men. In fact, the divine status of *dike* merely meant that there were more universal or natural laws with which any given human action might conflict. One *dikaios* path was to honor the gods (Eur. *Heracl.* 901ff.), but often it was not possible to honor them all at once. And one could easily be simultaneously *endikos* and not in right relation with the gods (Eur. *Supp.* 63ff.).

Thus, since *dike* could not be made supremely or even reliably attractive, it had to be weighed against other factors into the calculation of gain to be had from a given action. If possible, it was better to prevail with *dike*, for this would mean more honor for the house (Eur. *Andr.* 778ff.). There is no suggestion, however, that *dike* should ever be preferred to victory. In fact, *dike* could bring harm (Eur. *El.* 1041), and *dikaion* was certainly not as important as maintaining one's freedom or even as important as avoiding shame (Soph. *El.* 338, 559). Again, *dike* was clearly separate from the *kalon* which brought honor (Eur. *Or.* 194, 417). Given the importance of honor, even a judge, whose function was to dispense *dike*, would be so concerned with the opinions, praise, and blame of others, that he might choose to gain honor from the many rather than rule in accordance with the facts of the case (Eur. *Hec.* 852, 1240). In pursuing success, one might openly request help in an action conceded to be *adikon*, for even a very moderate Athenian could give the advice to do only such *adika* as would bring one no harm (Eur. *Or.* 646, *Supp.* 555). That is, there were other important ways of evaluating behavior besides in its relation to *dike*. Before considering the place of law or laws in enforcing limits on behavior, it will be useful briefly to consider some other Greek values.

3. General Values

The following sketch is meant as an introduction for those who have read little on the subject of Greek values. It is relevant for law and society and yet not crucial for the later analysis. This discussion is centered around the competitive emphasis in Athenian values with examples taken from fifth-century materials, concentrating on those plays and fragments of plays written mainly between 450 and 400. It stresses the distinctive importance of honor and shame in Greek culture as suggested by E.R. Dodds and developed by Arthur Adkins. Those who are not Hellenists should be warned that some have tried to play down the importance of this side of Greek moral values or even to reduce it practically to non-existence. However, despite disagreement as to details and extent, the balance seems to rest with those who see the Greeks as distinctly different from us in this area.[23] I do not wish to claim that feelings of cooperation and sympathy did not exist or were not esteemed. But it is important to establish the ways in which the balance between competition and cooperation was peculiar to classical Greek society. Instead of attempting to summarize all the complexities of popular values and ethics, I have concentrated on explaining what are sometimes thought to be important exceptions to a highly competitive ethic and on properly accounting for many passages which are often either considered peculiar or simply misinterpreted.

Two possible objections to the extensive use of passages from tragedy in exploring popular values might be, first, that the tragic stage and its situations and characters are different from everyday life, and second, that the context of the whole play is crucial for evaluating each passage. As to the first, I would give four fairly different types of reassurance. Most generally, although the situations of tragedy are extreme, human life is experienced as extreme, and great drama is always moving at least partly because the audience does not feel far removed from the types of dilemmas faced by the actors. More specifically, the second half of the fifth century in Athens was, as human history goes, a highly turbulent and critical time in which the citizens repeatedly faced plague and military disasters which threatened the collapse of life as they knew it and required the most painful and difficult choices year after year. This is partly why, whatever the original intent of the tragedians, modern interpreters have had little difficulty in drawing detailed parallels between political figures and events in Athens and the characters and plots of Sophocles and Euripides. The third point comes from roughly contemporary attitudes toward tragedy which indicate that the Athenians did feel quite close to the characters on stage. From the fourth century we have Aristotle's *Poetics* (especially Chapters 13–17) in which he insists not only on a certain realism and probability but also on the necessity of the characters being very much like ourselves. Discussions of tragedy in Plato convey a similar sense of identification with, rather than distance from, the plays. Perhaps the most convincing of such evidence comes in the debate between Euripides and Aeschylus in Aristophanes' *Frogs*, which again emphasizes the close involvement of the citizens with the values and examples set forth on stage.

The fourth reply relies on the most primary and objective evidence and is the most important for this study. Both the style and content of argument and deliberation found in Sophocles and Euripides differ very little from that which can be found in any other contemporary source, be it Herodotus, Antiphon, Thucydides, or Lysias.[24] In addition, if judgement can be suspended, at least briefly, it will be found below that a good part of Chapter 4 is devoted to illustrating the close connections between the stage and civic life and values.

This last point leads most naturally to the answer to the second objection, the importance of context. In part, I must ask the reader's trust in my assurance that I have always considered the context and have tried never to go against it. That is, I have not presented as valued or as positive any sentiment or choice which is undercut by the contextual dramatic devaluation of the character who expresses or makes it. Fortunately, most of the material which follows is guarded by a positive systematic approach. As a rule, I have sought groups of examples delivered by a variety of characters so that the sentiments acquire a certain independent weight. The point is to establish the outlines and general tendencies possible in ethical deliberation, and I believe the following exposition does this, and reveals that the accepted emphasis in fifth-century Athens often differs fundamentally from that which would be expected by someone working from various forms either of Judaeo-Christian or perhaps Kantian moral perspectives.[25]

Athenian politics was largely guided by men of high social standing who usually came from families which had long been wealthy and prominent. This group formed a sort of class called variously

agathoi (the good), *aristoi* (the best), and *kaloi kagathoi* (the fair/
fine and good, or noblemen). These men contributed the most to
the cultural and military well-being of Athens by financing civic
works of all sorts. They were paid with honor for the victorious
entries which they sponsored in athletic and cultural contests; but
they also expected, asked for and received recognition or payment
in the form of prestigious office or popular cooperation in the
assembly and courts.[26] Since talents and family fortunes inevitably
waxed and waned, not all sons of *agathoi* would equal their fathers'
greatness, especially not in all *aretai* (skills or excellences).[27] Still, it
was assumed that they and only they would be *agathoi* and display
the same types of skills and admired competitive competencies as
did their fathers.[28] Most tragic fragments which seem to support the
view that a low-born man can have great *arete* are from plays which
do not show this at all. These are plays of lost sons — especially lost
twins — which in fact assert that no matter how humble an
upbringing a child receives, if he is high-born, his nobility will come
through in the end (Eur. *Alexander, Melanippe Desmotis* fr.
495N[2]). Tragedy depicted the influence and advantages of wealth
much as they were in fifth-century Athens. An *agathos* has more
influence on the opinion of the many (Eur. *Hec.* 291). In time of
trouble his friends who provide help will be other *agathoi* and
therefore powerful (Eur. *Heracl.* 297). And if no powerful friends
are available, the *agathos*, merely by virtue of his birth, is more
likely to be pitied and spared (Eur. fr. 414N[2], *Or.* 784; Soph. *Trach.*
310ff.). An additional reason to claim pity or generosity was no
small advantage in Athens, for pity and generosity were not in
themselves *aretai* and therefore not in over-supply. Douglas
MacDowell has searched very thoroughly for uses of the word *arete*
in the fifth century which include the notion of generosity.[29] The
only instance before the end of the century is in an unsuccessful
attempt by the Spartans to attain a lenient peace (Thuc. 4.19).
They claim this would be an *arete* on the part of the Athenians,
who had the advantage. The Spartans carefully explain the advantages of this *arete* and promise to return it. But an *arete* does not
need its advantages explained and is not something one returns.
It is not surprising that they did not persuade the Athenians to
cooperate.

Since wealth was one of the chief means of acquiring the honor
and success so intensely desired in Athens, it is not surprising that
the Athenians had a considerable interest in gain. An Athenian did

not fool himself into thinking that wealth was a sufficient end. Heracles found that when wealth was powerless, friends could be preferable (Eur. *H.F.* 1425–6).[30] Riches might not help in illness (Eur. fr. 714N^2), and wealth was not the equivalent of and therefore not a substitute for wisdom or nobility (Eur. fr. 52N^2, *Tro.* 411–16). But even if it was not sufficient for success, it was certainly necessary. Because of traditional obligations to friends, no one wanted poor ones (Eur. *El.* 1130), and nobility could not erase the fact that poverty reduced one to nothing (Eur. fr. 142N^2, *Phoen.* 402, 438–42). The farmer who has married Euripides' Electra is an excellent illustration of just how limited the impoverished *agathos* became: the best he could do was to leave his wife alone and try not to reach above his humble position.

Obviously, wealth was a means to attain the end of success and prosperity only if it was stable. The loss of wealth not only impeded the pursuit of success, it signalled failure and brought shame and dishonor. Solon had voiced what men had long known, that wealth gained by force was liable to bring punishment (13W 7–8). Therefore, some care had to be exercised in the acquisition of wealth. But this was merely a rational calculation: only take that which will not cause grief later (Eur. *Kresphontes* fr. 77A). Wealth sought indiscriminately could lead to later misfortune (Soph. *Ant.* 312–14; cf. Eur. *El.* 938).

Although these sentiments have the ring of trite and vacuous generality, they were not merely empty commonplaces. For example, the Athenian attitude towards a bride's dowry vividly illustrates the concrete results of wariness in the acquisition of wealth. In the event of divorce, which the wife as well as the husband could request at any time, the wife's dowry had to be returned in full. Therefore, by accepting a dowry sufficiently large to raise one's status, one risked future shame through the loss of that status. This meant that a marriage to a woman of greater wealth could be viewed as a loss of freedom.[31] And, as a result, the immediate allure of gold and silver could be limited by far-sighted calculation of risk.

This concern over the dowry is merely one illustration of the great desire not to fail which followed naturally from the desire to succeed. Competition and proverbial envy meant that one's enemies were always ready to laugh at one's misfortune. And this laughter was always dreaded.[32] In fact, it was a commonplace of tragedy that if one could not live nobly, it was better to die.[33] If this seems to us merely a histrionic literary convention, we need merely recall that Paches stabbed himself to death in court in 426 BC when facing the shame of possible conviction (Plut. *Vit. Nicias* 61, *Vit. Aristides* 26.3).

It was in light of these values that the Athenian contemplated actions and evaluated events. It is therefore quite regular to find many aspects of Greek life frankly evaluated in terms of self-interest and personal advantage or gain. A Greek was likely to consider his own limited misfortune more grievous than the total destruction of those very close to him. It may have been that when Hecuba's lying enemy Polymnestor described the loss of his eyesight as a worse wound than the murder of his children, some Athenian spectators despised his self-centered attitude (Eur. *Hec.* 1168–71). But Hecuba, whose husband and sons have been murdered and whose daughters are being carried off to distant slavery, claims in language almost identical to Polymnestor's that her greatest grief is her enslavement (Eur. *Tro.* 489–90). Thus, although a modern reading can make Orestes' and Electra's exchange early in Euripides' *Orestes* sound like awkward but meaningful sibling affection, the statements should be taken as straightforward frank expressions of self-concern (310ff.). Similarly, we may imagine that Agamemnon and Pylades would mourn the loss of Menelaos and Orestes. But they emphasize their dread of returning alone and being shamed by the scorn and blame of others at home (*Il.* 4.169ff.; Eur. *I.T.* 674–86). Their declarations are to be read seriously and not just as covers for embarrassing affection.

Similarly, quite respectable men frequently evaluated a course of action solely in terms of the ultimate gain which might result. It is not a villain, but rather the honorable Theseus who moderately limits actions which would give others claims against one (or 'acting unjustly,' as *adikein* is often translated) to those which will not bring harm in return (Eur. *Supp.* 555–9).[34] Similarly, Sophocles did not present a shocking or base Orestes welcoming evil lies (as is often said) for the sake of profit (*El.* 61).[35] Rather, both he and Menelaos are willing to take the practical risk of an unlucky omen, being spoken of as dead, in order to regain a house or wife (Eur. *Hel.* 1050–2). Even in familial relationships, what has sometimes been called an unnatural and unfeeling concern over profit and loss is in fact perfectly regular for a fifth-century Athenian. The bitter calculations of Admetus after Alcestis' death are not worded to draw the audience's disapproval (Eur. *Alc.* 954–61). He merely expresses himself as do Heracles, Medea, Jason, and Amphitryon in similar situations.[36]

As we examine fifth-century literature more closely, a self-interested motive comes to seem almost a prerequisite for action. Careful explanations of personal advantage are made even when a deed or decision benefits someone else or seems self-sacrificing. For example, Oedipus' zealous investigation stems at least partially from self-avowed concern for his own safety (Soph. *O.T.* 139–41). And Menoikeus cannot bear the rootless shameful life which would be the alternative to sacrificing himself for the city (Eur. *Phoen.* 999–1005).

Once we accept the importance of this concern for profit and loss as a part of an extremely competitive value system, many passages from Greek tragedy lose what before seemed an odd tone. The whole point is to come out ahead on the balance sheet. Hence the concern when one item threatens the gain promised by another. A Greek will debate whether or not *sophia* (wisdom) is profitable and he will despair when it is not (Eur. *Med.* 294ff.; Soph. *O.T.* 316). Such concerns make it natural to wonder what use beauty may be to one who is not intelligent (Eur. *Oedipus* fr. 91A). And the perplexity of a Greek in the face of combinations of alternatives too complex to evaluate is probably more sincere than sophistic. Someone in Euripides' *Oedipus* asks, 'Is it more useful to be wise but not courageous or daring but not wise?' (fr. 95A). However a Theban might feel, an Athenian would genuinely want to know. Similarly difficult combinations of antitheses fill both the narrative and speeches of Thucydides, constantly requiring the reader to reason, calculate and compare. The historian's restless intellectualism grew logically from Athenian habit.[37]

One of the advantages most sought by Athenians was honor. In fact, praise and blame were so important that almost the entire importance of an action resided in other people's evaluation and opinion of it. So Antigone does not merely want Polyneices to be buried: it must be known that she buried him (Soph. *Ant.* 84–7). Heracles' daughter Makaria is not satisfied with the salvation of her family through her own self-sacrifice unless that sacrifice is totally voluntary and not produced through a lottery (Eur. *Heracl.* 547–51). The list of actions chosen or rejected in tragedy because of what people will say can be expanded almost indefinitely.[38] Even though individuals may acknowledge that the opinions of the despised crowd are based on standards less noble and judgements less capable, those opinions are of great importance (Eur. *I.T.* 674–9). Therefore, when urging someone else to act, one is likely to emphasize not how fine it *is* to do something, but how fine it *looks* to do it (Eur. *I.A.* 982–4).

Two other points, both more technical, will help demonstrate the extent of this Athenian concern. The first is an idiom. The Athenian is not so worried about being or becoming various ignoble things as about incurring the reputation for being any of those things, and to express this particular worry there is a particular verb and construction. To acquire the reputation for something is regularly *ophliskano* plus the abstract noun in *-ia*. Sometimes the more concrete verb *ktaomai* (acquire) is used, and other nominal forms, both abstract and concrete, are found as well. Such acquired public dishonor is a great annoyance, especially since it may bear no relationship to fact, as Antigone and Helen pointedly note.[39] The desire to avoid unfavorable opinion provided such powerful motivation that, despite the deepest pain and despair, Heracles agreed to go on living in order to escape the charge of *deilia* (cowardice) (Eur. *H.F.* 1348). Euripides seems to have been particularly fond of demonstrating the efficacy of this weapon, for in two plays his characters use the threat of a charge of cowardice to move a Hamlet-like Orestes to action.[40]

The second point is also one of usage. When it is used in tragedy, the verb *haliskomai*, which means 'to be caught' or, in the Athenian court 'to be convicted', is placed in the fifth and sixth feet of the line with a regularity approaching that of a Homeric formula. Such metrically fixed phrases are rare in tragedy, and the few that exist have obviously grown up around very basic concerns.[41] A character using this formula declares not that he or she will never do or be a certain thing but rather that he or she will never be caught or convicted of doing or being it.[42] In examining late fifth-century attitudes towards law and illegal actions, it is important to recall this standard, even trite, tragic resolution not to be caught or convicted.

There is one fifth-century passage which especially seems to assert the importance of something like conscience or an internal standard independent of outside circumstances:

But if one necessarily finds his life in peril, there is at least this, which I consider the greatest thing in such a circumstance: to be conscious that one has not erred, and if misfortune occurs that it is without baseness or shame, and through chance rather than wrong-doing. (Antiphon 6.1)

But the innocence, or even the knowledge of it, is not a good in itself. It is merely the best in a bad situation. Moreover, the situation is a murder charge which involves piety and pollution. As Chapter 2 will make clear in detail, matters of homicide are in a category entirely apart from all other actions.

Two things should be clear from the preceding survey. First, the Athenian desire for material success was so great that the end result often far outweighed the means in the evaluation of action. However, even though results and externality were so emphasized at this time that one might even say that man was entirely what happened to him (Hdt. 1.32.4, 7.49.3), there was an important sense in which this was not the complete Athenian attitude. Since we tend to take account of what we consider a man's internal qualities, a man in our society may feel that despite all the tricks of fate and all his outward failures, he has other types of greatness within him. Material circumstance was not final for Athenians either, but for a quite different reason. Whereas modern man may take refuge in an *alternative* inner standard, Athenians could not. And they were further burdened with an *additional* external factor rather than equipped with an alternative consolation. In Athens the idea of success included honor; and honor required not only material conditions but also the admiring recognition of others. At first this second point may not seem a significant mitigation of the orientation towards results, but in fact it provided an important brake on the individual striving for success.

Since public opinion often revolved around the good of the city, the individual who wanted honor for benefiting the city might have to forego some other form of success. He might aid the city directly and actively through some gift or sacrifice or less directly by limiting his competitive behavior and keeping down strife within the city. The subordination of the individual to the city is a frequent concern in tragedy.[43] Creon is the first in extant works to declare the necessity of a healthy state for individual prosperity (Soph. *Ant.* 184–90), but the sentiment was certainly a commonplace. We find it both in Thucydides (2.60.2–4) and Andocides (2.2–3). Public pressure was brought to bear on citizens not only through general honor or shame but also through the laws, *nomoi*. In other words, one of the main ends for which Athenians competed was public approval which was partly expressed through a cooperative legal system.

4. The Law or Laws?

The literature of fifth-century Athens contains a few striking passages in praise of law and democracy. If they are read out of context or in combination with fourth-century passages, they can give an impression of admiration for an abstract legal order and legality. However, as Gomme noted, 'it was in the fourth century particularly . . . that Athens adopted . . . measures . . . which were designed to secure the rule of law'.[44] And these institutional measures went hand in hand with theoretical developments in the questioning and defense of law and justice. Therefore, grouping statements from the two centuries together has one of two undesirable results. Either it reduces the fourth-century passages to statements equating law with freedom, or it tends to impart to the fifth-century passages a conceptual sophistication and a commitment to legality which they in fact lack.[45] The fifth-century statements about law must be carefully examined to see what sort of introduction they might provide to the nature of Athenian law in that century.[46]

In her recent book on the development of the concept of law in Greek thought, Jacqueline de Romilly claims that

> La Loi — et, plus précisément, la loi écrite — devient alors le symbole même de cette double opposition: elle incarna pour les Grecs la lutte contre la tyrannie, et l'idéal democratique, mais aussi la lutte contre les barbares, et l'idéal d'une vie policée.[47]

That the oppositions or contrasts she describes are commonplaces of fifth-century Greek literature is not in doubt, as will be shown below. However, it is wrong to find them symbolized by 'the law', especially written law.

De Romilly chooses as her strongest and most decisive statement a 'passage célèbre d'Hérodote'.[48] She quotes Demaratus' statement that

> Although they (the Spartans) are free, they are not free in all respects. They have a master, the law (la loi), which they fear

much more than your [the King's] subjects fear you. At any rate, they do everything that their master commands. (7.104)

But Demaratus' response is fuller. He explains just what it is that this *despotes nomos* enjoins the Spartans to do; and that is never to retreat in battle, but rather to stand and perish in formation. He is talking with the King, after all, solely about military bravery. This passage is not at all astonishing; and it is not about the law, especially written law. It is about *a* custom in Sparta which is very powerful. This is clear in the context of the entire conversation. But de Romilly quotes only part of Demaratus' response, and she thinks he is responding to Darius. One must read a paragraph in either direction to be reminded that it is Xerxes. Darius is dead. His ghost speaks at length elsewhere in Greek literature (Aesch. *Pers.* 681ff.), but not here. This passage contains the ghost neither of Darius nor of those implications which de Romilly finds.

What the discussion is related to is a passage which Aristotle tells us is a poetic commonplace (*Pol.* 1252b8). Fortunately the remains of fifth-century literature provide us with several examples of this topic. Broadly, freedom of self-rule under Greek laws and customs is opposed to the slavery of barbarian rule and tyranny. The antithesis was inspired by the threat from Persia and the Greek victories early in the fifth century. The contrast, however, between Greek communities with deliberative government and barbarian societies lacking such institutions is much older. We find it already in the *Odyssey* in the description of the Cyclopes:

. . . who have no meetings for counsel or traditional rules. They dwell in caves on the high mountain tops, and each one rules over his wife and children, and they do not care about each other. (9.112–15)

Maine, with his usual insight, realized the general implication of this passage and suggested it was 'Homer's type of an alien and less advanced civilization'.[49] It is not simply coincidence that Aristotle cites this passage almost immediately after a Euripidean example of the commonplace contrast between Greeks and barbarians, even though his emphasis is more chronological and developmental (*Pol.* 1252b22). The Homeric lines strikingly isolated what seemed characteristic of later Greek government: Plato had used them as well (*Leg.* 680b). In fact, the apparent simple contrast between slavery and freedom is really a combination of two comparisons.

The first juxtaposes Greeks, who are *not* ruled by a tyrant and who are therefore free, with foreigners — usually Persians or Trojans — who *are* ruled by a tyrant and therefore are slaves. Having lived abroad, Helen could report from experience:

> All the barbarians are slaves but one. (Eur. *Hel.* 276)

So Hellenic logic equates the perfumed eunuchs Helen brought back with Xerxes' finest men. Pylades (Eur. *Or.*) and Demaratus (Hdt. 7.104) are equally confident in the contemplation of battle involving barbarians: slaves are as nothing compared to free men (Eur. *Or.* 1115).

In other passages, imagination contrasts free Greeks with the same Greeks enslaved by tyrannical foreign rule. No Greek would have trouble choosing between these alternatives. So in the course of her defense Helen is able to re-enslave her husband partly with the very important, if very improbable, claim to have saved Greeks from slavery:

> So much did my marriage benefit Greece.
> You are not ruled by barbarians or a
> tyrant, nor do you bear arms for one. (Eur. *Tro.* 932–4)

Helen could be certain of the reaction to the prospect. The only question which could arise from contemplating foreign enslavement was purely rhetorical:

> Will we Greeks be slaves to foreigners? (Eur. fr. 717N²)

The distinction between these two oppositions of freedom and slavery has perhaps been unclear because the same passage will sometimes combine them. The Greeks are imagined as becoming slaves to foreigners whom they consider slaves. Now it would be unnatural and hateful for *any* foreigners to rule Greeks, as Menelaus explains:

> Will barbarians rule Greeks? Do you think
> I'm foolish hating what's unnatural? (Eur. *Andr.* 665–7)

Add to this the point that the foreigners are themselves slaves, and the state of affairs is totally unthinkable for a Greek:

> Mother, it's fitting for Greeks to rule
> barbarians, but not the barbarians Greeks,
> for barbarians are slaves, but Greeks
> free men. (Eur. *I.A*. 1401–2)

It should now be clear how important these passages are to an understanding of the one in Herodotus. They must be kept in mind whenever praise of the laws or law contrasts that which is Greek with that which is not. Such is the case in the following two passages:

> First, you live in Greece instead of a
> foreign land, and you know peaceful legal
> process and the use of law without force. (Eur. *Med*. 536–8)
> 'It's Greek always to honor one's own.'
> 'And not put oneself before the laws.' (Eur. *Or*. 486–7)

These passages clearly do not praise Greek legality either in contrast to other aspects of Greek life or as a good in itself. Instead they envision as alternatives the life of a free Greek (or even a newcomer like Medea) with Greek laws and customs on the one hand, and the life of a Greek (or even a foreigner) enslaved to a foreign tyrant and thus deprived of Greek laws and customs on the other hand.

There remain from Greek tragedy two passages extolling the free city Athens and its laws which do not contain a contrast with foreign, non-Greek rule or government. The first, from Theseus' debate with the Theban herald in Euripides' *Suppliant Women*, is perhaps as famous a locus for the praise of law as the Herodotean passage we began with.[50] Theseus explains that in the free city of Athens the *demos* (the people) rather than a tyrant rules (403–8, 429ff.). With written laws, the poor man and the rich can make the same legal claims, and the poor man can win if legality is on his side. A more eloquent and straightforward defense of a formal legal order has not come down to us from the fifth century. If it stood alone, we could almost wonder if there were any differences between the ideals of Greek law and modern Western law. However, it occurs in a context which modifies it somewhat and which points to another very similar passage that has further implications.[51]

In the previous episode Theseus explained that he freed the city and made the *demos* king (Eur. *Supp*. 352–3). But he is also absolutely certain that his wish alone is sufficient to ensure the city's action: whatever he wants will be done (350). Indeed, as soon as it is learned what he wants, the city joyfully acquiesces (393–4).

Now even if we join Paley in reading line 352 to mean that Theseus established the city as a monarchy with Theseus at the head (and I think this is a very unlikely interpretation of the Greek), lines 403–8 still remain. And *there* Theseus specifically states that the city is not ruled by one man but rather that the *demos* has kingly power (*anassei*). Even Paley (*ad loc.*), with all his gift for reconciliation, has felt a contradiction which leads him to comment as follows on the story of Theseus: 'The Athenians had at once a dread of kings, *basileis*, and yet a love for their royal ancestry of the heroic ages. And it was thus that they reconciled the two conflicting feelings.' Oddly enough, I think an Athenian would have felt less conflict here than did Paley. Furthermore, the situation was not at all confined to the memory of the heroic age. To be assured of this, we need look no further than the remaining passage most often cited in discussing fifth-century praise of democracy and law — Pericles' Funeral Oration (Thuc. 2.37).[52] Here is praise of democracy, of the equality of citizens and of the legal order almost as forceful as Theseus'. And it is delivered by a man whose control over Athens was almost as complete as that of the legendary king (Thuc. 2.65).[53] I do not believe that Euripides and Thucydides are representing Theseus and Pericles as insincere in their descriptions of Athens. It was possible at once to praise the full power and equality of the citizens and to have a man whose 'mere wish' (to quote Paley again) was virtually certain of enactment.[54] And it was certainly possible to praise the legal order and the equality it ensured, while using a system very much different from that which we would feel corresponded to such a description. The Athenians were confronted with a new creature. And we must be wary of their descriptions as of early drawings of beached whales or of animals newly brought to Europe. The creatures were greatly admired; but their total novelty somehow made them almost impossible even for quite capable draftsmen to a depict accurately.

A look at some of the aspects of Pericles' political and social career shows that his relationship to the law was in fact quite complex. Like other Athenians, Pericles rose to prominence partly by political use of the courts. That is, he gained leadership by prosecuting other leaders.[55] Eventually his enemies manipulated the courts for political ends in the same fashion by prosecuting and ostracizing his friends — Pheidias, Aspasia, Anaxagoras, and perhaps Damon.[56]

Another of these friends was Protagoras. And Plato makes Protagoras as eloquent a proponent of civic law as Thucydides does Pericles (*Prt.* 322–6). Fortunately, tradition gives us further evidence of these two men's commitment to law. Pericles introduced pay for jurors in Athens.[57] This measure coincided with and probably helped bring about a great increase in the importance of the popular courts in Athens.[58] Moreover, when Pericles arranged for the founding of Thurii, he made certain that a code of laws was drawn up. And the man he chose for the job was Protagoras (Diog. Laert. 9.50). However, Protagoras, like Pericles, did not simply institute laws and praise obedience. He claimed that there were two sides to every question. It did not matter if one of the sides initially offered poor prospects: he taught his students to make the weaker argument stronger.[59] It was felt with good reason that the masters of these doctrines could thwart the orderly application of the city's laws (Ar. *Nub.*). Indeed, the complexity of at least some areas of Athenian law left a good deal of room for elaborate argument. If Pericles and Protagoras really did spend a day discussing the case of an accidental death from a javelin (DK 80 A10), their intellectual and rhetorical resources surely filled it with speeches even more convoluted and dazzling than those in another fifty-century treatment of exactly the same type of case — Anthiphon's second *Tetralogy*. From this set of speeches composed by Antiphon we can see how the circumstances in such a case lent themselves to many ingenious — if strained — forms of defense and accusation and encouraged manipulation of law even in the matter of homicide.[60]

It may be that not all these testimonia about Pericles and Protagoras are true: the important thing is that they all could be. They help show that in the fifth century the praise of democracy and law does not imply a devotion to equality and an abstract ideal of justice, for Athenian democracy and Athenian laws were very peculiar and characterized by quite contradictory and conflicting elements.[61] That this was recognized by Plato we can see clearly from the *Protagoras*.[62] Although Protagoras upholds obedience to the laws as necessary for the very existence of cities, his whole speech defends a trade which aims at creating successful politicians. The ideal model is not left to be inferred: it is explicitly Pericles, the man who virtually ruled the city, and whose outstanding success is contrasted here (320a) as in the *Meno* (94b) with the failure of his sons. And Pericles, we remember, had risen partly through legal maneuvering — the prosecution of rivals. Again, I do not want to claim that Pericles and Protagoras were insincere in their attachment to laws. Rather, they knew that proper training and use of Athenian laws provided powerful competitive tools with 'implications which were far from democratic'.[63] Thus, if one wants to claim that the Athenians placed a high value on *the* law and equality, Pericles and Protagoras are not the most comfortable or convincing authorities. Nor is Theseus in Euripides' *Suppliant Women*, the speaker with whom this discussion began.

The remaining passage from tragedy in praise of Athens and its laws also comes from a speech given by Theseus to a non-Athenian Greek (Soph. *O.C.* 909ff.). All that has been said about Theseus, Pericles and Athens above applies to this passage as well. Indeed, Jebb found the language here suggestive of constitutional monarchy as implied in line 350 of *Suppliant Women*. But the exact wording of Theseus' praise here provides us with yet another point. Athens, he says, 'sanctions nothing without the law' (914). In some societies this statement might affirm that all civic life is regulated by a formal legal order. But having examined all the passages commonly cited as Athenian praise of legality, we have found no indications in the statements themselves that there existed in the fifth century such a concept of an abstract legal order and procedural justice. Moreover, in discussing Pericles we have glimpsed some evidence to the contrary. Jebb's translation of *krainousan* in this line as 'sanctions' reflects an over-willingness to see in fifth-century Athens such an attitude toward *the* law and legal order. The word is better translated 'accomplished'. One readily sees how close 'Athens accomplishes nothing except through law' is to 'in Athens, everything involves the courts'. And Athenian litigiousness is a commonplace in this period.[64] Theseus' statement differs in tone from an Aristophanean jibe at the courts, but it serves chiefly as a serious claim that law, not legality or justice, pervaded Athenian life.

As a further antidote to the view that the passages discussed in this section are evidence for Athenian respect for law and legal justice, it is important to note that Theseus ends his speech to Creon with a threat of violence. The legal standard is not persuasive on its own. And this is not merely because Creon is evil. Both Demaratus in Herodotus (7.104) and Pericles in Thucydides (2.37.3) cite fear as the element compelling obedience to the laws. Similarly, the necessity of fear was something on which even Aeschylus' Athena and Furies saw eye to eye, and on which Sophocles' Menelaos insisted as well.[65]

A final Thucydidean passage remains to be considered — a statement from a figure who frequently echoes Pericles. Cleon stresses the importance of obeying laws whether they are the best or not (Thuc. 3.37.3). Now Thucydides may have written this passage under the influence of the events of 411 and 403 BC; but it nevertheless expresses a concept which was current in the fifth century and for which there was an interesting word — *eunomia* often translated as 'good order.' Again, such a word might be thought to indicate the existence of a legal ideal. But it has been shown that it 'at all times refers primarily to the behavior of the citizens, and not directly to any sort of constitution'.[66] A passage of early Greek poetry, frequently imitated, made *eunomia* the child of Themis and sister of *dike* and peace. Together they all insured traditional civil order and legal obedience — but they did not define any formal ideals.[67]

As a group these passages from Athenian literature do indicate the basic importance of laws to Athenians in the fifth century. The speakers in prose and poetry express a belief that the laws and their workings distinguish their city from others. It has often been noted that law or the judiciary played a significant role in Athenian society.[68] But an understanding of the place of law will not be gained by examining the collection of general statements about law or the concept of law. Rather, we must turn to the peculiarities of Athenian legal administration and procedure and of particular laws.

Notes

1. The book is that of Hugh Lloyd-Jones, *The Justice of Zeus* (University of California Press, Berkeley, Los Angeles, London, 1983) rev. edn. On page 232 he notes the criticism by Jean -P. Vernant, *Journal de psychologie* 72 (1975) 237.

2. Roberto M. Unger, *Law in Modern Society: Toward a Criticism of Social Theory* (The Free Press, New York, 1976) 52–3.

3. This is the starting point for Jacqueline de Romilly, *La Loi dans la pensée grecque des origines à Aristote* (Les Belles Lettres, Paris, 1971) 1. The passages from the fifth-century literature which convey this pride form the basis of Section 4 below, p. 19ff.

4. In some ways the debate may be seen to begin with E.R. Dodds, *The Greeks and the Irrational* (University of California Press, Berkeley and Los Angeles, 1951).

However it took on more shape with the appearance of A.W.H. Adkins, *Merit and Responsibility* (Oxford University Press, Oxford, 1960) and Lloyd-Jones, *The Justice of Zeus* (first edition 1971). Other extended discussions can be found in K.J. Dover, *Greek Popular Morality in the Time of Plato and Aristotle* (University of California Press Berkeley and Los Angeles, 1974) and E.A. Havelock, *The Greek Concept of Justice: From Its Shadow in Homer to Its Substance in Plato* (Harvard University Press, Cambridge, Mass., 1978). There have also been a number of important articles with detailed arguments and extensive bibliography: Michael Gagarin, '*Dike* in *Works and Days*,' *CP* 68 (1973) 81–94, and '*Dike* in Archaic Greek Thought,' *CP* 69 (1974) 186–97; M.W. Dickie, '*Dike* as a Moral Term in Homer and Hesiod,' *CP* 73 (1978) 91–101; D.B. Claus, 'Defining Moral Terms in *Works and Days*,' *TAPA* 107 (1977) 73–84.

5. This and other relevant examples are collected and discussed by Gagarin, '*Dike* in *Works and Days*' and '*Dike* in Archaic Greek thought', and Martin Ostwald, 'Ancient Greek Ideas of Law,' in *Dictionary of the History of Ideas: Studies in Selected Pivotal Ideas* (Scribner, New York, 1973), 678.

6. Gagarin, '*Dike* in *Works and Days*', p. 87. The key term for approved behavior is *themis*. However, it certainly is not 'justice'. Rather, it condones traditional customs and behavior and religious ritual in Homeric society.

7. See both Dickie, '*Dike* as a Moral Term' and Claus, 'Defining Moral Terms'.

8. Dover, *Greek Popular Morality*, 184–5.

9. Robert Renehan, 'The Greek Anthropocentric View of Man,' *HSCP* 85 (1981), 250.

10. Eric A. Havelock, '*Dikaiosyne*: An Essay in Greek Intellectual History,' *Phoenix* 23 (1969) 50. This article collects and discusses the fifth-century uses of the word.

11. It is cited by Aristotle *Eth.Nic.* 1129b28 : *Dikaiosynas to chryseon prosopon*. We have no context for this phrase which comes, apparently, from *Melanippe Sophe*.

12. Soph. *O.T.* 1014, *El.* 1211; Eur. *Supp.* 746.

13. F.A. Paley, *Euripides: The Works*, vol. 1 (Whitaker and Co., London, 1857) p. 384 (on *Supp.* 186ff.). The words 'just' and 'justice' obviously have no relevance in this passage. Cf. Eur. *Heracl.* 142, 773.

14. See Pind. *Ol.* 2.35–40/55–60; Aesch. *Ag.* 202/215, 383–4/401–2, 416–19/432–6; Eur. *Med.* 431–8/439–45; Soph. *El.* 474–9/489–95.

15. Humphrey D.F. Kitto, 'The *Rhesus* and Related Matters,' *Yale Classical Studies : Greek Tragedy*, vol. 25 (Cambridge University Press, Cambridge, 1977) 326.

16. Eur. *Heracl.* 57, *Hec.* 1252, *H.F.* 733, etc.

17. Respectively Eur. *Hec.* 799; *Phaethon* 89ff.; *Hel.* 914, 944ff., *Heracl.* 104; *I.T.* 597.

18. Eur. *Supp.* 600, *El.* 583, *I.A.* 1034, etc.

19. So Reginald W.B. Burton, *The Chorus in Sophocles' Tragedies* (Oxford University Press, Oxford, 1980) 122. The conflict is well brought out by Jean-P. Vernant, 'Tensions et ambiguités dans la tragédie grecque,' in Jean-Pierre Vernant and Pierre Vidal-Naquet, *Mythe et tragédie en Grèce ancienne* (François Maspero Paris, 1981) 33, and Arthur W.H. Adkins, 'Law versus Claims in Early Greek Religious Ethics,' *History of Religion* 21 (1982) 234, 238.

20. Lloyd-Jones, *The Justice of Zeus*, especially 46, 128, 144.

21. Lloyd-Jones, *The Justice of Zeus*, 176.

22. The description is Jean-P. Vernant's, 'Le moment historique de la tragédie en Grèce: quelques conditions sociales et psychologiques,' *Mythe et tragédie*, 15.

23. Those who have not read Dodds, *The Greeks and the Irrational* are urged to do so. See also Adkins, *Merit and Responsibility*. Dover, *Greek Popular Morality* tries to de-emphasize the importance of shame as opposed to guilt, but see the sensible

remarks of John Gould in his review of Dover in *CR* 92 (1978) 285–7.

24. John H. Finley, Jr. has amply demonstrated this in 'Euripides and Thucydides,' *HSCP* 49 (1938) 23–68, and 'The Origins of Thucydides' Style,' *HSCP* 50 (1939) 35–84. I urge the skeptical reader to refer to these two articles which contain a wealth of detail.

25. The use of literature in examining moral values is admittedly an extremely difficult undertaking. Further difficulties have been suggested by Kenneth J. Dover in 'The Portrayal of Moral Evaluation in Greek Poetry,' *JHS* 103 (1983) 35–48. Some of his distinctions and qualifications are quite important. Without discussing his exposition in detail, I would simply say that I have tried to keep the use of my examples free from the problems he points out.

26. This claim or even, rather, social pattern is one of the most clearly attested in our public documents from the time. The legal consequences are discussed below in Chapter 3. The situation is concisely described and fully documented by John K. Davies in the first pages of his Introduction to *Athenian Propertied Families*: 600–300 BC (Oxford University Press, Oxford, 1971) xvii-xviii.

27. This was recognized in literature from *Od*. 2.276 through Eur. *Heracl*. 342–8. In Athens, Pericles' sons were an example which occurred to Plato if not to Socrates and Protagoras: Pl. *Prt*. 319e-320a, *Meno* 93a-94.

28. Eur. *Bellerophon* fr. 298N², *Diktys* fr.333N²; Soph. *Phil*. 874–6, 904–5, 1310–13, etc.

29. Douglas M. MacDowell, '*Arete* and Generosity,' *Mnemosyne* NS 16 (1963) 127–34.

30. There is a clear discussion in Arthur W.H. Adkins, 'Basic Greek Values in Euripides' *Hecuba* and *Hercules Furens*,' *CQ* 16 (1966) 219.

31. Eur. *Melanippe Desmotis* fr. 502N², *Phaethon* 158–9, *Erectheus* 53A; cf. Eur. *Rhes*. 168.

32. Eur. *H.F*. 731, Eur. fr. 460N², *H.F*. 282, 290 ff.; Soph. *O.C*. 900.

33. Soph. *Aj*. 479–80; Eur. *Heracl*. 200, 500, *Hec*. 371.

34. James Diggle in the new Oxford text sensibly prints Canter's *palin* in line 557. Theseus certainly knows civic concerns — hence the manuscripts' *polin*. But the advice of this passage centers more on the individual.

35. See, for example, J.H. Kells' edition of *Electra* (Cambridge University Press, Cambridge, 1973) 6. He finds this 'unprincipled statement' an expression of 'unscrupulousness' and 'baseness'. Milder misgivings are expressed by William Sale in his *Electra* (Prentice-Hall Inc., Englewood Cliffs, 1973) 12–13.

36. Soph. *Trach*. 1148; Eur. *Med*. 1029, 1347, *H.F*. 339.

37. The relation of Thucydides' antithetical style to his intellectual concerns is well described by Paul Shorey, 'On the Implicit Ethics and Psychology of Thucydides,' *TAPA* 24 (1893) 74, 83.

38. See Soph. *Trach*. 596; Eur. *Hipp*. 329, 419, *Supp*. 301, 324, 561, etc.

39. Soph. *Ant*. 924; Eur. *Hel*. 272. See Eur. *Med*. 218 and Page's other examples cited there; Soph. *O.T*. 512; Eur. *I.T*. 676, *Ion* 600, *Hec*. 327, etc.

40. *El*. 982, *Or*. 738. See Bond's note at *H.F*. 1348 for a discussion of these and other passages.

41. Perhaps the only one of more frequent occurrence is the use of the forms of *apallage* and *apallassomai* in the fourth and fifth feet of the line. This formula is used to voice the pervasive longing to be free of the burdens and ills which plague almost every tragic character.

42. For *haliskomai* see Soph. *Ant*. 46, *Aj*. 1267, *O.T*. 576; Eur. *I.T*. 1419, *Andr*. 191. Cf. Eur. *Med*. 84; Soph. *O.T*. 289; Ar. *Ach*. 659; and Eur. *Hipp*. 419, 426, 925, and 959. Compare also fr. 835.3 from Eur. *Phrixos*, often quoted in antiquity.

43. Soph. *O.T*. 634; Eur. *Erechtheus* 50A, 51A, *Supp*. 301, *Phoen*. 531, 993. This conflict or tension had been articulated as early as Solon 4W.

44. Arnold W. Gomme in Gomme *et al.*, *A Historical Commentary on Thucydides*, vol. 2 (Oxford University Press, Oxford, 1956) 112 (hereafter cited as *HCT* preceded by author responsible for cited volume or section).

45. So de Romilly, *La loi dans la pensée grecque*, p. 23 robs the later statements of much of their significance, whereas William K.C. Guthrie, *A History of Greek Philosophy*, vol. 3 (Cambridge University Press, Cambridge, 1969) 68–70 imports into the earlier texts meaning which does not belong.

46. The new developments of the fourth century are treated separately below in Chapter 5. Martin Ostwald in *Nomos and the Beginnings of the Athenian Democracy* (Oxford University Press, Oxford, 1969) has made an interesting case for the establishment of *nomos* in the sense 'statute/a law' in the late sixth or early fifth century BC. I would not question his assertion that the citizens are generally committed to the city's laws as binding. In this section I am more concerned to distinguish between laws/statutes and the more abstract ideal of law/legality.

47. Romilly, *La loi dans la pensée grecque*, 18.

48. Ibid.

49. Sir Henry Maine, *Ancient Law* (Dutton, New York, 1972), 74.

50. See Gomme, *HCT*, vol. 2, 110; Romilly, *La loi dans la pensée grecque*, 20ff.; Arthur W.H. Adkins, *Moral Values and Political Behavior in Ancient Greece : From Homer to the End of the Fifth Century* (W.W. Norton and Co., New York, 1972), 104, 112; Guthrie, *History of Greek Philosophy*, 69–70.

51. Yet another passage, Eur. *Phoen.* 535ff., is sometimes cited in this context, e.g., by F.A. Paley *Euripides* on Eur. *Supp.* p. 397 422; E.R. Dodds on Pl. *Grg.* 483c5, in *Gorgias: A Revised Text with Introduction and Commentary* (Oxford University Press., Oxford, 1959), 266. The discussion below on page 81 shows that this passage in context is little concerned with law and democracy.

52. Again see Guthrie, *History of Greek Philosophy*, 69–70; Adkins, *Moral Values*, 104–5; Gomme, *HCT*, vol. 2, 110 (on Thuc. 2.37.1) all of whom link this passage with Eur. *Supp.* 403ff. and or Hdt. 7. 104.

53. Gomme, *HCT*, vol. 2, 193–4 notices a certain tension between 2.37 and 2.65; but he indicates that 2.65 simply conflicts with Eur. *Supp.* 404. He does not consider the earlier lines in *Supp.* discussed above which show that it, as well as Thucydides, contains this 'double' description. Helen F. North, *From Myth to Icon : Reflections of Greek Ethical Doctrine in Literature and Art* (Cornell University Press, Ithaca, 1979), 152 in her discussion on *axioma* connects Thuc. 2.65.9 with the herald's speech in Eur. *Supp.* 423–5 as did Finley, 'Euripides and Thucydides,' 42–3. This additional similarity in the passages seems more interesting than it turns out to be. The concern with *axioma* is different, and the herald's claim can hardly be taken for Euripides' opinion.

54. Attacks on tyranny do not seem relevant. Thus Eur. *Supp.* 404 cited by W. Robert Connor, *The New Politicians of Fifth-century Athens* (Princeton University Press, Princeton, 1971), 116 is especially out of place. Nor does Ar. *Vesp.* 464–70 seem appropriate to Pericles. The only certain fifth-century attack on Pericles is the anonymous fr.60 (Edmonds) which comes from Plut. *Per.* 16.1.39 to end.

55. Anon. life of Thuc. Historian, Section 6; Plut. *Cim.* 14. *Per.* 10, *Ath.Pol.* 27.1; Stesimbrotus *FGrH* 107 F 5.

56. For Pheidias, Aspasia and Anaxagoras see Plut. *Per.* 31–2; Anaxagoras — Diog. Laert. 2.12; Aspasia — Diod. Sic. 12.39; Ath. 13.589e; Damon (ostracized) — Plut. *Per.* 4.1, *Nicias* 6.1, *Ath.* Pol. 27.4 (Damonides).

57. *Ath.Pol.* 27.3–4; Arist. *Poe.* 1274c8; Pl. *Grg.* 515e; Plut. *Per.* 9.2–3.

58. For its date soon after Ephialtes' death see Charles Hignett, *A History of the Athenian Constitution to the End of the Fifth Century BC* (Oxford University Press, Oxford, 1952) 342–3 (App. IX).

59. *Diog. Laert.* 9.51; Arist. *Rh.* 1402a23 = DK 80 A 1,20.

60. The authorship and date of these *Tetralogies* have come under rather heavy attack from time to time. Most recently see R. Sealey, 'The *Tetralogies* Ascribed to Antiphon', *TAPA* 114 (1984) 71–85. I remain convinced of their authenticity and so have used them, but they are in no way crucial for any of the claims of this study.

61. This is expressed by Arnold H.M. Jones in *Athenian Democracy* (Basil Blackwell, Oxford, 1957), 45: 'The Athenians were not . . . either in theory or in practice absolute egalitarians, but drew a distinction between different political functions. On one point they admitted no compromise — equality before the law . . .' Here, naturally, Jones cites Thuc. 2.37.1. But in setting Plato, his oligarchic bias and the oligarchic revolutions against the democracy, he underestimates the oligarchic, aristocractic and competitive features of the democracy itself and of its laws.

62. See Arthur W.H. Adkins's excellent discussion in '*Arete, Techne,* Democracy and Sophists: *Protagoras* 316b–328d', *JHS* 93 (1973) 3–12, especially pp. 9 and 12. This same tension is also well analyzed by James Redfield, 'Plato and the Art of Politics' (Ph.D. dissertation, University of Chicago, 1961), 51, 86.

63. Adkins, '*Arete, Techne*', 12.

64. Pseudo-Xenophon *Ath. Pol.* 3.6; Ar. *Av.* 39–41. Later see Xen. *Mem.* 3.5.16.

65. See Gomme, *HCT*, Vol. 2, 111–12 (on Thuc. 2.37.3). Aesch. *Eum.* 517–23, 690–3; Soph. *Aj.* 1073–6.

66. Antony Andrewes, 'Eunomia', *CQ* 32 (1938) 91.

67. See *Theogony* 901–3 for the original genealogy of these concepts. It may well not be Hesiod (see West *ad loc.*), but early imitations suggest a well-known text: see Bacch. 15.55, Pind. *Ol.* 13.6–8.

68. For example, Robert J. Bonner, *Aspects of Athenian Democracy* (University of California Press, Berkeley, 1933) 26.

2 The Courts

1. Introduction

Law, Montesqieu claimed, is so closely connected with national religion and government that none of the three can change independently. If this were true of Greece, we should expect to learn much about law by examining the very large amount of information we have about Greek religion and mythology. And, in fact, no less a scholar than Nilsson asserted that 'no such unity as we find in Greece between state and religion has ever existed elsewhere.'[1] Certainly the Greek household cult and ritual were based on and exclusively maintained by the family; and Gustave Glotz needed a large book to describe the importance of the family — and therefore, by implication, of religion — in Greek criminal law.[2] Yet others have described Greek society quite differently, emphasizing either that laws were secular and recognized by the Greeks themselves as human convention or, similarly, that the Athenians neither explained justice in terms of piety nor regarded it as piety.[3] At its most extreme, this view of Athenian law as ultimately secular removes even homicide law from the sphere of religion.[4]

Why does Athenian law admit of such divergent descriptions? Is it merely because, just as with the Romans and all other peoples, law and religion were not originally differentiated and remained mixed in many spheres?[5] Or were laws and morals even more extensively and persistently entangled in Athens than in Rome?[6] No. These are merely restatements of Montesqieu's claim that law and religion are related.

These conflicting conceptions of Athenian law are possible because although in fifth-century Athens some laws were still closely related to religion, other large discrete areas of both legal procedure and substantive law were dramatically more secular. This isolation of much of Athenian legal life from the religion and mythology which otherwise pervaded the society had resulted from recent political and economic developments, and it accounts for much of the peculiar nature and function of law in that society. In order to demonstrate this, the discussion below begins with the claims which have been made for the religious origin of Athenian

31

law and the general place of law in the city which such analyses posit. Criticism of this position brings out the isolated position of homicide law and the homicide courts. This in turn leads to an examination of the newer popular courts and their contrasting secular nature. Finally, the chapter closes with a reconsideration of the ways law and religion were related in the city.

2. The Religious Origin of Athenian Law

The most ambitious claims for the religious derivations and character of Athenian law are still to be found in one of the doctoral theses of Louis Gernet, a student of the Durkheim School.[7] Beginning from the idea that the history of words can reveal the history of social change and development, Gernet examined the growth of concepts such as crime, individuality and responsibility by focusing on words used for wrong-doing and penalty. He posited three important periods of usage: the first coincides with the time of the total social unification of the family; the second, intermediate stage came as the family and family beliefs were breaking up; and the final period began when the city had established itself as the new significant group. In Gernet's analysis the city takes over or inherits the feelings and ways of thought with which the family originally responded to offenses against its members. Thus it protects the citizens in a spirit of self-defense, maintaining an intense religious sense of outrage at an attack against its well-being. The originality of Gernet's seemingly countless insights stemmed from what he called the sociological viewpoint, an assumption of relations and connections between a culture's intellectual products and its forms of social structure and organization.[8] However his work shares the almost exclusive preoccupation with values of the group and clan which characterized and weakened Durkheim's work on the sociology of religion and development of penal law.[9] It is the repeated failure sufficiently to consider the individual which most often produced distortions in Gernet's description of the development of Athenian law and legal thought.

Gernet's examination of the words used for wrong-doing and crime such as *hybris* (self-indulgent or outrageous behavior), *kakegoria* (slander), and *hamartema* (fault) begins with discussions of their use in relation to the family.[10] Since the family or clan was united by the ancestral cult with sacred obligation to relatives both dead and living, crimes against its members from either within or without were invested with a religious significance. Then, Gernet argues, as family solidarity and function steadily dissolved in the face of the rapidly developing city-state, the city simply replaced the family, and the feelings of solidarity and sacredness passed from the smaller to the new and much larger group. As he says, 'De fait, la cité, en succédant à la famille, se conçoit elle-même comme une vaste famille.'[11] Therefore crime in the city has religious significance just as it did in the family. This is the basis for his treatment not only of homicide but also of private suits in general. He analyzes the development of the legal apparatus and various procedures as a response to a sense of crime against the group or community.

The problems that arise in moving analogously between the city and the individual in the search for justice in Plato's *Republic* are notorious. Gernet's move is no less precarious. The family is sufficiently small that a crime against one of its members or against its property whether from within or without clearly constitutes a crime against the family unit; but this is only partially true at the level of the city, for it is so much larger that the possibilities for types of wrong-doing are greatly increased. An assault on the city from outside — usually war — is a crime of religious significance, for it threatens the city's gods; and a crime against the city from the inside — treason — was treated severely indeed. In fact, as Gernet correctly points out, treason in Athens was treated like the most serious forms of impiety, since the penalty for both was death and confiscation of property.[12]

But crime within the city was not necessarily crime against the city. In fact, an enormous part of legal activity in Athens centered on private suits. It is no good to say, as Gernet does, that such suits were based on a feeling of crime against the group or city rather than the individual. For example, the city's finances involved considerable sums of money and were quite separate from the property and finances of individual citizens. In the case of theft from or indebtedness to the state, the procedures, penalties, and manner of executing judgement were entirely different from those involving theft or debt between private citizens. Private debtors were liable to seizure of property by the citizen to whom the debt was owed; but a public debtor, that is, one whose crime was against the city, suffered disenfranchisement which even in its mild form could be a severe liability.[13]

Gernet's emphasis on community and collective interest leads not only to the neglect of large areas of law and legal activity but also to distorted explanations of specific laws. In considering *hybris* and the formal legal action against it, Gernet underemphasizes the parallel private suits for assault, slander and violence which were apparently almost always used instead.[14] He stresses the sense of public outrage argued by Demosthenes in his speech against Meidias (Dem. 21.45–6). But this is an obviously biased attempt by Demosthenes to gain the sympathy of the audience; and he is merely using one of the two most common antitheses in both forensic and deliberative oratory — (harm both) private/individual and public/common. Moreover, Gernet passes over Aristotle's explanation of *hybris* which singles out the damage to individual pride and honor through self-display and personal exaltation (*Rh.* 1374a13–15, 1378b23–25).[15] Yet it is Aristotle's description which fits better with all we know of traditional Greek values and concerns. Similarly, Gernet ascribes the great seriousness attached to theft from an individual in a public place to community solidarity, but the more probable motivation, as with *hybris*, is the acute shame and embarrassment suffered by the individual in front of his peers.[16] Finally, it should be noted that Gernet's description of the city as a family with collective concern to protect itself does not account for the prevalence in Athens both of public and private arbitration — attempts to handle legal disputes between individuals with as little civic or citizen involvement as possible.

The other major work on family, religion, and law in Greece preceded and influenced Gernet's thesis. This is Gustave Glotz's *La Solidarité de la famille dans le droit criminel en Grèce*. Although Glotz was deeply concerned with family solidarity and the sacred obligations and religious values bound up with it, he was not a Durkheimian.[17] He too saw the family dissolving and its power being taken over by the developing city-state. But in Glotz's analysis the family in fact gives way to the individual, for the city's laws, especially in democratic Athens, fostered individual responsibility at the expense of family solidarity.[18] The extensions of group responsibility that Glotz did envision were much more limited than those claimed by Gernet. A passage from *Works and Days* cited in Glotz's chapter on neighbors shows what one would expect — that in fact although communal solidarity was hoped for in Hesiod's society, it was not taken for granted.[19] And when Glotz outlines group solidarity at the city level, unlike Gernet he limits himself to effects involving conflict between cities.[20]

Moreover, Glotz is less concerned to demonstrate the spread of group responsibility than to detail the limitations imposed on family solidarity. His systematic discussion of sixth-century Athenian legal developments carefully isolates the one exceptional area in which family, religion and law remain tightly bound together: murder and the related homicide laws.[21] In fact, much of Glotz's book is devoted to this topic, for vengeance against the murderer is the greatest act of family solidarity, a religious obligation, and the murderer is religiously polluted.[22]

It is the exceptional nature of homicide law in Athens — its continued direct relation to family solidarity and religion in contrast to the rest of Athenian law — which created the second major problem for Gernet's treatment; for rather than separating homicide, Gernet takes it as the typical case in private law and the general model for legal procedure.[23] This ignores the explicit fifth-century emphasis on the fact that homicide suits and their procedures greatly differed in all ways from other legal actions (Antiphon 5.88, 6.6). His vision of the religious solidarity of the city and its importance in law is kept alive by his continual emphasis on homicide.[24] Gernet made his choice quite consciously: murder is tied to religion and religious sentiments are collective sentiments.[25] This, he believed, was the area in which to find the development of moral and legal thought rather than in historical, political or economic events and influences.[26] Thus, Gernet adopted a circularity by which he cut himself off from the extensive legal developments of Athens having little to do with religious moral concepts. Yet he and Glotz point the way to understanding the extent and nature of the ties between law and religion in Athens.

3. Homicide Law and Homicide Courts

The Athenians themselves singled out their chief homicide court, the Areopagus, both in speech and in deed. Not only did they praise it as the best court in Athens or even in Greece, but the most varied and radical governments in Athens refrained from depriving it of its power to treat homicide cases, even when they disbanded all the other courts.[27] Now Attic reverence usually had its practical side, and in this case the Areopagus and other homicide courts benefited the community by diminishing the threat of pollution arising from murder.

It has recently been suggested that pollution may have had no importance in Athenian homicide law and that secular grounds may be found for all its provisions.[28] However, there are additional religious concerns involved in Athenian provisions for murder, such as vengeance (Dem. 37.59) and the public declaration against the murderer, which was patterned after the curse at the tomb (Dem. 47.68–73).[29] And in any case, there can be no doubt about the concern with pollution in the fifth and fourth centuries. The evidence ranges from poetry to the fact that homicide trials were held in the open air so that no one would have to share a roof with the accused.[30] Even earlier, in Solon's amnesty law, the exclusion of those condemned by the Areopagus on charges of homicide was almost certainly an attempt to avoid pollution.[31] The Athenian amnesties during the Persian Wars and at the restoration of the democracy in 403 also refused to include those who had been found guilty of homicide.[32]

Maine was correct, then, in singling out the religious nature of the laws administered by the Areopagus.[33] But it is neither this nor the importance of the offense to the family or even both combined which make the greatest contrast with the rest of Athenian law.[34] For example, although maltreatment of parents involved tradition, religion, and family in a law suit, it was not tried by the court of the Areopagus. The treatment of homicide held a special place in Athens not merely because the offense had religious significance but because the courts which handled it were themselves a part of the religion and mythology of the culture.

The author of the Aristotelian *Constitution of Athens* thought it worth noticing that the homicide courts were held at sacred sites with sanctuaries which, as a rule, gave the courts their names. The Areopagus was exceptionally weighted with religious tradition: it not only was sacred to Ares but had an altar for Athena Areia and a sanctuary of the Eumenides as well (Paus. 1.28.5, *CIA* 2.333). Cases of unintentional homicide were tried at the Palladium, a temple for Pallas Athena which served for the worship of Athena and Zeus.[35] The sanctuary of the Delphinion with its temple for the worship of Apollo and Artemis of Delphi provided the site for hearing cases in which the defendant claimed the homicide was lawful.[36] Finally, cases in which the 'killer' was either not human or simply unknown took place at the religious center and sacred hearth of the city itself, the Prytaneion.[37] In keeping with their sacred sites and religious names, the homicide courts had a firm place in Greek mythology; and although the writers of modern handbooks on Athenian law have chosen not to emphasize this, Demosthenes did (23.65–6). As he says, he chose merely two of the many legends about the Areopagus. The latter, the story of the trial of Orestes accused by the Furies (as told in Aeschylus' *Oresteia*), gives the court an origin quite ancient and august, but other accounts made the founding of the Areopagus even older and more exclusively divine. In Demosthenes' other legend, the court's first defendant was Ares in the trial for the murder of Poseidon's son Halirrothius, who was unfortunately caught violating Ares' daughter.[38] Presumably some of the legends omitted by Demosthenes are about the trials of Cephalus for the murder of Procris and of Daedalus for the murder of Talos or Kalos.[39] These legends had a local immediacy for Athenians which others lacked: on the short walk from the theater where Aeschylus first staged the trial of Orestes to the Areopagus itself, a citizen would pass both the fountain where Halirrothius made his fatal attempt and the graves of Talos and his mother.[40]

Similarly, legend linked the very founding of the sanctuary of Pallas with the incident which gave rise to a court for involuntary homicide — the mistaken slaughter of the Argives returning from Troy. Pausanias knew several versions of the story, and there were other variations current at least as early as the fourth century BC (1.28.8).[41] Again, Theseus' justified slaying of the Pallantidai furnished the occasion for his visit to Delphi, after which he supposedly founded the Delphinion.[42] Whatever the ultimate origin of the title 'Delphinion,' to the Athenians it inevitably suggested the cleansing aspects of Apollo and the importance of Delphi in purifying the killer.[43] Theophrastus recorded the Athenian tradition that homicide trials for inanimate objects began with the first ox sacrifice to Zeus Polieus in the time of Erechtheus (Ael. *VH* 8.3; Paus. 1.28.10). And finally, even the obscure, unlocated court of the Phreatto can claim Teucer or Telamon as a founding defendant according to Pausanias.[44] Thus name and legend tied the homicide courts of fifth-century Athens to the gods and heroes and therefore to the religion and history of the city.

What archaeological evidence there is reinforces this picture. The preliminary hearings for homicide trials will have been heard by the archon basileus and his assistants in his 'office', the Stoa Basileios.[45] The earliest history of this building at the north-west corner of the agora is lost, but at least by the middle of the sixth century, a simple but apparently lovely Doric structure occupied the spot. Probably within a decade or two of the Persian sack of the area the stoa was rebuilt incorporating much of the archaic material. The structure, with its precise ashlar masonry, was well maintained: soon after the middle of the fifth century the roof was repaired with decorated terra-cotta tiles, and elaborate terra-cotta acroteria were added. Indeed, the stoa seems to have been lovingly protected and periodically repaired well into the Christian era.

After preliminary proceedings here, the vast majority of those cases which did not go to the Areopagus were assigned to the court at either the Delphinion or the Palladion. These were both in what is now called the Ilissos area, a section of Athens south-east of the acropolis. In the fifth century this was thought of as the site of the city's earliest history in the time of Theseus and even before, as opposed to the agora area north of the acropolis which began to be more developed around the time of the Peisistratids (Thuc. 2.15). Although neither of these courts has been conclusively identified, excavation has produced excellent candidates for both. The temple of Apollo Delphinios and the associated court were said to have been near the Olympieum, and the two buildings just south of the temple of Olympian Zeus containing potsherds with the first letters of Apollo's name are now generally thought to be this temple and court. The construction of the classical temple wiped out any evidence of its predecessor, but the older court building is archaic, its solid polygonal walls probably dating to around 500BC.[46] Ancient sources also put the Palladion and legendary events associated with it in this section of the city. This important sanctuary, which included temples of Zeus and Athena as well as a lawcourt, is now placed with a fair amount of confidence at a site just east of the Delphinion ruins.[47] The older building which dated from the late sixth or early fifth century was later replaced by an impressive stoa; but the earlier building would seem to have been venerable at least by virtue of tradition — remains at the site indicate that there had been some structure there since at least the seventh and perhaps even eighth century. Thus the archaeological evidence tallies with the literary testimony about the homicide courts — they were a long-established and solidly marked part of the city's past. As we shall see, all these elements set them distinctly apart from the rest of the city's courts and laws.

4. The Popular Courts and Their Secular Nature

By the fifth century in Athens only scattered and often obscure elements of religion can be found in the laws not dealing with homicide. Feet and footwear, for example, seem to have had some ritual significance in the assumption of property, as the legends of Theseus, Jason and Orestes coming into their inheritance all indicate. Athenian legal terminology for inheritance and taking possession of property (*embateusis, embateuein*) faintly reflects this ritual concern.[48] The religious element is more obvious in several of Solon's legal reforms such as those dealing with funerals and inheritance; yet these laws with their provisions for dowries, wills and debts had motivations and consequences that were much more political and economic than religious. If anything, these measures somewhat threatened religion in the family and family cult, since in many ways the laws encouraged the break-up of large estates.[49] In fact, it was the secular, human nature of Solon's laws which impressed the Athenians in the fifth century. No one would question the ancient, unwritten laws of piety whose author was not even known (Lys. 6.10), but Solon's statutes were the imperfect work of a fellow citizen. Both in the fifth and fourth centuries practical criticisms were made which aimed at removing the ambiguities in Solon's laws; reformers merely differed as to whether the lack of clarity in the laws was due to the intent or the incompetence of their human author.[50]

Other Athenian laws also came from men whose names were known: Drakon and Solon were the distant ones; the rest were much more recent. Often Athens is likened to other cities which also traced their legal codes to specific lawgivers.[51] But the similarity is much less important than the contrast, if we consider the role of religious authority in the two cases. It was never suggested that Solon or even Drakon sought or accepted the advice or blessing of gods or oracles in their legislative work. Yet the legends of other cities regularly claim such sources for the choice of lawgivers and the origin or approval of their codes. Most of the divine influence came through Pythian Apollo and his Delphic servants. Such was the undisputed tradition of the Locrians.[52] Similarly, Herodotus tells us that when the people of Cyrene sent to Delphi for a constitution, they were assigned a legislator (4.161). And although opinions differed at Sparta, the story of Lycurgus' dependence on Delphi was asserted early and ultimately prevailed.[53] Other gods lent help as well: Athena followed up Apollo's appointment of Zaleucus as Locrian legislator by sending him the law code in a dream (ΣPind. *Ol.* 10.17). And the brothers Minos and Rhadamanthys were said to have been so fortunate as to have Zeus as a close helper in establishing legislation (Pl. *Leg.* 624ff., 632d); Homer himself was authority for the close, perhaps even regular association of Minos and Zeus (*Od.* 19.178–80). Yet our traditions for Athens, by far the fullest, provide not even the hint of a parallel. And this is all the more striking since the account of Solon's legislative activity seems to have certain stock elements common to the tales of these other early lawgivers.[54]

This secularity is also indicated by the fact that, in contrast to the homicide courts, none of the other Athenian courts had names of ritual or legendary significance.[55] Some of the names must be lost, for these courts were never as famous as the homicide courts (Paus. 1.28.8). Even now modern handbooks of Athenian law sometimes omit the names we still know. Yet because of their thoroughly secular nature, the names of the popular courts reveal as much about law in the fifth century as those of the homicide courts or more. The *Trigonon* (Triangular) and *Meizon* (Greater) apparently took their names from their shape and size. Others bore some mark of their location in the city, although no source tells us either what the *Meson* was in the middle of or where the *Parabyston* was inserted except that it may have been in an out-of-the-way place perhaps near the walls (Paus. 1.28.2, Ar. *Vesp.* 1108ff.).[56] There was a New Court (*Kainon*), of which we know little more than that it was far from alone in its newness; for in the matter of abrupt foundation we can connect three of the other courts with leading figures of the mid-fifth century. The Archon heard cases relating to grain and perhaps guardianship at the *Odeion*. This court, built by Pericles, was sufficiently complete by 443 BC to enable Cratinus to make a joke at Pericles' expense (*Thraittai* fr. 71K).[57] And two of Pericles' friends gave their names to the courts they built during his reign — the *Metiocheion* of Metiochus and the *Kallion* of Kallias. Such is the list we can make from the final cavalier clippings of what was probably an already wounded and ragged treatise by Telephus on the Athenian courts.[58] But even these scraps indicate how quickly these institutions arose, much like that Infernal Court built in an hour for a host even more quarrelsome than the litigious Athenians, as if to the musical strains from Pericles' *Odeion* itself.

Just as the archaeological evidence reinforced the picture of the homicide courts conveyed in the literary sources, so the evidence from excavations in Athens confirms this situation in which many new popular courts were hastily constructed. In the north-east corner of the agora are the ruins of a number of buildings which, because of both the concentration of lawcourt equipment found in them and because of the details of their composition, are sure to have been various courts. The buildings seem to date from the late fifth and early fourth century. No name can be assigned to the oldest; but it is bounded on either side by two others, the shapes of which may provide clues to their identity. The triangular one seems likely to have been the *Trigonon*. And one jammed against the center court is attractively — if hesitantly — identified as the *Parabyston*. Besides the evidence of its shape there are two roof tiles with inscriptions which might have designated them for this court: each have what might be parts of letters of the label *to Parabysto*. Whatever their names, all of these courts 'were put together out of second-hand material, and all, so far as one can judge from their remains, were of shoddy construction.'[59] Later in the fourth century a more ambitious replacement structure was begun on the same site and apparently used into the second century BC even though it was never finished.

This large colonnaded building may have housed one or both of two additional courts in Pausanias' list: the *Batrachioun* (Frog-green) and the *Phoinikioun* (Red), which had kept their names to his time (1.28.8). At the writing of the Aristotelian *Athenian Constitution* the courts were designated by colors which figured in assigning jurors to them (*Ath. Pol.* 65.1–2). A painted lintel or rafter marked the entrance. This associated various courts, and thereby laws, with different colors, an oddly literal realization and perhaps even the source of Plato's metaphor of dyes and laws (*Resp.* 429 ff.). Jacoby may be correct in dating the color courts from the fourth rather than the fifth century, but for the purpose of my argument either alternative will serve.[60] It may be that these color names, like the ones used for the new non-homicide courts, were assigned in the fifth century for secular architectural rather than religious reasons.[61] Otherwise, they must, in the fourth century, have replaced such names as we have described — those of recent architects, size and shape — because the names they displaced were not of sufficient traditional and legendary significance to be maintained. In any case, these scattered bits of information seem to confirm the general differences between the homicide courts and the popular courts. The history of the court buildings, their location in and around Athens and the attitude towards them, apparently reflected in the nature and quality of the architecture, all point to the sharp contrast of the old and the new, venerated history or foundation mythology as opposed to new business procedures to accommodate problems and institutions stemming from recent civic growth.

Diverse factors helped create this great civic need for the new courts Pericles and his friends were building and naming. After Ephialtes had relieved the Areopagus of a great deal of its jurisdiction, he (or someone soon after his death in 461) eased the burden on the single popular court, the *Heliaia*, by dividing it into several courts or *dikasteria*.[62] More important than this redistribution of power, however, was the fact that both the city of Athens and its empire were growing rapidly. Even if the number of cases transferred to Athens from its allied cities has sometimes been exaggerated, it was nevertheless at least a significant new factor, and meanwhile the growing population and economic activity in Athens and the Piraieus amply increased local litigation.[63] This apparently led to the reinstitution of deme judges in 453/2; but it seems that even these thirty traveling officials eventually proved insufficient to handle the growth of legal activity.[64] Thus the 440s saw the creation of a series of new civic courts.

The addition of more popular courts was followed by other innovations which likewise contributed to the secular, civic character of Athenian law. Pericles instituted payment for the jurors, and, soon after his death, Cleon probably had it increased.[65] Other cities may have consulted oracles for legal codes; Athens took a different approach to legislation. When Pericles appointed a man in 443 to write a code for the new colony of Thurii, he chose not a priest but Protagoras, the sophist with whom he and Socrates discussed the laws and for whom all things took their measure from man. And then there were new laws for Athens itself in this period as well. If it was Alcibiades' opponent the demagogue Androcles who asserted that the laws needed a law to correct them, his call for legislation will have been made before his assassination in 411 BC.[66] This may also be the period in which the comic poet Plato joked that an Athenian who had been away from his city for three months would not be able to recognize it because of the changes in the laws (fr. 220). In any case, there were certainly major legal reforms such as Pericles' new citizenship law of 451/0, and it would be surprising if there were not many smaller ones as well.[67] Thus, although fifth-century Athens inherited some of its laws from men of the past, other laws, the city's legal apparatus, the courts, their buildings and the pay for the jurors who filled them were conceived, legislated and built by the politicians and citizens who walked its streets.

In some ways, Pericles and his predecessors in governmental reform put more distance between Athens and its past than there was between the mother city and its colonies. The massive presence of the democratic courts went far to dissolve what remained of the close correspondence which had once existed between the city's social structure and the government and organization of the gods in traditional mythology. In the *Iliad* the world of men is closely and repeatedly reflected in the world of the gods, and even upheaval and change had their place in the history of the divine community.[68] But whereas in Athens aristocracy and then democracy pushed the kings of men further and further into the past, heaven retained its final monarch, Zeus, and even the mythological hints at his replacement intimated no constitutional changes.[69]

Of course, the development of democracy did not isolate Athens from its gods. A political mythology included genealogies which linked the city's families to legendary heroes and ultimately to divine ancestors.[70] Even some institutions of community government stayed remarkably the same in their new setting: the men and gods of the *Iliad* had Agamemnon and Zeus, but they also had meetings where action was discussed and debated. Though a Thersites or a Hephaistos might occasionally speak and provide laughter for the assembly or relieve tension, the meetings were mainly opportunities for the noble and fair to put forth their various proposals and seek support for them. Thus the agora provided great continuity, and by the fifth century, the greatest single change was that Alcibiades and Nicias made their speeches before the citizens in prose.[71]

Against the background of these continuities, however, the strangeness of the judicial procedures stands out even more vividly. The gods simply had no popular courts for resolving their disagreements and conflict, for such courts, though a significant part of society, were too new to have any place in traditional mythology. Gernet tried to bring the gods into court indirectly by taking the words used to describe offenses for suits in the popular courts and tracing their use in association with the gods.[72] He then claimed that their basic or original tone was a religious one which also applied when they were used to describe human conflicts. But this semantic methodology is far too general. Since the Homeric society of the gods more or less duplicates that of man, the same vocabulary, with a few notable exceptions, describes the behavior of both groups. The Homeric poems and later literature not only provide but usually feature conflicts with characters in all combinations of immortality and mortality and with outcomes ranging from silent sulking to the most varied violence. An insulted man or god might choose either to pout or attack. Neither response was particularly religious or secular. The one alternative which does distinguish men and gods is recourse to courts, and the men who resorted to them were engaged in one of the very few activities entirely confined to mortals. Among the gods, the alternative to responding with violence or force for offenses such as adultery and theft was personal and familial negotiation rather than the standard court procedure an Athenian would use. So Hephaistos comes to agreement with Ares and Poseidon when his wife is unfaithful (*Od.* 8.325–59), and Zeus settles the dispute between Apollo and Hermes over stolen cattle even though it is discussed in the presence of other gods (*Hymn.Hom.Merc.* 327ff.).

The significance of this absence of court procedure in heaven is perhaps more evident when stated a little differently: the Athenian popular courts had no legendary connections with the gods. Gernet himself noted that there was a minimum of mythical imagery and elements in Athenian judicial punishment and the contemporary discussions of it.[73] Euripides drew attention to this great divorce between heaven and earth by ridiculing even the possibility of a divine legal bureaucracy and system of records for offenses and penalties (fr. 506N^2). The *thesmothetai*, archons who presided in court, and their secretaries and scribes had no immortal counterparts. Hesiod's Thrice Countless Legal Guardians were never admitted to Athens where, as Thirty Thousand, they would conveniently have equally the traditional number of male citizens, the men who made up all juries.[74] Since at Athens only the homicide courts could claim mythological foundations, one might expect that any exception to the Olympians' lack of formal judicial apparatus would come in the area of murder. In fact, only one legend gives the gods a court with voting stones. With these they tried Hermes for the murder of Argos. And even this story will date to the fifth century only if its ascription to Xanthus is legitimate.[75]

Even though the popular courts had no historical mythology or parallels among the gods, it is often claimed that they had a general connection with Apollo and Delphi. This would have significant consequences for the sacred character of the law, especially on the view that Apollo is the god of the highest social, civic and intellectual life, and that he is crucial in the development of political morality and civic organization.[76] However, the scholars of Greek religion who assert Apollo's authority in Athenian civil law conveniently provide the refuting evidence as well. Nilsson immediately follows his claims of Apollo's general involvement in legislative activity with the admission that even though we know most about legal matters in Athens, the connection with Delphi seems 'less prominent' there.[77] What he lists as 'very real signs' of involvement are not at all related to Athenian popular courts: Apollo's ties to homicide law, courts and purification; the festival calendar; and the interpreters of religious law.[78] In the same way Farnell combines claims of Apollo's legal significance with admissions of the absence of specific connections in Athenian laws and courts.[79] However, he adds the much stronger assertion that in Athens Apollo became 'the god of the law courts and the government.'[80] First, Farnell makes him god of the law courts because the jurors took their oath in his name. But Apollo did not stand in the oath as a god of truth and justice nor did he stand alone. He appears in a standard list along with Zeus and Demeter.[81] Since any serious business or promise among the Athenians required one or more oaths, the inclusion of Apollo here has no particular juristic significance.[82] Second, Farnell names Apollo the god of government because it is Apollo 'to whom the archons dedicated votive offerings commemorative of their office.'[83] He would seem to have had in mind Plato's Phaedrus, who mentions the archons and the dedication of golden statues of 'equal measure' at Delphi (*Phaedrus* 235d). Indeed this passage provided Plutarch or whoever was responsible for the text of *Solon* 25 with material which was combined with a section from *Athenaion Politeia* (7.1) on the archon's oath. But it is not at all clear that Phaedrus, especially in the matter of equal measure, was referring in detail to the specifics of bureaucratic procedure, and in any case we learn from a later passage in *Athenaion Politeia* (55.5) that any offerings were 'commemorative' of offices archons would rather have forgotten; for what the magistrates swore was to donate such a statue if convicted of taking bribes while in office. No source mentions Apollo as the recipient of the votive statue, and neither the writer of the *Athenaion Politeia* not Heraclides nor Pollux saw fit to mention Delphi; the *Suda* disperses the gold more generally through Greece; and, in the end, neither Delphi nor Apollo seems to have appeared in the original oath at all.[84] But even if either of them had, Apollo's function as recipient of penance from convicted bribe takers would hardly establish him as the god of Athenian government.

If Apollo had any relationship to the lawcourts, it had to do with their ambiguous, unpredictable power either to save or to destroy. By chance, his name provided a pun for both alternatives, as Phrynichus, the writer of comedies, must have seen when he wrote the line describing the two voting urns: one to acquit, and the other to convict:

> idou, dechou ten psephon; ho kadiskos de soi
> ho men *apolyon* houtos, ho d' *apollys* hodi. (fr. 32 Kock)

In fact, these voting urns were the one element of the popular courts which did have rich connections with mythology. Even within their own setting, they were vivid symbols of the judicial procedure. The discs which the jurors dropped into them determined the outcome of the dispute with virtually no chance of appeal. In the *Wasps*, Philocleon is duped into placing his vote into the urn for acquittal; in the *Agamemnon*, hope vainly approaches the urn which would acquit Troy and save it from destruction. This appearance of the urns in Aristophanes is literal and comic (*Vesp.* 987); in Aeschylus metaphoric and lyrical (*Ag.* 816ff.). But they were always the end, temporarily unknown but soon to be fixed, toward which the whole process moved.[85]

The images in earlier literature which bear resemblance to these urns were equally powerful and well-known and may well have added greater depth to their symbolic significance. In the *Iliad* Zeus dispenses good and ill to men from two jars. The gods, it is emphasized, have a life without cares; the contents of the jars affect men only and are given apparently without regard to individual acts or merit (*Il.* 24.527ff.). Although Hesiod's myth is entirely different, the elements are almost identical (*Op.* 83ff.). Zeus sent a jar to man which, when opened by Pandora, filled mortal life with various ills. But hope remained in the jar to comfort men.[86] Here, as in the *Iliad*, man's fate contrasts sharply with that of the gods. Each case argued in court, settled in the end by the contents of urns, represented in miniature man's peculiar condition. He could receive good or ill, but with no guarantee that it would correspond to innocence or guilt. Although judicial process distinguished man from the animals (Hes. *Op.* 279ff.), it isolated him just as surely from the gods: it was a means, a compromise; and as such, it was irrelevant to the divine world. Gods, who had no reason to count their days, very seldom troubled to count their possessions.[87]

This is the lonely position of judicial process and the laws in the culture of fifth-century Athens. If we simply call it secular, we are sure to misperceive it. Most aspects of our lives are secular; almost no aspect of Athenian life was. Their gods feasted and wove, made weapons and fashioned musical instruments; they met together in council and hunted alone; they hated and they loved; but they did not litigate.[88] Athenians went to war and to work accompanied by gods in order to fight and create like gods; but to court they went alone.

The great public courts had grown and multiplied before the eyes of the citizens of the new empire. Like some exotic species, they evolved too late to share in the rich mythical cultural code which connected every traditional aspect of Greek life through generations of shifting and developing legend. As a result, legal institutions were cut off 'vertically' from divine aetiologies, models and parallels. In turn, this severely limited the 'horizontal' associations through which law could be defined against or in relation to the rest of society. Impoverished and youthful, it borrowed what trappings it could and learned to mimic its more established relatives.

This cultural transparency of the courts and their functioning had resulted from their exaggeratedly late and rapid growth. In the case of Athens this amounted more to a lack of metholodogical autonomy in law than to a broad failure in formalism. As will be seen in the next chapter, the courts adopted many formal patterns and fixed rules both in procedure and substance, but these patterns and rules came from other areas of culture. There was no distinctive legal method or type of discourse to offer resistance to other strong forces.[89] The result was what Maine saw as the dangerous elasticity and laxness in the Athenian administration of justice.[90] It has been claimed that it was the absence of both a court of appeals and a superior power to pardon which made the juries susceptible to the great variety of arguments admitted in legal oratory.[91] But this diagnosis depends on a contrast with non-Greek institutions and misses the surer explanation which, as we have seen, lies in the character of the courts and their history.

These oddities attracted attention. Some observers, such as Protagoras, could carefully take the measure of man and then, when called on, either create laws or fashion stories about the gods' gift of judicial procedure to man, as the situation required (Pl. *Prt.* 322cff.). Others reacted less calmly. In a fragment from a fifth-century satyr play called *Sisyphus*, the speaker pointedly asserts that laws are an artificial limitation entirely of man's devising. Any claims of divine concern for justice are mere deceit for the purpose of bolstering these laws (Critias DK B25). Fortunately for the present purpose it does not matter that we lack both the context of the fragment and certainty as to its author. For it is either by Critias, in which case it harmonizes neatly with the author's demonstrated contempt for the law of Athens, or else it comes from Euripides' *Sisyphus* which was staged in 415 with *Alexander, Palamedes* and the *Trojan Women*.[92] And these plays, especially the *Palamedes*, create a heroic world in which judicial process produces vivid injustice; the conviction and death of an innocent man, brought about through intentional deception, remains unpunished by the gods.[93]

This chapter began with a search for the relationship between religion and law in Athens. The examination of the development of the popular courts has helped clarify how very limited their connections with religion were. It will now be easier to understand both the relative general importance of religion and law and why the city used this secular law to handle religious matters the way it did.

5. Law, Religion and the City

The nature of the interaction of law and religion took its shape largely from the peculiarities of the latter, since they were much more established and revered than the relatively new and characterless features of Greek law. In order to illustrate this phenomenon, it will help first to take a specific religious matter which often came up in the courts. This in turn will point to a more general consideration of why certain elements of Greek religion were the subject of frequent and sometimes grave litigation.

Athens required its wealthy citizens to undertake public services called liturgies. In the fifth and fourth centuries, they called for the appointment of around one hundred citizens each year, and they fell into two main groups, although the discussion below should make it clear that the two were very closely related.[94] First there were the processions, music, drama, athletic training and other activities and expenses involved in each year's religious festivals.[95] Time and again in extant speeches a litigant proudly emphasizes his own or tries to discount his opponent's fulfilment of these great civic and religious obligations.[96] Usually the liturgies cited had no direct connection with the action being tried, but the rituals they served were often far older than the courts where the trials were held. The festivals maintained the Athenians' ties with the gods, whereas the courts were a reminder of human limits. No wonder the liturgies commanded respect from the law.[97]

Second, in addition to these directly religious liturgies, there was the care and finance of the navy without which Athens could not have survived. The fact that this liturgy was mentioned in court as often as any other is indirectly explained by religion, since Greek beliefs made the city's welfare a matter of especially deep anxiety. Tradition led many Greeks to expect an afterlife practically without perception or pleasure. So bleak was this underworld existence that, after tasting it, Achilles, the great proud figure of the heroic world, desired to be the lowliest servant on earth rather than rule the dead (*Od.* 11.484ff.). This view of human fate had many consequences. One, it has been claimed, is 'the recurrent melancholy of all Greek literature.'[98] On an individual level, it intensified the competition and desire for immediate material success.[99] By the fifth century, man's fate was so completely dependent on that of his city, that the state acquired an importance which must have approached that of religion. There was no Christ for salvation in the hereafter. There was only the state for salvation here and now. Even though the Athenians were increasingly turning to the mystery religions, there seems to have been little confidence in a very desirable afterlife. Accordingly, reverence was fully due those who financed the fleet.

The Athenians' attitude toward their leaders further reflects the almost sacred status of the city itself.[100] A *prostates* could be either a divine or a human protector, but as Athens' existence grew increasingly precarious in the second half of the fifth century, the word was used more and more of the city's political leaders.[101] The comparison was not merely implied: a character from a play by Eupolis describes how the citizens revered the generals as gods and thereby were saved from disaster (fr. 117 Kock).[102] Tradition made the identification familiar: any student of Homer knew Agamemnon, Achilles, and other leaders had been honored as gods in their time (*Il.* 5.78, 10.33, *Od* 11.484, 14.205).

Leaders alone, however, could not save the city. Any of the gods could help or harm as they pleased. So every effort was made to carry out rituals and festivals properly, to avoid impiety and to punish any acts which might anger the gods. Three archons — the eponymous archon, the polemarch and the basileus — had responsibility for the festivals, liturgies and sacrifices. The trio neatly embodies the complex relation of religion and law in the city. The duties of each were mainly religious and judicial; but in each office the balance or connection was quite different.[103] Old Athens survived in the basileus, its king, whose judicial duties were as sacred as his ritual and festival responsibilities, for he had charge of homicide and impiety — legal matters which were thoroughly religious. The eponymous archon's legal and sacred activities were generally quite separate, but they overlapped when he presided over litigation arising in connection with disputes over liturgies. Finally, although their original close relation could be reconstructed,the two spheres of the polemarch's office had diverged completely. On the one hand he managed sacrifices and games related to war, but in court he presided over cases involving *metics* (resident aliens). Thus with duties in both areas, the archons bridged law and religion.

Measures to avoid and punish religious offenses brought the courts and the sacred into even more direct contact. Not only did the courts accept suits for offenses connected with festivals; the attempt at a festival to recover property or money, even if it was legally owed, was grounds for a court action any citizen could bring (Dem. 21.175–80). Here law subordinated itself to religion and enforced its own secondary status. The legal relationships and rights of one individual with regard to another were simply less important than the relationship of the citizenry and the city to the gods. These provisions and the importance accorded to liturgies in trials have not been sufficiently considered by those who object to the idea that in fifth-century Athens 'man's relation to the state and law overshadowed his relation to fellow individuals' or who feel that only 'immoralists and authoritarians' were sufficiently perverse and corrupt to minimize the 'importance of the relation between individual and individual.'[104] The Athenian was not bashful about his individual business, but he lived in a city which put itself and its safety first and enforced this hierarchy with law.

Although some forms of impiety, such as various ritual infractions, merely drew fines, serious offenses were equivalent to betrayal of the city.[105] Whether or not one law actually included both these civic threats, Athenians regularly mentioned treason and impiety together as the most terrible crimes.[106] The two became practically indistinguishable in the great furor over the mutilation of the herms and profanation of the Eleusinian mysteries in 415. It did not matter that Hermes himself was a trickster, liar, thief and god of the night *par excellence*, nor was it important that neither the vandalism nor the mockery had physically harmed a single Athenian. Eleusis, unconcerned with men's relations with other men, promised the possibility of a more pleasant afterlife simply in exchange for participation in ritual. Since the attractiveness of the promise was greatly stimulating devotion to the irrational ritual among the citizens of the democracy, they mobilized all the resources of the law and the courts to convict and execute as many of the offenders as possible.[107] The incident forms an excellent conclusion to the consideration of law and religion in Athenian democracy. The laws and their new courts had few connections to cultural tradition and mythology. Moreover, as we have seen, even traditional Greek views of the gods had little to offer to encourage the avoidance of human disputes or conflicts with which the courts dealt. The new popular religion was even further removed from such concerns: the hopes it held out for man did not depend on the ethical nature of his deeds or even on his success in this life. The popular courts were a new tool for men to use, and the nature and limits of their use derived from other spheres of values and cultural patterns.

Like most new tools, the judicial apparatus worked smoothly, but it had little character of its own. If it was wanted for the service of religion, no independent legal values or traditions stood in the way. The next chapter examines the various cultural patterns which were adopted by the laws and legal procedures.

Notes

1. Martin P. Nilsson, *A History of Greek Religion* (W.W. Norton and Co., New York, 1964), 242.

2. Gustave Glotz, *La Solidarité de la famille dans le droit criminel en Grèce* (Arno Press, New York, 1973).

3. The former, for example, can be found in Jacqueline de Romilly, *La Loi dans la pensée grecque des origines à Aristote* (Les Belles Lettres, Paris, 1971), 126; the latter in L. Pearson, *Popular Ethics in Ancient Greece* (Stanford University Press,

52   The Courts

Stanford, 1962), 32. He cites Pl. *Euthphr.* 12d.

4. George Thomson, *The Oresteia*, vol. 1 (Cambridge University Press, Cambridge, 1938) 8–9. He describes law as developing in response to 'the interests of property and trade,' and he cites A.S. Diamond's argument in *Primitive Law* (Longman's, Green and Co., London, 1935) 151–4, 161–9 that law is 'based on simple economic necessities.' The secular nature of homicide law has recently been asserted at more length by Michael Gagarin. See the discussion below on p. 36.

5. See H.J. Jolowicz, *Historical Introduction to the Study of Roman Law* (Cambridge University Press, Cambridge, 1954), 99.

6. Fritz Schultz, *Principles of Roman Law* (Oxford University Press, Oxford, 1936), 20.

7. Louis Gernet, 'Recherches sur le développement de la pensée juridique et morale en Grèce: Étude sémantique' (Ph.D. diss., Ernest Leroux, Paris, 1917). A very helpful outline of Gernet's connection with Durkheim giving many helpful references is S.C. Humphreys, 'The Work of Louis Gernet,' *History and Theory* 10 (1971) 172–96.

8. Gernet , 'Recherches,' xvi, 32,

9. The approach derives from the work of W. Robertson Smith. For his enormous influence on Durkheim see Steven Lukes, *Émile Durkheim: His Life and Work : A Historical and Critical Study* (Penguin, New York, 1975) 238–44. Smith's work was also used by Glotz (for whom see below pp. 34–5). This shared concern partly accounts for Gernet's acceptance of Glotz even though he was not of the Durkheim school.

10. Gernet, 'Recherches,' respectively 6–7, 84, 94, 234–5, 345.

11. Gernet, 'Recherches,' 156.

12. Gernet, 'Recherches,' 58–9. See Alick R.W. Harrison, *The Law of Athens*, vol. 2 (Oxford University Press, Oxford, 1971) 178–9 (hereafter cited as *LA* followed by volume and page).

13. Harrison, *LA*, vol. 2, 172–3, 186–7, 208ff. Douglas M. MacDowell, *The Law in Classical Athens* (Cornell University Press, Ithaca, 1978) 147–9 (hereafter cited as *LCA*).

14. Gernet, 'Recherches,' 183–97. MacDowell, *LCA*, 129–32.

15. These are both cited in MacDowell, *LCA*, 130.

16. Gernet, 'Recherches,' 191.

17. However, like Durkheim he was interested in the work of Robertson Smith. See Glotz (above, note 2) 159–61, 211, 268.

18. Glotz, *La Solidarité de la famille*, x-xi, 238–9, 404–6.

19. Glotz, *La Solidarité de la famille*, 198–208; Hes. *Op.* 340 ff.

20. Glotz, *La Solidarité de la famille*, 209–22.

21. Glotz, *La Solidarité de la famille*, 340–400, especially 370–80, 400.

22. Glotz, *La Solidarité de la famille*, 48–9, 76, 194, 227–9, 271, 284, 425.

23. Gernet, 'Recherches,' 79, 93.

24. Gernet, 'Recherches,' 108, 146–7, 156, 169–70, 362–79, 407.

25. Gernet, 'Recherches,' 301–2.

26. Gernet, 'Recherches,' (above, note 7) 426–9.

27. Lys. 3.2; Aeschin. 1.92; Lycurg. *Leoc.* 12. See Xen. *Mem.* 3.5.20; Dem. 23.66. Some have thought that the Thirty disbanded the homicide court. There is no reason to think that they did and good reason to think they did not. Besides the present discussion and the testimony of Demosthenes see *Ath.Pol.* 35.2 which shows, as one would have guessed, that the Thirty, far from dismantling the Areopagus, were adding to its prestige. See also Sir John Edwin Sandys, *Aristotle's Constitution of Athens* (Macmillan, London, 1912), 152 (on *Ath.Pol.* 39.5) and Robert J. Bonner's excellent 'Note on Aristotle *Constitution of Athens* xxxix.5,' *CP* 19 (1924) 175–6.

28. Michael Gagarin, *Drakon and Early Athenian Homicide Law* (Yale University Press, New Haven, 1981) 164–7. But pollution as a factor cannot be argued away. The evidence for concern with pollution in Athens is collected and, one hopes, finally presented in irrefutable fashion by Robert Parker in *Miasma: Pollution and Purification in Early Greek Religion* (Oxford University Press, Oxford, 1983) 104–130.

29. Douglas MacDowell, *Athenian Homicide Law in the Age of the Orators* (Manchester University Press, Manchester, 1963) 141–8. Louis Gernet, 'Droit et prédroit en Grèce ancienne,' *Anthropologie de la Grèce antique* (François Maspero, Paris, 1968) 227–9.

30. Soph. *O.T.* 236–42; Antiphon 5.11, 3.1.10; Pl. *Leg.* 871. See MacDowell *LCA*, 119; MacDowell, *Athenian Homicide Law*, 145–7; and P.J. Rhodes, *A Commentary on the Arisitotelian 'Athenaion Politeia'* (Oxford University Press, Oxford, 1981) 641, 648 (on *Ath.Pol.* 57.3, 59.4). (This work hereafter cited as *CAAP.*)

31. This is argued by Robert J. Bonner and Gertrude Smith, *The Administration of Justice from Homer to Aristotle*, vol. 1 (University of Chicago Press, Chicago, 1930), 54 (hereafter cited as *B and Sm* followed by volume and page). Gagarin, *Drakon and Homicide Law*, does not mention this evidence or the argument from it for legal concern with pollution.

32. For the amnesty of Solon, see Plut. *Sol.* 19. It is also discussed in *B and Sm*, vol. 2, 104–5 and by C. Hignett, *A History of the Athenian Constitution to the End of the Fifth Century BC.* (Oxford University Press, Oxford, 1952) 311–13, who, despite his usual skepticism, accepts it. For the later amnesty laws see Andoc. 1.77–9, and *Ath.Pol.* 39.5.

33. Sir Henry Maine, *Ancient Law* (Dutton, New York, 1972), 218.

34. The debate still continues as to whether or not relatives could prosecute for homicide. See Mogens H. Hansen, 'The Prosecution of Homicide in Athens: A Reply,' *GRBS* 22 (1981) 11–13. The uncertainty originates in classical Athens itself, as MacDowell's careful discussion of Dem. 43.47 and *IG* i²115.20–3 makes clear (*Athenian Homicide Law*, 13–18). In any case, the concern and activity centered almost entirely around the relatives.

35. For the trials see *Ath.Pol.* 57.3; Paus. 1.28.8. For the sanctuary *IG* i²324 lines 78–95, *IG* i²1096, 3177, 5035. These inscriptions are cited by MacDowell, *Athenian Homicide Law*, 58.

36. *Ath.Pol.* 57.3; Dem. 23.74; Paus. 1.28.10; Poll. 8.119.

37. Dem. 23.76 and scholiast; Poll. 8.120; Paus. 1.28.10. See *Ath.Pol.* 57.4. The most complete and up-to-date collection of references for the Prytaneion and its religious significance is now found in Rhodes, *CAAP*, p. 105 (on *Ath.Pol.* 3.5). In this account I omit the Phreatto. Not only are its name and location in doubt, but Aristotle indicates it met seldom, perhaps even never to his knowledge (*Pol.* 1300b28 ff.). See MacDowell, *Athenian Homicide Law*, 82–4.

38. For the first trial of Ares see also Eur. *El.* 1258ff., *I.T.* 943ff., *Or.* 1648–52; Apollod. *Bibl.* 3.14.2; Paus. 1.21.4, 1.28.5.

39. Σ Eur. *Or.* 1648, originally from Hellenikos. See Jan Bremmer, 'The Importance of the Maternal Uncle and Grandfather in Archaic and Classical Greece and Early Byzantium,' *ZPE* 50 (1983), 178. For more on the importance of the mother's brother see Chapter 3 p. 86.

40. Paus. 1.21.4; Lucian *Piscator* 42; Apollod. *Bibl.* 3.15.9; Diod. 4.76; the *Suda* and Photius *s.v. Perdikos hieron.*

41. The Atthidographers Clidemus and Phanodemus each had a different account. See Harp. *s.v. Bouleuseos* and *epi Palladioi*; the *Suda s.v. epi Palladioi*; Poll. 8.118 ff.

42. Paus. 1.19.1, 1.22.2, 1.28.10; Poll. 8.119. This legend is the basis of Eur. *Hipp.*

35ff. See the scholiast there, which = Philochorus *FGrH* 328 F 108.

43. For speculation about the origins of the title see Lewis R. Farnell, *The Cults of the Greek States*, vol. 4 (Oxford University Press, Oxford, 1907) 145–7. For cleansing see Louis Gernet and André Boulanger, *Le Génie grec dans la religion* (La Renaissance du Livre, Paris, 1932) 176.

44. For the Phreatto, which tried exiles on additional homicide charges see note 37 above. See also Paus. 1.28.11, 2.29.10.

45. For the excavation and interpretation of this stoa see T. Leslie Shear, 'The Athenian Agora: Excavations of 1970,' *Hesperia* 40 (1971) 243–55 and 'The Athenian Agora: Excavations of 1973–1974,' *Hesperia* 44 (1975) 365–70, and Homer A. Thompson and Richard E. Wycherly, *The Athenian Agora*, volume 14 of *The Agora of Athens : The History, Shapes and Uses of an Ancient City Center* (The American School of Classical Studies at Athens, Princeton, 1972) 83–9; Homer A. Thompson, 'Athens Faces Adversity,' *Hesperia* 50 (1981) 346. There are archaeological rumblings about the dating of this stoa, but even the latest proposed foundation will make it early in comparison with the popular court buildings. Similar disagreements attend the identification of the Delphinion and Palladion discussed immediately below. Fortunately, the argument for the established respectability of the homicide courts will not be affected negatively if these are not (the) archaic buildings. Literary testimony firmly places these courts in the sacred precincts. The necessary contrast this entails with the popular courts is made clear in the following section.

46. See Rhodes, *CAAP*, p. 644 and John Travlos, *Pictorial Dictionary of Ancient Athens* (New York and Washington 1971) 83 with illustrations 84–90 and 291–3.

47. See John Travlos, 'The Lawcourt ΕΠΙ ΠΑΛΛΑΔΙΩΙ,' *Hesperia* 43 (1974) 500–11; Rhodes, *CAAP*, p. 643.

48. Gernet, 'Droit et prédroit,' 223–6; Pind. *Pyth.* 4.70ff., Aesch. *Choe.* 172ff., Soph. *El.* 909ff.; Plut. *Thes.* 3.5, 12.2–3.

49. The relation to religion is noted by Gernet and Boulanger, *Le Génie grec*, p. 159. The limits and other consequences by Glotz, *La Solidarité de la famille*, 340–400 *passim*, especially 340–3, 348. See *B and Sm* vol. 2, 168–9.

50. *Ath.Pol.* 9.2, 35.2. See Rhodes, *CAAP*, p. 162.

51. There is a very helpful collection of these traditions in the chapter, 'The Lawgivers,' *B and Sm* vol. 1, 67–82.

52. For Locri see Σ Pind. *Ol.* 10.17 which = Arist. *Lokron Politeia*.

53. Tyrtaeus fr. 4 West; Isyllos lines 74–6 in J.U. Powell (ed.), *Collectanea Alexandrina* (Oxford, 1925) 134. For more on Lycurgus see Chapter 5, p. 140.

54. See Andrew Szegedy-Maszak, 'Legends of the Greek Lawgivers,' *GRBS* 19 (1978) 199–209. In light of these facts Athenian law is carefully to be distinguished from that of other cities and exempted from the claims of den Boer who states that 'law rested in the base formed by religion and was sanctified by it' 'Aspects of Religion in Classical Greece,' *HSCP* 77 (1973) 19; his evidence is exclusively from cities other than Athens.

55. The most complete recent discussion is F. Jacoby's on Androtion of Athens *FGrH* 324 F 59 (IIIb Supp.i, pp. 164–7; ii pp. 146–53). But Douglas M. MacDowell on Ar. *Vesp.* pp. 120, 389, and 1108 is also useful and has even more recent bibliography: Aristophanes, *Wasps*, edited by Douglas M. MacDowell (Oxford University Press, Oxford, 1971).

56. A possible location is suggested below.

57. See plates 237 and 258 in Marguerete Bieber, *The History of the Greek and Roman Theater* (Princeton University Press, Princeton, 1961) 58, 67.

58. Telephus of Pergamon *FGrH* 505 (F. Jacoby IIIb pp. 482–3). Franz V. Fritzsche, *De sortitione judicum apud Athenienses: Commentatio* (August Lehnhold, Leipzig, 1835) 34–40, and Alan L. Boegehold, 'Philokleon's Court,' *Hesperia* 36

(1967) 111–20, have closely examined the evidence for a court near a shrine of an Athenian hero named Lykos. Boegehold makes it quite clear how little to be trusted are the late references about which Fritzsche was overly optimistic. The court near the statue may have been one of those discussed above or one we know nothing else about. In any case, there is no evidence of anything sacred about the court itself.

59. Thompson and Wycherly, *The Agora of Athens*, p. 59. For this group of buildings, see this volume pp. 52–60. For the *Parabyston* see Homer A. Thompson, 'A Lawcourt at the Northeast Corner of the Agora,' in 'Excavations in the Athenian Agora: 1953,' *Hesperia* 23 (1954) 58–61.

60. F. Jacoby *FGrH* IIIb Supp. ii pages 146–7.

61. LSJ claims, entirely without authority, that the Phoinikioun was named for the color of its walls, but is less daring in the case of the Batrachioun. In fact, the only evidence is that of *Ath.Pol.* 65.2 for the lintel or rafter.

62. Hignett, *History of the Athenian Constitution*, 216–17. *B and Sm* vol. 1, 195ff. M.H. Hansen has recently debated this point with P.J. Rhodes. Hansen's argument is that several dikasteries of sworn jurors date from the time of Solon: *Eisangelia* (Odense University Press, Odense, 1975) and '*Demos, Ecclesia,* and *Dikasterion* in Classical Athens,' *GRBS* 19 (1978) 127–46. His case rests on Arist. *Pol.* 1274a and *Ath.Pol.* 7.3. Rhodes's arguments appear in *The Athenian Boule* (Oxford University Press, Oxford, 1972) 169 note 5, 197–200, '*EISANGELIA* in Athens,' *JHS* 99 (1979) 103–6, and *CAAP*, 160, 318 (on *Ath.Pol.* 9.1, 25.2). The last is particularly rich in citations of related sources and discussions. Hansen's main supporting evidence for earlier dating is Hdt. 6.104.2 and *Ath.Pol.* 25.2 on the trials of Miltiades and the reforms of Ephialtes. Macan is rightly quite hesitant about Hdt. 6.104 (also 6.136), and the state of government even at the time Ephialtes began his reforms has little significance for the time of Solon. As Hansen admits, evidence of any sort between Solon and Pericles is scarce. Each person must decide for himself; but the arguments of Hignett, Rhodes and others who favor late dates for plural *dikasteries* seem more persuasive in themselves. I, of course, believe the picture I present strongly supports the late date.

63. On litigation connected with the empire much has been said from the fifth century through the present. See Thuc. 1.77.1 and Pseudo-Xenophon *Ath.Pol.* 1.14–18. There is much information in Arnold W. Gomme in Gomme *et al.*, *A Historical Commentary on Thucydides* (Oxford University Press, Oxford, 1956), vol. 1, 236–44 (on Thuc. 1.77.1: hereafter cited as *HCT* preceded by author responsible for volume or section) and a clear discussion by G.E.M. de Sainte Croix, 'Notes in Jurisdiction in the Athenian Empire,' *CQ* 11 (1961) 94–112, 268–80. For local growth see Hignett, *History of the Athenian Constitution*, 218–19, F. Jacoby *FGrH* IIIb Supp. i p. 167.

64. For the deme judges see *Ath.Pol.* 16.5, 26.3, 53.1.

65. Hignett, skeptical as ever, has made the case for the earliest institution of pay; but even he does not take the measure out of Pericles' hands: *History of the Athenian Constitution*, App. IX, 342–3. For Cleon see Σ Ar. *Vesp.* 88.

66. Arist. *Rh* 1440a9. The name is common, however; it could be a different Androcles than the one noted by Thuc. 8.65.2.

67. *Ath.Pol.* 26.2 and Rhodes, *CAAP, ad loc.*

68. Hes. *Theog. passim*; Aesch. *Ag.* 168ff.; [Aesch.] *Prometheus Vinctus* 956 ff.

69. See Martin P. Nilsson, *Greek Piety* (W.W. Norton and Co., New York, 1964) 2–3 for divine monarchy versus Athenian democracy. The hints at Zeus' overthrow are found at Pind. *Isthm.* 8.31ff.; [Aesch.] *Prometheus Vinctus* 908ff., 956 ff.

70. Nilsson, *History of Greek Religion*, 236–7.

71. Democracy did not mean that beauty, wealth and good family were no longer advantages to the public speaker, as even Plato's Socrates affirms *Prt.* 319c.

72. Gernet, 'Recherches,' Part II, passim.

73. Ibid. 157–8.

74. Hes. *Op*. 249ff. For thirty thousand citizens see Hdt. 5.97.2, Ar. *Eccl*. 1132, Pl. *Symp*. 175c.

75. The story can be found as Xanthus fr. 9 *FHG* (Müller) 1.38. It is taken from *Etym. Magn. s.v. hermaion*. For the problem of ascription to Xanthus see Ath. 12.515d.

76. See especially Farnell, *Cults of Greek States*, 98, 113, 152–3, 183.

77. Nilsson, *History of Greek Religion*, 190.

78. Ibid. 190ff.

79. The claims are in Farnell, *Cults of Greek States*, 98, 113, 152–3, 183. The admissions Farnell, *Cults of Greek States*, 118, 198–9, 217.

80. Ibid., 154.

81. In our fullest text of the oath, Dem. 24. 149–51, Poseidon has taken Apollo's place. But Apollo should almost certainly be restored as in Poll. 8.122, Ar. *Eq*. 941, Dem. 52.9. Many oaths used this set trio.

82. For a general discussion see *B and Sm* Chapter 7, especially 145.

83. Farnell, *Cults of Greek States*, 154, 157.

84. See the *Suda s.v. chryse eikon*. See especially Sandys *Aristotle's Constitution*, 25 (on *Ath.Pol*. 7.1) and Rhodes, *CAAP*, p. 620–1 (on *Ath.Pol*. 55.5).

85. Some details in the procedure for using the urns changed from the fifth to the fourth centuries. See Harrison, *LA*, vol. 2, 164–6. In the fifth the juror had only one *psephos* which he dropped into the urn for acquittal or the one for conviction. In the fourth century, the juror had two bronze discs, a solid one for acquittal, a perforated one for conviction. These are illustrated in Sandys' frontispiece (*Aristotle's Constitution*). A juror dropped the one he wanted to count into a bronze urn, the other into a wooden one. See Aesch. *Ag*. 816 and E. Fraenkel *ad loc*. and the commentaries on *Ath.Pol*. 68.2ff. I find this wooden urn quite mysterious, although no one else comments on it. The author of *Ath.Pol*. calls it a wooden amphora (68.3). A wooden urn or amphora would have been quite impractical, and I can find no trace of a reference to another one in classical Greece. (The large wooden jars or barrels smeared with pitch to store wine are quite different and much later. Strabo 5.1.12.) LSJ claims that a third-century inscription from Delphi refers to a wooden voting urn or box (*SIG* 418 A 7). The inscription is difficult; but I cannot make sense of *kiboton* if it is for voting. It seems rather a treasure chest or coffer as in Ar. *Eq*. 1000, *Vesp*. 1056. If, then, this wooden urn in the courts was so unusual, it must have been especially significant; but I cannot account for the symbolism.

86. See Martin L. West on *Op*. 96 in *Works and Days* (Oxford University Press, Oxford, 1978). It is a different, vain hope which approaches the voting urn at Aesch. *Ag*. 816ff. But in both, hope is the antidote in the face of possible ills.

87. Pl. *Resp*. 359ff.; Arist. *Eth.Nic*. 1137a26ff. There were exceptions such as Apollo's cattle in *Hymn. Hom. Merc*. But these instances are quite rare and atypical.

88. Nor, properly, did they legislate or enforce the laws. Such references as there are to these activities are collected by Kenneth J. Dover in *Greek Popular Morality in the Time of Plato and Aristotle* (University of California Press, Berkeley and Los Angeles, 1974) 255–61. However, the references to divine legislation apply to cities other than Athens or to homicide law. As for divine enforcement, it is important to consider Dover's passages in combination with the various motives of the gods and considerations of the types of activity which draw their intervention. See Chapter 1.

89. See Roberto M. Unger's excellent analysis of the elements of law in *Law in Modern Society : Toward a Criticism of Social Theory* (The Free Press, New York, 1976) 52–3, 195–205.

90. Maine, *Ancient Law*, 44–5. These remarks come in a remarkable analytic passage in which Maine rightly noted their connection with rapid development of law.

91. Robert J. Bonner, *Aspects of Athenian Democracy* (University of California

Press, Berkeley, 1933) 45–6.

92. See Ruth Scodel, *The Trojan Trilogy of Euripides* (Vandenhoeck and Ruprecht, Göttingen, 1980) 124ff.

93. See especially Scodel, *Trojan Trilogy*, 43–4, 60–1.

94. The evidence is all conveniently collected, evaluated, and tabulated by John K. Davies, 'Demosthenes on Liturgies: A Note,' *JHS* 87 (1967) 33–40.

95. In the mid-fourth century, Demosthenes tried to limit the class of liturgies which were strictly religious. But the argument he makes is extraordinarily convoluted and difficult in many ways. When he closes his speech by asserting his certainty that all is clear to the jurors, one feels the opposite must be the case. See Dem. 20 especially 125ff. In his edition, *The Speech of Demosthenes against the Law of Leptines* (Cambridge University Press, Cambridge, 1890) ii–xi, John Sandys makes some helpful and entertaining observations on the liturgies.

96. For more on the significance of this practice, including bibliography and references to examples, see the discussion in Chapter 3, p. 62.

97. For the importance of the religious side of the liturgies as part of the political strategy of an individual see John K. Davies's review of W. Robert Connor's *The New Politicians of Fifth-century Athens* in *Gnomon* 47 (1975) 377.

98. William B. Stanford, *The Odyssey of Homer* (Macmillan, London, 1965) 398 (on *Od.* 11.488–91).

99. See Chapter 1.

100. The citizen's duties to Athens were sworn in explicitly religious language in the ephebic oath. See Tod *GHI*² 204 which is related to Lycurg. *Leoc.* 76, Stob. 43.48, Poll. 8.105–6. See Gernet, 'Recherches,' p. 58 who did not have the benefit of the Acharnae inscription found in 1932.

101. Soph. *Trach.* 209. W. Robert Connor, *The New Politicians of Fifth-century Athens* (Princeton University Press, Princeton, 1971) 112–13.

102. Cited by Connor, *New Politicians*, 159.

103. See Rhodes, *CAAP*, p. 612 on *Ath.Pol.* 55–9.

104. These passages are from Pearson's defense of the individual against the voice of the state: *Popular Ethics*, 33.

105. Jean Rudhardt, 'La définition du délit d'impiété d'après la législation attique,' *Museum Helveticum* 17 (1960) 87–105. Glotz's simple statement that treason and impiety were treated in the same way is impecise: *La Solidarité de la famille*, 453–4. Discussions of impiety are complicated by the fact that the action *graphe asebeias* was not used for many acts of impiety which could be prosecuted under various other actions. As in other areas of Athenian law, there is uncertainty about the relationship between the general designation and more specific descriptions of offenses and what terms constituted formal indictments. But the general outlines, as usual, are satisfactorily clear.

106. Xen. *Hell.* 1.7.22 suggests one law for sacrilege and treason, but Antiphon 5.10, while equating the two, seems to indicate separate laws. See also Lycurg. *Leoc.* 147, Ar. *Thesm.* 327.

107. On the growth of these beliefs see Gernet and Boulanger, *Le Génie grec*, especially 134–6. Dover gives a very helpful list of those charged in the affair of the herms and the mysteries in *HCT* vol. 4, 277–82 (excursus on Thuc. 6.27.9).

3 The Administration of Justice

The true problem is not to study how human life submits to
rules — it simply does not; the real problem is how the rules
become adapted to life.

B. Malinowski[1]

1. Introduction

As we have seen, Greek religion provided little or no basis for the
Athenian democratic legal order. Moreover, this religion
encouraged traditional, intensely competitive aristocratic ideals. In
such an atmosphere, 'an ideal of formal equality, and together with
it a commitment to generality and autonomy in law' were slow to
develop.[2] Instead, since the rules and the courts which enforced
them largely lacked historically independent forms, they reflected
the society around them all the more. The peculiar outcome was a
legal apparatus finding models in traditions and institutions which
were themselves indifferent or even antagonistic to cooperative
ideals and the fair administration of justice. It may seem odd, then,
to claim that the law court was 'the model institution of the
Athenian democracy.'[3] But having taken form late and relatively
quickly, the courts were in many ways a pure distillation of the city's
values. Greek mythology, literature, and ritual all have the richness
of an oil painting gradually built in successive layers in which the
elements, repeatedly shifted and varied, finally attain a complex,
subtle and almost mobile relationship. The Athenian legal system
represents the same culture, but it is a fast sketch in clean clear lines.

Greek culture and social organization were replete with figures of
competition and combat. In general, this was as true of the form of
poetic figures of speech as of athletic and military struggle. More
specifically, considerations of quantity often dominated in contests
where we would expect qualitative judgement to have a greater
effect on the outcome; and there is a related obsession with dividing
the matter at hand in any situation into balanced, symmetrical
oppositions. By the time the Athenians turned to the courts and
began to develop their procedures, they possessed a rich stock of
institutions and images of rivalry already mimetic of each other and

easily brought into a new and natural fighting arena.

This chapter first examines Athenian law generally as a contest and then focuses on the elements of quantity and symmetry. Each of these sections begins with a description of these phenomena in Greek tradition and culture and then turns to their manifestations in the laws and legal procedure of fifth- and fourth-century Athens. Finally, there is a consideration of the various ways that the place of women in Athenian society and the attitudes of that society toward them are reflected in the law and legal materials.

2. The Contest

'Pour les Grecs de l'époque classique, la guerre est naturelle.'[4] The frequent wars of classical Greece are ample evidence for Vernant's stark statement. The violent struggles between the city-states had more peaceful counterparts in the great panhellenic games which brought together the same men from the same cities for safer competition.[5] The combative spirit, a regular part of daily life in Athens, inspired both the words of the assembly debates and the deeds of athletic training.[6]

The earliest monuments of Greek literature provided models of word and deed for training the minds and bodies of Athens' youth. The *Iliad* contains not only mêlées but also great duels between the outstanding warriors. It even has its own games with hotly disputed outcomes in which athletics and adjudication become inextricably interwoven.[7] The poem also presents debates and disputes in assembly. These activities were sufficiently attractive to draw a warning from Hesiod, who urged the expense of time and energy in more productive competitions, peaceful and professional rivalries between neighbor farmers and fellow craftsmen in the city (*Op.* 20ff.). The advice did not fall on deaf ears, as the products of Athenian artists amply testify. The painter Euthymides even found his own words for this Hesiodic attitude and left the confident cry of triumph over his rival on a vase — 'as never Euphronius' (*hos oudepote Euphronios*).[8] Young aspirants to Athenian generalship would know Archilochos' critical comparison of captains, even if their standards differed (fr. 114 West). Meanwhile, they faced each other in daily wrestling, an activity which provided a metaphorical vocabulary for war and rhetoric. For a Greek trained at the palaistra, the image of a whole country brought to its knees was both vivid and natural (Aesch. *Pers.* 929ff.). One army could weigh down another's limbs as they grappled in the dust (Aesch. *Ag.* 63ff.).[9] But a skillful speaker, using the clever turns and twists, could wriggle out of the most difficult position.[10] Defeat was well avoided, for even a mighty god could enter oblivion through the metaphor of a loss in wrestling (Aesch. *Ag.* 167–75).[11]

Nor was the importance of athletic competition at all confined to metaphor. The greatest athletes won at the greatest games and were immortalized in song by the greatest poets who used syntactic devices mastered at school along with wrestling. Clauses were carefully balanced with the words *men* and *de* and related phrases which created a quiet rhetorical competition within the sentence. And the supreme frame for excellence was a figure of speech now called priamel which selected and crowned the best of the best with a series of superlatives.[12] But competition was relentless at every level in the Greek world; if Pindar used the priamel for the athlete, Xenophanes could just as easily turn it against him (fr. 2W).[13] One could never be certain of supreme victory in the estimation of another. There was no possible end for the competition which was — as this brief survey has tried to convey — embedded early in the culture and in education, and which spread to all areas of human activity.

Moreover, competitive opposition and conflict did not even cease with the world of man but rather extended upwards through a sort of cultural priamel to the world of the gods. Their battles were sometimes quite literal, as in the *Iliad*. In other instances, their competition, as, for example, that of Aphrodite and Artemis for Hippolytus, reflected a more abstract opposition of attributes and concerns, the contrasting categories of the culture which worshipped them. At a final philosophical remove the whole cosmos was conceived by Empedocles as the product of a great struggle between *neikos* and *philia*; and even in this highest conflict one of the striving elements was strife itself.

When we turn to the courts, the military and athletic aspects of confrontation emerge clearly. The two litigants competed before a large audience of jurors just as Menelaos and Paris or Ajax and Hector did when dueling before the Greeks and Trojans. The terminology of the courts came from man's most basic struggles. The verbs of prosecution and defense, *diokein* and *pheugein*, were those used to describe pursuit and flight in the hunt and in war.[14] The two activities fused in Achilles' deadly chase after Hector before the walls of Troy. Every Athenian boy would learn the lines of the *Iliad* which described the two fighters now as dog and deer, now as men, in the frantic but seemingly frozen flight and pursuit of an anxious dream:

> hos d'en oneiroi ou dynatai pheugonta diokein
> out' ar' ho ton dynatai hypopheugein outh' ho diokein.
> (*Il*. 22. 199–200)

As an athletic counterpart to the military, the boxing of Epeius and Euryalus and the wrestling of Ajax and Odysseus at Patroclus' funeral games were more controlled.

The Athenians themselves described their court battles as wrestling and boxing matches. Aeschines warns against old wrestling tricks of the courtroom and compares the struggle there to boxing contests (3.205–6). The metaphor came easily since the same words for 'contest' (*agon*) and 'contend' (*agonizesthai*) were commonly used for war, athletics and litigation. And just as the twists and turns of the limber wrestler could describe the clever rhetorician or sophist, so Plato applied them to the artful and confident lifelong litigant.[15] Finally, to finish off an opponent in debate is to give him the third fall just as in wrestling (*hosper palaisma*, Pl. *Euthydemus* 277d). Triple failure had even more serious consequences in the courtroom: a third conviction for proposing an unconstitutional law (*graphe paranomon*) or for perjury (*dike pseudomartyrion*) added disenfranchisement (*atimia*) to the penalty for the crime itself.[16]

But the Greek fighting spirit came out most vividly in the Olympic contest which followed wrestling and boxing.[17] Xenophanes understandably called the pancratium a terrible contest (fr. 2.5): the rules for this event, which combined wrestling, boxing and kicking, permitted strangling, kicking in the stomach, jumping on or hitting a fallen opponent and twisting the joints. Only gouging and biting were disallowed; and the sixth- and fifth-century vases show that the athletes often disregarded even those restrictions.[18] Athenian values and attitudes towards rivals made it natural, as Aeschylus noted, to kick a man once he had fallen (*Ag*. 884–5). Certainly legal assaults on political figures were frequently planned and launched at times when the defendants were already in difficulty.[19] In the following passages from Plato, the descriptions of skill at the pancratium and in court virtually fuse the two activities into one.

Before I did not know what true pancratists were. For these two [Euthydemus and Dionysodorus] are absolutely ready for any battle. They're not like the two Acarnanian brothers who are pancratists, for those two are only able to fight with their bodies. These two are first of all most formidable physically; they are quite skilled at fighting in arms and can teach anyone who pays. Second, when it comes to the battle in the courts, they are most strong both at contending and at teaching others to speak and to compose court speeches. They were already incredible, but now they have put the finish on their pancratistic skill. The only remaining type of combat they had not touched they have now worked out completely so that no one can oppose them.So skilled are they at fighting in speech and refuting any assertion that it makes no difference whether it is false or true. (*Euthydemus* 271c–272b)

Such was the Athenian perception of the legal struggle.

If a witness to be used in the contest managed to escape, the trial had nevertheless to proceed (Dem. 49). But the failure to appear and testify was so much felt to resemble flight from battle that the legal term was modeled directly on the set of words for military desertion. From words such as *lipostratia* (desertion from the army), *lipotaxia* (desertion), and *liponeos* (deserting the fleet), there came *lipomartyrion* (non-appearance as a witness).[20] And as one might expect, in Athens such behavior provided grounds for further litigation.[21]

For awarding a final decision, the athletic games of the *Iliad* again provide a very important model. We have already mentioned that the verdict in the popular courts could be influenced by many considerations, especially the liturgies and achievements of the defendant and even of his ancestors.[22] There was no need to be delicate and indirect about the matter. A speaker could simply state to the jurors that he had spent large sums on the city 'so that I would be thought better by you, and if anything should happen to me, I might have a better case in court' (Lys. 25.13). Disappointed critics claim that justice failed, formalism was lacking and equity was promiscuous. Others see here the origin of a higher justice, the dynamic judicial corrective which culminates in Aristotle's definition of equity.[23] But this aspect of Athenian legal behavior is neither injustice nor superior justice. It is a deep Greek tendency which simply allows the competition to be removed to a higher and more general level.

The negative version of this phenomenon begins very early in Greek literature when Odysseus refuses to consider the substance of Thersites' assertions and complaints. It is not that they are incorrect or unwarranted: Thersites' low social status simply disqualifies him from effective speech (*Il.* 2.248ff.). He was apparently expected to remain quiet and merely cast his vote when it was called for. Solon seems to express much the same attitude towards the lower classes.[24] Likewise (but conversely), the education of an Athenian gave him good reason to expect that even if he had done what he was charged with in court, he could ask to be acquitted or to win the case on the basis of past excellence in achievement and service. Eumelus finished last in the chariot race at Patroclus' games. But since he was in fact the best charioteer, he won a prize all the same (*Il.* 23.289, 532ff.). By the same reasoning, Agamemnon takes the prize in javelin without even having to throw the spear. A specific instance or trial would not count against the fact that he *is* the best javelin thrower (*Il.* 23. 884ff.). Even in a culture obsessed with results and success in competition, the most immediate victory or failure might not be the most relevant.

It is seldom recognized how regularly Greek law operated along these lines, which were completely conventional in the society.[25] Although we may not think it ideal, we can easily imagine that the ugliness of a Thersites was a hindrance to success in the Homeric assembly. Much more astonishing is the fact that in the fifth century, forcing a defendant to undergo bodily harm could cause his friends to desert him and to testify falsely for the opposition. Even if Euxitheus' friends had other motives or were loyal in the end, his description of this disadvantage had at least to be plausible (Antiphon 5.18). Similarly, it is not possible to know whether Isocrates deserved on purely financial grounds to lose the case of *antidosis* or liturgy exchange in which he was defeated. In point of law, the decision rested exclusively on the relative wealth of the two opponents in court. But Isocrates' successful challenger apparently based his case more broadly on Isocrates' teaching profession and its effects on society; and Isocrates certainly felt that those arguments had found a receptive audience (Isoc. 15.4ff.). Again, when Simon saw that an old enemy was suffering defeat in litigation, he found confidence to prosecute for a totally unrelated incident from four years in the past (Lys. 3.20).[26] Having lost once, a man was more liable to be defeated again in Athenian society even if he was innocent or on equal ground with his opponent in the new matter.[27] The priamel worked in court just as in poetry and the palaistra. Facts were not necessarily denied, but a litigant or competitor might claim a victory at one level only to lose in the final consideration to a more important, if technically irrelevant, superlative.

Even conviction of the defendant did not end the duel in most cases. Most suits, both public and private, were *timetoi*, which meant that the penalty was not set by law, but varied from case to case.[28] Like to combatants or athletes casting their spears in turn, the prosecutor and defendant continued for another round each proposing a penalty, and the jurors voted again to choose the 'winner' at this stage of the process. In important public cases, this part of the process could take one-third of the day's trial.[29]

In order to see clearly how the courts facilitated individual competition, it is necessary to consider how the various divisions or groups in Athenian society were relevant to the operation of the judicial system. By far the most significant distinction in Athens, directly articulated and reinforced by the courts, was that between citizen and non-citizen.[30] Only citizens could own land, vote, hold office, bring all types of cases to court and serve as jurors. This 'allowed even the poorest Athenian citizen to be conscious that he was a member of an elite, a minority of the total number of adult males who lived within the boundaries of Attica.'[31] The traditional aristocratic emphasis on excellence and the desire to achieve as high a status as possible did not diminish under democracy. As a result, the litigants and jurors in Athenian courts generally shared a unifying pride in their status and rank above other men. In short, Athenian law both defined and exclusively served a group so privileged that the courts had little chance of becoming an arena for 'class' conflict.[32]

It is true that money could be a very useful commodity in court; but such usefulness must not be mistaken for a struggle between the rich and poor *per se*. Death would have protested against Athenian law as he did against Apollo's law in *Alcestis*: it was made for the rich (Eur. *Alc.* 57). Fines were best paid immediately since imprisonment could be imposed until they were taken care of, and prison could be a most unpleasant place: one can imagine that an Athenian gentleman would be willing to part with a great deal of money to avoid such incidents as having his nose bitten off and swallowed.[33] Those who failed to pay fines or debts by the ninth prytany incurred *atimia* and all the liabilities involved in loss of citizen rights (Andoc. 1.73ff.). But wealth could be even more useful before conviction: litigants frequently and successfully bribed juries.[34] To bribe so many jurors will have been not only difficult but also quite expensive if the price per juror was at all considerable. Nevertheless, because jurors received long-term assignments in the fifth century, it was possible to identify more or less which citizens might be involved. In response to what apparently became a considerable problem, the procedures for selecting jurors were substantially altered, ending pre-trial assignment to a given court, and a law or laws were instituted to punish attempts at bribery. Yet fourth-century references make it clear that even the threat of the death penalty could not end the practice. If the rich were willing to continue to use their money in this way and at such risk, it would seem that the less wealthy jurors, even if they in some way resented the wealthy who were seeking to escape punishment with bribes, did not resist financial persuasion in a spirit of 'class conflict.'[35]

Related, but somewhat different in emphasis, is the view that the rich and prominent were victimized in the courts. Their frustration at bearing the burden of the Peloponnesian War and suffering the attacks of sycophants is supposedly exhibited in the early action of the Thirty Tyrants against these professional litigators.[36] But the Thirty had broad support in these prosecutions.[37] The sycophants were widely despised and could be tried annually by a special popular procedure (*Ath. Pol.* 43.5).

Not only were those who attacked the rich hated; there are indications of a general attitude in court of contempt for the poor. This is all the more remarkable since the jurors themselves were comparatively less well-to-do. The cloak (*tribon*) and shoes (*embades*) apparently most typical of jurors signalled relative poverty.[38] For an Athenian gentleman, such as Cephisodotus, to be reduced to going about in such clothes was a sad fate meant to arouse great indignation among the jurors (Isae. 5.11). We have no examples of speakers defending themselves on grounds of poverty or boasting of it, as if not having access to luxury were something admirable which united them with the jurors. Rather we find a rich man ridiculing his less wealthy opponent for his less privileged social position, in which lack of fortune required him to work for a living (Dem. 18.265–6). And thus when a speaker suggests that his opponent will try to defend himself on the grounds that he is poorer than the speaker, it seems highly doubtful that the less wealthy opponent will at all have intended to draw these facts to the attention of the jurors (Isae. 6.59).

There was a line of attack to be used against the rich, but the charge was not the mere possession of wealth. The appeal was to the greed of the jurors on the grounds that the opponent had concealed his wealth in order to avoid having to spend any of it in the service of the city.[39] In fact, it was the claim to have acted in the opposite manner that provided the rich with one of their most commonly used court defenses — the past performance of liturgies — as we noted above. Thus, although rich men inevitably became involved in litigation and did not hesitate to use their money in or out of court to protect themselves and their fortunes, the courts were not the site of a conscious social battle between the rich and the poor.

Nor did 'oligarchic' and 'democratic' parties find an arena at law. Connor has carefully shown how such broad party divisions oversimplify Athenian politics and fail to account for events and activities in the fifth century. Traditionally, there were many small family and friendship groups whose leaders acted by forming powerful if often brief coalitions.[40] In the second half of the fifth century, this political style was challenged by men such as Cleon who drew their power from broader popular support.[41] The old methods had produced leaders with greatly differing oligarchic and democratic tendencies who nevertheless cooperated on occasion. Rivals like Nicias and Alcibiades could work together tactically — if only very briefly — to achieve something like the ostracism of Hyperbolus.[42] But the power of the assembly was so great that most leaders, whatever their connections and background might be, found that success required popular support. Nicias and his son may have remained aloof, but even Critias and Theramenes joined Cleon in seeking popularity with the people.[43] Ambitious men, vying with each other to lead groups of aristocrats and oligarchs, had to compete for popular approval and political power on an individual basis as well. This is not to claim that Athenians were not divided into ideological groups — oligarchic and democratic, imperialist and anti-imperialist. But these various factions within the community were often more the assistants and audience for personal power struggles than the independent elements of factional strife. During the revolutions, of course, party lines hardened and group antagonisms were transformed into vivid and horrible actions. But that was not the normal state of affairs.

In any case, the domination of politics by individuals, described above, stands out even more clearly and regularly in legal activity. The courts provided a perfect forum for both traditional and newer methods of political competition. At least from the beginning of the fifth century, Athenians prosecuted rivals to advance their own standing (Hdt. 6.136). Ephialtes pursued his politics and Pericles began his career with such attacks (*Ath.Pol.* 25–8). And once these two men had accomplished their reforms in the administration of justice, 'the power and prestige of the popular courts increased and the use of litigation as a political weapon became prevalent.'[44] The clubs (*hetaireiai*), small associations of friends and relatives, coordinated their manipulations of the courts with money and influence to achieve greater effects than isolated individuals could often manage.[45] Since the opportunities which stemmed from Athenian laws and procedures themselves were open to any litigant, the clubs were most helpful outside the actual trial in organizing bribes and related suits, some of which are discussed below. One of their pretrial activities vividly points up how close the courtroom and trial voting approached to popular elective politics. Before a trial, club members canvassed jurors. As Calhoun noted, the Athenians themselves described these efforts with words such as *paraggellein* (to canvas) which were used for assemblies and elections.[46]

Inside the new dikasteries, it was the new method of politics which was more important to the litigant. The process was frightening for many reasons. One of these was the danger arising from the frequent unexpected turns of events in the popular courts, a subject on which the defendant against Simon is quite eloquent (Lys. 3.2). The innocent were so uncertain of acquittal that they readily paid sycophants not to bring suits against them.[47] The Greek commonplace said that *chronos* (time) would reveal the truth; and the figures of tragedy frequently warned against quick action before time could establish true innocence or guilt.[48] But only homicide suits provided a long discovery period with a public pronouncement and three monthly pre-trials before the trial itself.[49] During the proceedings, the only testimony a speaker could hope for from time was the cumulative record of past time (Hyp. *Lyc.* 14), for even as he spoke, the water clocks were quickly emptying, and the jurors would soon choose a winner. From Achilles (*Il.* 9.312ff.) to Demosthenes (18.282), Greeks professed hatred of lying speeches; but without the benefits of time and truth, citizens turned to tricks of litigation to win the popular approval of the jurors. 'So notorious were the vagaries of the dicasts that litigants constantly feared a miscarriage of justice and even innocent men were led to defend themselves by unlawful means.'[50] Very like addressing and controlling the assembly, court speaking was a technical skill for the mastery of which citizens were willing to pay great sums.[51] As detailed below, the laws themselves frequently directed the choice of a preferred victor rather than the determination of an abstract right. But aside from considerations of legal formalism, the Athenians were more eager to be entertained and dazzled by the best and cleverest than to render consistent and careful decisions (Thuc. 3.37–8).[52]

Mixed motives for litigation did not trouble the jurors. For example, although a challenge to undertake a liturgy, *antidosis*, should have depended on a completely objective comparison of wealth, the action was used to create inconvenience and could be cited in court as proof of personal hostility (Lys. 4.1–2). Athenians frequently opened their court speeches with the explanation that the present prosecution was a convenient way to avenge past personal and even hereditary grudges and hostilities in no way connected with the immediate charge.[53] A prosecutor had hope of winning a private suit by reminding jurors of their own old grievances against the defendant's father. Thus, when Tisias brought a private suit against the younger Alcibiades for horses his father allegedly stole, the son was faced with all the bitter resentment against his infamous father that Tisias could arouse in the jurors (Isoc. 16.1–3). And even in defending himself on a homicide charge, Euxitheus found it necessary to try and clear his father's reputation. It is unlikely that the digression was superfluous: the speech was a product of the astuteness and expertise of Antiphon (5.74–80).

The Athenian legal system itself encouraged the subjective and personal approach adopted by litigants and jurors. As Gernet has noted, every judgement in Athenian law merely awards a preference which does not imply any pre-existing or abstract right.[54] The adjudication of heiresses (*epidikasia*) and estates (*diadikasia*) makes this especially clear. Precisely parallel rules applied to the award of an heiress with her attached estate and to the inheritance of an estate.[55] If there was only one claimant, the award went to him automatically.[56] When more than one citizen made claim, the court had to choose one as the winner. It was not possible to declare that no claimant had the right, nor did the judgement establish any absolute right of the victor to the heiress or the property. The decision merely meant that he had defeated his opponent or opponents in this particular contest.[57] The successful litigant throughout his life, and his heirs for up to five years after his death, could be brought back into court not only by new claimants, but even by those who lost the original decision as long as they made their challenge on new grounds.[58] As with determination of penalties (*timesis*) described above, no complicated solutions involving compromise or independent evaluation could come from the jury. The vote chose one litigant (or penalty in *timesis*) simply and without qualification.

Athletic victors carried off tripods and other valuable objects as awards. In Athens the victory prize was carried over even into public cases.[59] A successful prosecutor received one-third of the fine in a conviction for usurpation of citizen rights (*graphe xenias*), one-half when denouncing violation of certain trade regulations and guardianship rules (*phasis*), and an enticing three-fourths in the recovery of property owed to the city (*apographe*), not surprisingly the most frequently used of these actions.[60]

If Athenian juries accepted arguments and evidence not properly related to the charge before them, there were also ways in which the Athenian legal system allowed for less connection between cases than logic requires. This tended to isolate each trial as a separate battle and to make many cases a matter more of vengeance than of evaluative redress. Perhaps the most extreme form this independent treatment took was the countersuit (*antigraphe*).[61] Suit and countersuit could go on simultaneously, the separate trials usually dealing with related but different claims on the same estate (Dem. 40, 41). Although many of the facts would be relevant to both cases, the decisions were in no way coordinated and could have the effect either of a sort of mutual cancellation or of doubling the success of one of the litigants. Although such suits arose naturally from frustration over the severely limited and inflexible rules for inheriting or dividing an estate, even the Athenians felt that these related but separate tests came somehow improperly close to contending twice over the same issue (Dem. 41.12ff.). In fact, it seems that this procedure allowed exactly that: when an Athenian (whose name we do not know) was trying to take some property from Theophemus as security for the payment of a previous court judgement against Theophemus, the two men came to blows. They each proceeded to prosecute the other for having struck the first blow, and the cases were entirely independent throughout — from separate arbitrators to separate trials ([Dem.] 47). How or if conflicting verdicts could be reconciled in such instances is not clear; but in this instance the tactic seems to have been very useful to Theophemus in one stage of a long, complicated legal struggle.

Other procedures for which we have more information show this same pattern. So, for example, cases for false evidence were oddly disconnected from the trial in which the original testimony was given. Conviction did not insure reopening of the old case. It was, again, a separate contest, an opportunity for vengeance against a witness.[62] Precisely parallel were actions against alleged witnesses to a summons (*graphe pseudokleteias*) or the summoning litigant (*dike kakotekhnion*) who had won a judgement by default. The suits provided a means of retaliation against the opponents, but they did not cancel the original decision; they were merely preliminary requirements for yet another trial which might annul the default judgement.[63] Finally, magistrates could impose limited fines which citizens could not appeal. In order to avoid arraignment as a public debtor and the dangerous liabilities attendant in the *apographe* procedure, a citizen might well choose to pay the fine, even if he felt it was not legal.[64] But he could avenge himself on the magistrate by charging him with misconduct at his *euthyna*, the examination at the end of his term of office.[65] There was no mechanism in any of these sets of actions by which the courts adjusted early decisions in light of the new charges or tried to make a more inclusive, final determination of the respective rights of the litigants at the original point of disagreement. Instead they judged or refereed a series of blows between the contestants.

At times Athenian legal procedure surrendered completely to the spirit of political election and athletic competition. It is somehow fitting that this approach was actually prescribed for the prosecution of those whose regard for the law was lowest. No matter how many sycophants stalked the courts of Athens, only the three most troublesome citizens (and perhaps metics) could be proposed for trial in each sixth prytany (*Ath. Pol.* 43.5).[66] Thus the procedure was not so much an establishment of absolute innocence or guilt as a negative election. Since the candidates for conviction as sycophants were chosen somewhat like winners in a race, the author of the *Athenaion Politeia*, in noting the custom, aptly mentions ostracism in the same sentence. Both procedures created a sort of inverse priamel by finding the worst rather than the best.

Although ostracizing a powerful politician might ease tension in the city, the annual conviction of six sycophants could not limit litigation. Threatened suits spawned countersuits to delay them, and every trial produced a loser anxious to pursue his victor in subsequent suits.[67] If a direct assault seemed unpromising, he could attack his enemy's friends. Witnesses were charged with false evidence; and most court speeches contained enough personal criticism to motivate further suits for defamation. Thus one Theomnestus, after successfully defending himself on a charge of speaking publicly after having thrown away his shield, brought a perjury suit against Dionysius, one of his prosecutor's witnesses. But in the process of winning this case, he called someone else a parricide and so wound up in court a third time defending himself against a charge of slander (Lys. 10). As a result of such extended battles, the dikasteries grew like the city-state itself with more and more contests to decide. One of the most unusual and persistent elements which emerged in the settlement of these disputes was an emphasis on quantity. The next section explores the cultural basis of this preoccupation and the eventual extent of its legal application.

3. Quantity

It was entirely logical for quantity to be of great importance in a success-oriented society: a comparison of measurements or amounts is one of the simplest ways to gauge achievement. However, the Athenians carried this concern into many areas where we would not expect find it, and a dependence on a quantitative approach explains various oddities in Greek literature, science and philosophy. Thus, in a comic vein, Aristophanes could stage a poetic competition in which the quality of a verse depended on its weight, and its weight depended on the size and number of objects it mentioned (*Ran.* 1379ff.). Yet despite the absurdity here, this fixation on quantity found a place in much more serious arguments. In the fifth and fourth centuries, some medical theories held that the sex of a child could be determined by the relative quantities of seed contributed by the father and mother. Similarly, whatever the sex of the child, in each of its parts it would resemble whichever parent had contributed the larger amount of seed from that corresponding part.[68] Again, Socrates' introduction of the hedonisitic calculus in the *Protagoras* (356c–e), reducing the choice of actions to the art of correctly measuring pleasure and pain, should be seen as part of this tendency. And although this argument in the *Protagoras* may include a certain amount of irony, Aristophanes' comic exaggeration comes close to everyday attitudes.

In fact, the verse-weighing in the *Frogs* closely reflects the Greek competitive spirit which produced an obsession not merely with number but with the superlative number. This fascination helped shape Thucydides' first sentences, which resound with superlatives like the opening of a Pindaric ode. If he needed a model, he could have found it in Nestor: 'They were the mightiest, and against the mightiest they fought' (*Il.* 1.267). When one superlative could not express the exceptionality the historian wanted to describe, he simply used two, creating sentences which often will not even translate into idiomatic English.[69] This preoccupation found expression in poetry as well as in prose. In fact, a common if unnamed (and perhaps until now unnoticed) figure of speech relied on taking what was already an impressive number or multiple and increasing it, as is always possible, by one. Achilles first does this when struggling for status against Agamemnon (*Il.* 1.128), and the device often has the competitive air of forceful assertion.[70] Aggressive comparison can quickly drive the numbers from tens to countless millions, as when Achilles rejects imagined offers in imaginary quantities (*Il.* 9.379ff.).

Such imaginary numbers became quite real during the Athenian empire. Tribute poured into the treasury creating massive surplus, and the scale of everything from the grain trade to temple architecture increased as well. Pericles' vision of magnificence emanated partly from this mass itself. Somehow the conclusion of his last speech in Thucydides manages to translate quantity into quality. Athenians spent the most men and labors in the greatest wars. They ruled the most Greeks. They were the richest and the mightiest. And when all these things were counted and measured, it was clear, at least to the Athenians, that their name and their city were superior to all others (Thuc. 2.64).

Long ago Gernet maintained that measurement was characteristic of Athenian law as it increasingly evaluated offenses and set penalties in economic terms.[71] But in fact quantity and measure had a much deeper and broader base in the dikasteries. In many cases the arithmetic is reasonable enough. Although the details were complicated, court fees generally increased, either in set increments or proportionally, as the value of the claim or disputed property rose. The fee called *prytaneia*, payable in some financial suits, was three drachmas if the money claimed from the defendant was less than a thousand drachmas, thirty if the claim was for more than a thousand. In inheritance cases a deposit called *parakatabole* might be required: it was either five or ten per cent of the property under settlement.[72] Similarly, the fine exacted from an unsuccessful plaintiff was often one-sixth of his original claim, that is, one obol per drachma or *epobelia*.[73] Finally, the number of jurors varied in relation to the significance of the trial: two hundred for small private suits and twice that for those involving more than one thousand drachmae (*Ath.Pol.* 53.3). Public cases, to which significantly more time was also allotted, required multiples of five hundred jurors up to as many as six thousand in the most important trials.[74]

But sometimes what began as reasonable considerations of quantity led to less logical ends. For example, law provided that an Athenian assigned a liturgy could challenge a wealthier citizen to assume the burden. If the challenged party brought the issue to a dikastery, the sole criterion for determining the obligation was, in theory, their relative riches. So far so good. But if the challenged party both refused the liturgy and feared the courts (as he reasonably might), his only alternative was to exchange estates with the challenger.[75] With this, the complications attained the absurdities of Aristophanean verse-weighing. Careful study of the procedure led Goligher to pronounce it clumsy, absurd, stupid and inane. He declared, in exasperation, that, 'The Athenians were emphatically stupid in the realm of legislation,and the particular stupidities of the antidosis appear in other institutions where no one thinks of denying them.'[76] The present study undertakes rather to find comprehensible patterns than to label 'particular stupidities'; but certainly a cumbersome dependence on quantity alone caused many oddities in Athenian law.

The importance of a suit or the amount of money it involved affected more than the size of the jury, fees and fines. In private suits the evaluation of the dispute in drachmas rigidly determined the maximum length of each speech. Thus, for each litigant in cases of over five thousand drachmas, the water clock ran approximately forty minutes for the first speech and twelve for the second. Lesser matters to the lower limit of a thousand drachmas deserved first and second speeches of thirty and eight minutes. Arguments for less than one thousand drachmas needed careful wording or fast delivery; they were probably limited to twenty minutes and eight minutes (*Ath. Pol.* 67.2).[77] If the jury voted to convict and penalties needed to be proposed, the litigants in private suits may have had as little as two or three minutes for their proposals. However, it seems more likely that at this stage too they were allotted time in proportion to the quantity of drachmas at stake — perhaps half the time allowed for the original main speech (*Ath. Pol.* 67.3, 69.2).[78]

Only in trails for the maltreatment of parents, orphans and heiresses were speeches exempt from the limits of the clock.[79] And this class of cases, which constituted a small percentage of lawsuits in Athenian courts, was a matter more of sacred custom than of daily law. By the fifth century, Athenian legislation embraced both positive, general law and traditional, family obligations. The separate treatment of these offenses parallels the distinction between the homicide and popular courts.[80] But, aside from these specially protected relationships, the precision of the clock governed all grievance.

Now the elements of Athenian family, finance and trade frequently wove themselves into terribly intricate webs. Although it is easy to imagine a case for nine hundred drachmas with endless complexities and of immense consequence for less wealthy litigants, the Athenian courts were not concerned and would not consider allowing the extra ten minutes of speaking time that another hundred drachmas would have insured. Even so long ago, time was money; or rather, money entitled one to time. In this instance, one objective measurement matched another, and no other factor, subjective or qualitative, was considered.

I present this neither as evidence of stubborn callousness nor, as does Goligher, of emphatic stupidity. It was simply natural in Athens where tangible measurement mattered so much, even to those who thought quite abstractly. Of this there could be no more dramatic demonstration than Plato's treatment of false evidence and the reopening of a trial. Although the precise requirements for retrial on grounds of false evidence in Athenian courts remain uncertain, Book Eleven of the *Laws* closes with precise instructions for reopening such a case.[81] The decision depends on the impeachment neither of critical evidence nor even of evidence from a key witness. Indeed, these might be insufficient. It is simply a matter of amount. Even though the courts received testimony on matters quite varied in their relevance to the immediate dispute, if half — any half, but no less than half — of this information could be disproved, it was time to begin again (*Leg.* 937c–d).

Cleverness could turn such rigid quantities to considerable advantage. In inheritance cases, speakers could take as long as about fifty minutes for their first speech and ten for the reply (Dem. 48.8).[82] But Theopompos persuaded three friends to enter claims when he opposed Phylomache (Dem. 43.7). The four attacked with a great quantity of concerted and repeated lies which the bewildered opponent could not hope to answer in his precise but unnegotiable fraction of time (Dem. 43. 7–10,30). Thus mere mass brought victory. It was an extraordinarily shrewd tactic which destroyed the quantitative equality the water clocks were supposed to provide. Even to Athenians, it must have seemed unsporting once the prior complicity was revealed, for competition requires at least an initial balance of symmetry at some level. At the games, rules applied equally to all athletes. And, as the Athenians bluntly reminded the Melians, without some basis of equality, claims simply had no point (Thuc. 5.89). However there was seldom any danger for a Greek that a basis for competition would be lacking since the culture tended relentlessly to balanced symmetries and oppositions. In fact, so much attention was devoted to particularly matched quantities or entities that the various cultural and legal consequences of this concern deserve separate treatment.

4. Symmetrical Balance and Oppositions

The Greeks imposed many different sorts of binary divisions on their world. Some were contrasting, competing oppositions; other were merely alternatives or doubles; but all were carefully matched and balanced. Some of the following examples may seem somehow unnatural or merely forced, but this is precisely what makes the phenomenon so important. The pattern was so prevasively applied that it appears in areas where it is not at all appropriate and forces or creates 'false' symmetries or oppositions when they do not naturally exist.

Long before the Mediterranean knew the words and deeds of Greeks and barbarians, its plants and animals lived and died by day and night on the land and in the sea. There is neither room nor reason to list all the regular pairs the Greeks found and named in their world. These, like the sands and the benefactions of Theron, elude all number. But the Greeks worked this double pattern from nature into their own creations with elaborate artifice. There were

men and *de*, particles to emphasize either the balance or the opposition of two words, phrases, sentences, or even longer expressions,
matched in Gorgian antitheses. But these were absurdly simple
compared with the complexities of choric responsion. Each antis-
trophe reflected the rhythm of its strophe like a mirror. This precise
metrical repetition made it possible to bind two elements in
comparison or contrast merely by placing them in corresponding
positions of two sections.

Binary division so dominated Greek thought that it did not even
require two objects or ideas. A concept could simply supply its own
double. Hesiod knew not one *eris* (strife) but two (*Op*. 11–26). And
if he did not explicitly divide *aidos* (modesty, *Op*. 317–19),
Euripides certainly did (*Hipp*. 385–6). In each case, as with the first
sons of Adam, one was good, the other bad. Not surprisingly, love
— either as Eros or Aphrodite — took the same two forms.[83]
Eventually this self-contained twinning faded into the mechanics of
rhetoric like our 'on the one hand' and 'on the other.' Thus in his
orderly way Aristotle, using *men* and *de*, describes the two aspects
of very many things, including justice (*Eth.Nic*. 1162b21–2). But the
process could be quite vivid: it is one thing to think of two varieties
of *philia*, quite another to confront two Helens. Menelaos' reaction
to such unexpected duplication was purely Greek: double everything else. Perhaps there were two Spartas, two Troys, even two
Zeuses (Eur. *Hel*. 483ff.).

This is not simply Euripidean vaudeville. In the late sixth century,
vase painters began the mastery of an entirely new technique,
replacing black figures with red. Some of them, the bilingualists,
responded much like Menelaos and left us vases with two of everything: Herakles and Kerberos, Herakles and the bull, trees and
clubs, Ajax and Achilles, spears and game boards. The scenes with
all their objects are painted once in each technique. Each object
finds its chromatic opposite in itself.[84] Moreover, the bilingual
rendition of the Ajax and Achilles scene by the Andocides painter
carries a further sign of the relentless tendency to symmetrical
production. The scene seems to have been originated by Andocides'
teacher. Exekias created a carefully composed contrast between the
helmeted Achilles and bare-headed Ajax. But his pupil and the
other painters who reproduced this scene, of which more than a
hundred specimens survive, chose almost without exception to
make both heroes either helmeted or bareheaded. It seems that
both the alteration of Exekias' scene and its popularity can be laid to

the opportunities for emphasizing centralized symmetry.[85]

A vision so unlimited was not always logical. Perhaps it is not surprising in myth when two eagles flying from the earth's farthest reaches meet at its exact center.[86] But at the level of phrase, the failure of reason could be more jarring. Greek possessed a large stock of paired words and phrases now called polar expressions. Variously taken as mutually exclusive or collectively exhaustive, they were frequently presented disjunctively to pose alternatives or jointly to emphasize totality.[87] But as these pairs began to appear promiscuously in tragic speech, the second member often limped behind the first, sometimes merely irrelevant, often stunningly out of place. Obviously, when one is trying to emphasize completeness, the complement for the first phrase should be of the collectively exhaustive rather than the mutually exclusive type. But great tragedians, or their characters, were not always clear logicians. 'Come servants, both men and women!' or 'old and young!' would have served Creon's immediate urgency much better than his own, 'Come servants, both present and not present!' (Soph. *Ant.* 1109ff.).[88] Very similar in both language and logic is Electra's lament that Orestes, by delaying, has destroyed the hopes she had and the ones she did not have (Soph. *El.* 305); and the idiom even finds a precarious place in Plato's *Symposium* (209c).

Finally, this illogical love of symmetry extended from word to deed. It is sometimes doubtful in Thucydides whether a polar expression such as 'neither slave nor free' has entered in the service of ornament or of information (2.78).[89] There are puzzles such as his description of the building and width of the Peiraeus walls (1.93.3–7). The strange explanation that 'two wagons opposite each other brought up stones' is bracketed by many editors, and those who defend it have very different explanations of what it means. In any case, like the very similar passage in Aristophanes' *Birds* (1124–9), it seems to illustrate a tendency to conceive action at the moment of symmetrical meeting of opposites and to use this image as a measure of static width. In a similar manner, the historian records an odd and unambiguous military manoeuver (4.23.2) which must have been the product of someone's aesthetic affinities for balanced opposites. The two Athenian ships circled Sphakteria in opposite directions like carefully balanced tendrils painted up either side of a scene on a vase. But although Thucydides seems as blissfully unconcerned as the Athenian commander has to have been, this allowed the Spartans twice as much time for machination at the points where the ships' paths crossed than if the boats had flouted bilateral symmetry and trailed each other separated by a semicircle.[90] But in this society, eagles, servants, and ships were called to their courses in inevitable, balanced elegance.

It would be strange if the courts had eschewed the practices common to poets and generals. The city's institutional heirs to duel and combat could not have avoided paired oppositions; they incorporated them, as the rest of the culture had, with varying degrees of logic. Competing litigants went before the jurors as human embodiments of disjunctive polar expressions. Just like the terms of the rhetorical figure, they often expressed positions which were not really mutually exclusive but rather tangled, overlapping, or only superficially balanced. Yet the courts had to treat them as clean contradictions; the vote which chose one simultaneously rejected the other. And although the irregularities of human life could produce positions for which there would seem no natural diametric opposition, the artifice of sophistic rhetoric could almost always correct the defects of sublunary asymmetries. Protagoras may have been the first formally to teach that there were two opposing arguments for everything, but he soon had fellow professors.[91] The existence of these *dissoi logoi* is asserted in Euripides' *Antiope* and vividly demonstrated there by those most antilogical of twins Amphion and Zethus (fr. 189N[2]).[92] In Aristophanes' wonderland, the opposing arguments actually come to life and speak for themselves (*Nub.* 889–1114).[93] Although in Athenian courts the litigant or his writer had to devise the speech, argument and counterargument arose almost automatically. A well-trained Athenian had technical competence equivalent to that of the bilingual vase painter: he could depict any scene in either set of colors. The Andocides painter has left us his Herakles amphorae, Antiphon his *Tetralogies*.[94]

The court arguments contain the same balanced phrases found in other prose and verse. The polar expressions vary in relevance and logic, as do those of the tragedians. Wilamowitz, in his commentary to line 1106 of *Herakles*, cited two examples from the orators: one is entirely for emphasis rather than for any contrast. 'Neither a larger nor a lesser transaction' means simply 'no transaction *at all*' (Dem. 33.13). Practically any speech of Isocrates or Demosthenes will yield examples of this device used for stylistic fullness and antithetical balance. It is particularly prevalent with the stock antitheses in phrases such as 'neither public nor private' and 'neither in speech nor in deed' and their many variants.

Wilamowitz's second phrase from oratory is 'those who do or suffer something voluntarily' (Antiphon 3.2.6). This rather complex and unusual phrase trades on two simpler, commonplace antitheses: the distinction between voluntary and involuntary has significance in Athenian law both in homicide and in damage suits, and 'doing and suffering' are regularly joined in Greek both as a universalizing doublet, like 'land and sea,' and as an expression for a form of *lex talionis*.[95] If the two terms of the two antitheses are combined, four new pairs are possible; but only three of them correspond to any relevant concept. Involuntary action (or doing) and voluntary action are standard legal categories, and the latter is often opposed rhetorically to 'involuntary suffering,' a phrase which accurately described the experience of the victim of a crime. In fact, Anthiphon uses this contrast himself (1.27). But the remaining rhetorical product of these combined antitheses, 'voluntary suffering,' has no proper place in Athenian law, even though it might possibly be used of a protagonist in a tragedy of self-sacrifice. Nevertheless, this phantom category has not entered Antiphon's speech through careless inadvertence or merely for ornament.

Antiphon creates and exploits this odd antithesis as an artificial 'hard-line' position which he can then abandon for one apparently more moderate but still to his advantage; and the clever way he does it is as follows. Athenians distinguished broadly between voluntary (*hekon*) and involuntary (*akon*) homicide, and cases of the latter came before a separate court and drew milder penalties. The defendant in this speech, charged with unintentional homicide, admits that those who err in action are nevertheless responsible for accidental results. Now he twice hints that whether the part of the deceased in his death is to be called acting or suffering, it was willing or voluntary, thus suggesting *voluntary* suffering. Then, however, the defendant seemingly retreats to a more moderate position, strengthening his claim by graciously allowing that the deceased boy erred *involuntarily*. But then the boy must at least be responsible for (his own) involuntary homicide — and the defendant, as a consequence, must be innocent of the involuntary charge. The other main type of homicide is deliberate, with which the defendant is not even charged. So the defendant cannot be guilty of homicide at all (3.2.6–9). The Athenian habit for balanced antitheses had so filled its rhetoric and laws with oppositional pairs that elegant speech could combine and recombine them for almost any desired effect.[96]

This skill, which Antiphon so cleverly demonstrated in his models, was put to use in fourth-century court oratory. Demosthenes, for example, uses it to make a rather weak contrast, involving the permanent and the temporary, seem clearer and more relevant then it actually is (20.65). But the true master and most frequent manipulator of these oppositions in his extant works is Isaeus. He will try to heighten the shamefulness of relatives wrangling over property by pointing out antithetically that it would be disgraceful even for those who were not related to contest the case — but, of course, the contrast is absurd since inheritance was contested exclusively by relatives (1.5).[97] Isaeus repeats this illogical contrast in another context in the speech *On the Estate of Menecles*: the uncle is trying to block an adoption whereas even those who are not relatives never try to do so (2.24–5) — as if they would! The same device reappears almost immediately: the opponent and his brother are divided by a *men/de* contrast which is entirely verbal and misrepresents the opponent's actions. So in the tangled case of Philoctemon's estate, Isaeus simultaneously works two contrasts — the capacity or incapacity to make a will and the existence or non-existence of a will. The result is that in his alternatives he can shift the grounds and the emphasis of his contrasts so as not to have to suggest with any vividness the possibility claimed by the opponents — that a will was simply not written (6.52–3). This sounds somewhat confusing; that, of course, was the point. The oppositions sound convincingly orderly and logical, yet they mask difficulties and embarrassments.

Not only the litigants' speeches, but the laws of Athens as well were cast in carefully balanced form. The chiasmus is an extremely artificial prose device especially when it inverts subjects and verbs to maintain mirror symmetry between clauses. In the less than twenty-five still legibly inscribed lines of Drakon's homicide law the pattern is repeated five times.[98] The effects of such arrangement have pleased writers and readers of various languages for centuries. Here, the use of the chiasmus organizes and clarifies the basic intent and provisions themselves.[99]

The balanced equality of chiastic apportionment had its counterpart in Athenian inheritance law which gave equal shares of an estate to each son (Isae. 6.25). This solution, so in keeping with Athenian aesthetics, would certainly have been welcomed by others elsewhere. Hesiod suffered at the hands of judges who did not understand that the virtues of an even half could make it more valuable than a larger, unequal portion (*Op*. 39ff.). Greek tradition found models in nature to help persuade rivals peacefully to share equal quantities. Day and night most frequently made this division of the world both in literature and in life.[100] If stubbornness blocked settlement on equal terms, brothers might find another sort of balance in mutual annihilation. Such was the fate of Eteocles and Polyneices when Jocasta's attempt to mediate failed.[101] Outside the theater, fraternal violence might be somewhat less symmetrical but just as fatal. Disagreement over the division of an estate eventually led Thoudippus to kill his brother Euthycrates, an event recounted in a court speech written for a half-brother of Euthycrates' son when family members in the next generation were again quarreling over an estate settlement (Isae. 9.17). Anything *other* than absolutely equal division could lead to great complications in Athens. Asymmetrical settlement required a separate suit which was quite likely to generate a matching countersuit to restore the balance (Dem. 40).[102]

Sometimes the formal equalities imposed on Athenian legal procedure had a fair face. Something could be said for giving opponents equal time to talk. But inflexible limits could prevent either side from presenting all the relevant material. Litigants had as much time to present cases of the simplest outlines as to explain those involving traders from Byzantium with successive levels of complexity and intrigue fully worthy of the Court which would arise there far in the future. In the speech *Against Apaturius* (Dem. 33), the defendant has only a few minutes to explain the negotiation of multiple loans, the mortgage of a ship, the failure of a bank, attempts to seize slaves and to sneak the ship out of a harbor, transfer of the mortgage, disagreements leading to violence, the disappearance of a key figure to a site serving as a temporary home during exile from Byzantium, earthquakes which bring loss of both property and family, and the arbitration and suits which had grown out of these events. The speech demonstrates how all this can be presented with arguments woven in; but it also shows us how something in the way of clarity and legal precision is lost in the process. Moreover, with equal allotments, prosecutors soon learned regularly to put the defendant at a disadvantage by making accusations and damaging suggestions too numerous and complicated for him to answer adequately.[103] Opponents might even indicate possible diversionary lines of attack well before the trial in hopes of forcing the other side to have to *plan* to waste part of its time refuting the irrelevant or outrageous suggestions (Dem. 27.53). Fear that silence would imply consent forced the defendant to try and address every point (Hyp. *Lyc.* 10). With great skill, a defendant could turn this handicap to advantage. This is one of Demosthenes' particular triumphs in *On the Crown*. Although he claims he is forced to defend himself against the irrelevant accusations of the prosecution, he in fact uses the opportunity to speak at great length on personal matters equally irrelevant but almost certain to capture the sympathy of the jury (18.9, 34).[104] If we can trust Thucydides, precisely this tactic had been used successfully almost exactly a century earlier by Alcibiades in his debate with Nicias over the desirability of a Sicilian expedition. Alcibiades opened his reply to Nicias with a personal defense brilliantly constructed simultaneously to create admiration for the glory he had imparted to Athens and to whip up the desire for more. In the end his speech and Nicias' are almost identical in length: they each occupy 108 lines of the Oxford text. There is more to be said about Thucydides almost immediately, but this brings us back to the point which initiated the discussion of strategy — the enforced equal length of speeches.

This discussion has emphasized certain oddities and irrationalities that the time allotments created. And yet we saw that illogical polar expressions and outlandish *antidosis* procedure were in fact so much related to traditional ways of speaking and acting that Athenians accepted and used them without complaint. Formalities of rhetoric and procedures of law grew from what was culturally common and familiar. So the court's water clock, with all its intricacies, really reflects a completely regular Athenian approach to speaking and argument. Athenians engaged in dispute insisted on their own chance to speak and be heard, and they made their demands with the special antiphonal verbs *antilegein* and *antakouein*. They appended phrases such as *isa* (equally) to emphasize that the opportunity should be equal.[105] If we had only the specific examples of choric responsion, exactly matched strophes and antistrophes, we might still hesitate to find in the maxim a desire for equal length. But fifth-century Athens has left us many literally equal speeches. Paley collected all the pairs of speeches in Euripides of matched length. And even though his numbers for exact correspondence owe their magnitude partly to his own precision surgery, any text of Euripides will yield an impressive set of very close agreements.[106] Likewise, Thucydides' personal passion for precision and balance found a realistic outlet in the carefully measured speeches delivered in democratic Athens and Syracuse. Although only Nicias and Alcibiades and Hermocrates and Athenagoras express themselves in exactly the same number of Oxford lines, each speech in a given pair agrees quite closely with its companion. This is all the more remarkable in view of the fact that the lengths vary considerably from pair to pair.[107] The debate over Sicily seems even more like a trial since it is followed by a version of *timesis*.[108] Nicias tries to set the price or 'penalty' of an expedition so high that it will be rejected. But oddly like Socrates, whose equally extreme and more famous timetic proposal was rejected, Nicias lost his gamble when the assembly accepted his figure (Thuc. 6.24): Nicias' death was more delayed, Socrates' less pathetic.

If we ask of the proverb, the tragic speeches, the debates in Thucydides and the courts with their water clocks, which influenced which, it will be difficult to give an answer both specific and convincing. Finley faced the same problem with the rhetorical connections both in content and form between Euripides and Thucydides. His conclusion is sensible: rather than either borrowing from the other, they came to similar ideas and methods as a result of the intellectual climate and developments of their time.[109] It may be unprofitable and even impossible to treat cultural elements like manuscripts in a fantastically interwoven stemma. But the conclusion of this section should serve the reader as a warning and a foretaste of what is to come in the next chapter; for speeches of equal length are among the simplest and most straightforward of the connections between the theater and the courts.

But before turning to drama, where the women's roles were always taken by men, we will see what can be learned of the social roles of women by examining some of the ways in which they figure in Athenian laws, legal administration, courts, and court speeches.

5. Women and Law

Almost every discussion of Athenian women makes reference to the statement of Thucydides' Pericles: as to the excellence of women, their great glory is to be least spoken of (2.45.2). Every such discussion is limited by the extent to which the society was guided by this sentiment. Evidence is hard to come by and, once found, perhaps even harder to make speak in an unbiased fashion. The lead tablets of Attica, for example, with their fascinating curses frequently have unkind words for legal opponents and their courtroom assistants (*syndikoi*).[110] And one includes among the cursed enemies Aspasia and her 'lawyers' or legal helpers.[111] Just what events lie behind this inscription we cannot say; nevertheless, it suggests the possibility that women had legal connections involving some tension and power, even though they were barred from speaking or acting directly in the courts. Court speeches refer explicitly to some ways that women might influence litigants and jurors: it is said that some women could prevent their husbands from giving false evidence (Isae. 12.5), and claimed that jurors should bear in mind how their wives would react to a given verdict (Dem. 59.110–11).[112] Yet besides the fact that both these claims are highly tendentious, the types of influence they single out are relatively limited and superficial. There are other more profound connections between women and the law, and they indicate a position for women like that which they occupy in Greek mythology and broadly in Athenian society — a position now agreed on by a number of people. That is, Athenian men and their laws simultaneously place women in a position of 'total dependence' and treat them with 'obsessive fear and revulsion.'[113] Much fruitless disagreement about the status of Athenian women arose in the past from the failure to recognize the basic ambiguity of their position — in some ways powerless, in other ways highly powerful.

Some of the passive, powerless aspects of a woman's lot in Athens were elaborately codified in the laws. A woman, like a piece of property, was always under legal control of some man; and if he should die in her lifetime, she and whatever was attached to her passed to the next male relative in the same elaborate order of succession used for any other property. If the woman was heiress to an estate, the estate went to the appropriate male relative whose wife she necessarily became; she had no more choice in the matter than would a tripod or a vase.[114] One would imagine that, like property, a woman could be maltreated and discarded; and the speeches seem to bear this out. A woman was at the mercy of a husband's caprice (Andoc. 1.124–7). Moreover, if a husband caught his wife in adultery, he had to divorce her on pain of disenfranchisement (Dem. 59.87); hers was an offense against the property in that it might bring bastard children into the line of inheritance (Lys. 1.33). If an adulteress — proven or, it seems, even simply alleged — were found participating in any public cult, she could be insulted and maltreated in any way which did not result in death. And, as Harrison importantly pointed out, all these provisions apparently applied as much to the victim of rape as to the most willingly unfaithful.[115]

Despite so vulnerable a position, a woman was not entirely unprotected under the law, and her single greatest security was her dowry. The dowry or its financial equivalent was returnable on divorce absolutely without exception and could be claimed exempt by the wife if her husband's goods were confiscated. There were special suits both to enforce the return of the dowry (*dike proikos*) and to secure payment of eighteen per cent interest on it for support of the woman until it could be returned (*dike sitou*). Such protection could be made substantial even for a woman from an unwealthy family through the mechanism of a fictitious dowry, a sum agreed to by the husband at marriage to be forfeited in case of divorce.[116]

It may or may not be that the seclusion of Athenian women resulted partly from an attempt to protect what was such an important element in the transmission of the estate and continuation of the family: the whole topic is difficult. But even though one can make a list of times and places for acceptable and even expected public appearances of Athenian women, there is ample evidence that they were generally confined to the inner quarters of the house — and the wealthier the house, the more the servants did away with any need for the mistress to go outside.[117] Women did not even accompany their husbands to dinner parties in other houses or appear for dinner in their own home in the presence of their husband's guests (Isae. 3.13–14).

The results of such an exclusively private existence are evident in the courts. Painstaking argument and massive testimony are needed at times merely to establish the identity or even existence of a given woman after long years inside the home.[118] Such a task was all the more difficult in that women were not only seldom seen, but also, in accordance with Pericles' dictum, seldom spoken of. This was true not only in daily life but also in court, so that even in cases in which women were the key elements, or a large number of women had repeatedly to be referred to, orators went to great lengths to avoid using the names of the women involved. They might, it is true, name the dead, prostitutes, slaves, or with a certain relish — the female relatives of their opponents; but if at all possible they would designate their own relatives by various periphrases — even if this required a profusion of men's names.[119]

With the evidence which has now been marshalled, it would seem difficult to claim that the lives of Athenian women were not subject to extensive public restrictions. However, no matter how inclusive and severe those restrictions were, they could be compatible with a very different private situation in which these same women might exercise considerable power.[120] In fact the court speeches show that this was precisely the case sometimes: there were women who were quite knowledgeable and active in details of household finance and estate management.[121] These speeches are also one of the main sources of indications of what seems to have been a more general and pervasive sphere of female influence: the men who were important in the lives of the family's children were apparently almost exclusively the mother's not the father's relatives — particularly the mother's father and brothers.[122] The laws of adoption reflect the strength of these maternal ties. Although adoption broke all legal connections between the child and natural father, it had absolutely no effect on the ties to the natural mother — including, of course, the rights to potential inheritance from her father.[123]

Part of the property and potentially the vehicle for its transmission, the source of heirs and the provider of relatives helpful to them, the woman as a center of power and importance in the house became the focus of certain anxieties as well. She was, for example, liable to prosecution for abortion: the destruction of an embryo — especially in cases where the father-to-be had died — could secure property claims for relatives who might never have had a chance to profit had the child been born.[124]

There seems to have been anxiety for much more than the embryo. Many things might come under the control of a woman at the heart of the house. In fact, sufficient control might even give her power over her husband — with potentially disastrous results for him. Aeschylus' depiction of Clytemnestra with her man-planning heart seems at least related to this male fear (*Ag.* 11), and it must have gained effect from the fact that such role reversal was not confined to literature and imagination. At least this is what Euphiletus wanted the jurors to believe on his day in court (Lys. 1). In recounting the chain of events which led him to the discovery of his wife's adulterous liaison, he creates a narrative in which the depiction of women is quite consistent and always disturbing.

Of the two apparently standard arrangements for a Greek house — women's quarters inside and men's out, or women's upstairs and men's down — Euphiletus made use of the latter until he allowed the spatial order in his home to be reversed. The new arrangement decreased the inconvenience associated with the care of a new-born child, but it also made possible a reversal in sexual roles. The wife took advantage of her freer position to carry on an affair with another man. The servant girl conveyed messages to the lover and arranged simple but devious nocturnal signals to the wife. In the end, the tissue of lies and tricks created by these women was dissolved only through the agency of another woman's destructive hatred: a jealous female rival of the wife denounced the affair to Euphiletus. Throughout this vivid account the most striking element is the persuasive speaking of the wife. She uses clever words first to obtain the changes in the household and then to maintain her husband's blindness — she even teases him about his unfaithful desires when she is on her way to meet her lover. Her ruinous persuasive skill brings us to our last legal point.

We have seen several ways in which the estate, its management and transmission were tied to the woman. The apprehension over a woman's power in inheritance was explicitly codified by including among grounds for invalidating a will the persuasion of a woman. Cases could turn on this problem or seek desperately to avoid it (Isae. 2.19, 6.9). It must have been an effective line of attack. First, if there had been a woman in the life of the deceased, it would be difficult to prove that he had not made his will 'thinking improperly since he was persuaded by a woman' — *gynaiki pithomenos . . . paranoon* ([Dem.] 46.14). Besides being difficult to disprove, the charge must have had a powerful emotional effect. The jurors were moved by tragedies which turned on the catastrophes which developed from yielding to women's persuasion: Jocasta at least tried to tempt Oedipus not to trust oracles; Medea succeeded in persuading all the men she met; and after reasoning with Agamemnon at length, all Clytemnestra had to say to get her way was *pithou* — be persuaded (*Ag.* 943).[125]

It is not surprising that law and tragedy should both reflect the society's concerns. But when they mirror each other so closely, as in the case of the anxiety over female persuasion, each seems more intelligible, and the combination seems to bring out more clearly the outlines of the problem they address. The next chapter is devoted entirely to the ways these two cultural institutions — law and tragedy — intersect.

Notes

1. Bronislaw Malinowski, *Crime and Custom in Savage Society* (Littlefield, Adams and Co., Totowa, 1976), 127.
2. Roberto M. Unger, *Law in Modern Society: Toward a Criticism of Social Theory* (The Free Press, New York, 1976), 124.
3. James Redfield, 'Plato and the Art of Politics' (Ph.D. diss., University of Chicago, 1961), 90.
4. Jean-Pierre Vernant, *Mythe et société en Grèce ancienne* (François Maspero, Paris, 1974), 31.
5. Vernant, *Mythe et société*, 45.
6. See Vernant, *Mythe et société*, 31. Drama is omitted here not because it was exempt from the spirit of competition but because, as a phenomenon of the democracy, it developed in parallel with the courts rather than serving as part of their cultural base. All this is discussed in Chapter 4.
7. *Il.* 23. Specific examples are discussed below. The continuity between games and law is noted by Louis Gernet, 'Jeux et droit: remarques sur le XXIIIe chant de l'*Iliade*,' in *Droit et société dans la Grèce ancienne* (University of Paris, Paris, 1955) p. 17. His claim that community approval of the decision is necessary cannot be correct (p. 16). The Homeric assembly is not a democratic one, as *Il.* 1 demonstrates.
8. John D. Beazley, *Attic Red-figure Vase-painters*, 2nd edn (Oxford University Press, Oxford, 1963) 26.1. John Boardman, *Athenian Red Figure Vases: The Archaic Period: A Handbook* (Oxford University Press, New York and Toronto, 1975) plates 33.1 and 33.2 (hereafter cited as *ARF Handbook*).
9. Eduard Fraenkel (ed.), *Agamemnon* (Oxford University Press, Oxford, 1962) *ad loc.* notes that wrestling, in Greek, is a general term for athletic or military contests.
10. Soph. *Phil.* 431ff.; Ar. *Ran.* 775, 877. *Ran.* 775 strongly suggests a courtroom proceeding. Certain explicit uses of this metaphor in that context are discussed below.
11. For the importance of wrestling metaphors in the *Oresteia* see Michael Poliakoff, 'The Third Fall in the *Oresteia*,' *AJP* 101 (1980) 251–9.
12. Pind. *Ol.* 1.1ff., 3.42ff. A truly excellent bibliography and discussion on the priamel is now to be found in Anne Pippin Burnett, *Three Archaic Poets: Archilochus, Alcaeus, and Sappho* (Harvard University Press, Cambridge, Mass., 1983) 281ff.
13. And Sappho could turn it against practically anything in a characteristically elegant and clever way: fr. 16.
14. The verbs were used for erotic battle as well: *kai gar ai pheugei tacheos dioxei* (Sappho 1.21). Poetry and painting continued through the centuries to blend wrestling with war and love.
15. See note 10 above. Pl. *Resp.* 405c.
16. Alick R.W. Harrison, *The Law of Athens* vol. 2 (Oxford University Press, Oxford, 1971), 172, 176 n.2 (hereafter cited as *LA* followed by volume and page). The most important passages are Andocides 1.74, Hyper. 4.12 and Dem. 51.12.
17. For the regular order of the events see Paus. 6.15.5.
18. All aspects of the pancration are clearly discussed and amply illustrated in E. Norman Gardiner's two books *Greek Athletic Sports and Festivals* (Macmillan and Co., London, 1910) 435–50 and *Athletics of the Ancient World* (Oxford University Press, Oxford, 1930) 212–21.
19. George Miller Calhoun, *Athenian Clubs in Politics and Litigation* (University of Texas Bulletin, Austin, 1913) 103. Aristophanes claimed not to kick Cleon while he was down (*Nub.* 550), but this showed rare restraint for an Athenian — which is, of course, part of the point in making the claim. It was a thousand years before

Sopater would assert such generosity to be a general Athenian trait. See *Rhetores Graeci*, edited by Ch. Waltz, vol. 4 (J.G. Cottae, Stuttgart, 1832–6) p. 550. It was regular to discourage kicking or gloating over a dead man, but that was an entirely different matter. (See Soph. *Aj.* 1348. There is something of this at *Od.* 22.412 where the scholiast gives us also Archilochus fr. 134 West.) And even the dead were far from the respect of their enemies.

20. The poets coined other words for culpable desertion. Sometimes they were literally military, as Aeschylus' *liponaus*; sometimes only metaphorically, as Euripides' *lipopator*. The other class of compounds in *lipo-*, clearly not relevant here, was for defects, usually physical.

21. Dem. 49.19ff. The actual details are murky. See Harrison, *LA*, vol. 2, 141–2 and more fully Robert J. Bonner and Gertrude Smith, *The Administration of Justice from Homer to Aristotle*, vol. 2 (The University of Chicago Press, Chicago, 1938) 139–44 (hereafter cited as *B and Sm* followed by volume and page).

22. See especially Andoc. 1.141–3, 147–8, 2.26. Other examples and discussions will be found in Kenneth J. Dover *Greek Popular Morality in the Time of Plato and Aristotle* (University of California Press, Berkeley and Los Angeles, 1974), 293; Arthur W.H. Adkins, *Merit and Responsibility: A Study in Greek Values* (The University of Chicago Press, Chicago, 1975), 202ff. There is a perceptive discussion with many citations by Wyse in his note to Isae. 4.26. This commonplace of court rhetoric is also noted and discussed (with additional references) by John K. Davies, *Athenian Propertied Families: 600–300 BC* (Oxford University Press, Oxford, 1971), xviii.

23. See especially Max Hamburger, *Morals and Law: The Growth of Aristotle's Legal Theory* (Bible and Tanner, New York, 1965) 89–102.

24. Fr. 6 West. See P.J. Rhodes, *A Commentary on the Aristotelian 'Athenaion Politeia'* (Oxford University Press, Oxford, 1981), p. 141, 173 (hereafter cited as *CAAP*).

25. However Adkins, *Merit and Responsibility*, 56 does note the similarity of criteria in the games of *Il.* 23 and in the Athenian law courts and assembly.

26. The concise Greek at this point leaves it unclear whether the speaker's recent defeat was merely in *antidosis* or *antidosis* followed by other defeats. The latter, fuller pattern is the one envisaged by Robert J. Bonner, 'The Legal Setting of Isocrates' *Antidosis*,' *CP* 15 (1920), 194.

27. '[A]t Athens . . . the legal and political were intertwined, so that the movement of an individual up and down the scale of status, power and influence in the community was determined by the outcome of *dikai* as well as *graphai*.' Kenneth J. Dover, *Lysias and the 'Corpus Lysiacum'* (University of California Press, Berkeley and Los Angeles, 1968), 171.

28. Harrison, *LA*, vol. 2, 81–2 gives a convenient list of cases certainly or probably *timetoi* with the evidence for each type. See also Louis Gernet, 'Sur la notion du jugement en droit grec,' in *Droit et société*, 78–9.

29. Aeschin. 3.197–8. *Ath. Pol.* 67.3, 69.2 and Rhodes, *CAAP, ad loc.*

30. Moses I. Finley, *The Ancient Economy* (The University of California Press, Berkeley and Los Angeles, 1973), 48.

31. Dover, *Greek Popular Morality*, 34. There were complicated divisions within the group and Attic Greek had terms such as *agathos* and *poneros* to express them. However, although writers such as Aristophanes, the 'Old Oligarch,' and Thucydides vividly express the perception of class differences, the courts do not seem to have served as an arena for hostilities based on class differences. See the discussion below.

32. Dover, *Greek Popular Morality*, 37–41; Finley, *Ancient Economy*, 47–51; Unger, *Law in Modern Society*, 123–4.

33. For the provision of imprisonment see Dem. 21.47, 24.105, 33.1, 35.46–7,

90   *The Administration of Justice*

56.4; for loss of the nose — Dem. 25.60–2.

34. *Ath.Pol.* 27.5. See Rhodes's comments here: the first bribery must be well before 409 BC. See [Xen.] *Ath.Pol.* 3.7, Isoc. 18.11. Calhoun, *Athenian Clubs*, 66–72 presents the evidence and reasons from it very clearly. Other references cited by Calhoun include Lys. 29.12, Isoc. 8.50, and Aeschin. 1.86–7.

35. For the law see [Dem.] 46.26. Its authenticity, with the exception of the clause on anti-democratic conspiracy, was accepted by Gernet, who dated it, in his edition *ad loc.*, near the end of the fifth century. For the new juror allotment procedures see Harrison, *LA*, vol. 2, 239–40. As evidence of their failure to end the activity see Lys. 29.12, Isoc. 8.50, Aeschin. 1.86–7. Rhodes accepts *dekazein* in all these as 'bribe' jurors: *Ath.Pol.* 27.5. Dover, *Greek Popular Morality*, 38–9 gives a fairly balanced picture but perhaps overestimates 'class division.'

36. S.C. Humphreys, 'Politics and Private Interest in Classical Athens,' *CJ* 73 (1977/8) 103–4.

37.Xen. *Hell.* 2.3.12, 2.3.38; *Ath.Pol.* 35.2. Caution is required here because of the lack of precise fifth-century information on sycophancy. It is not clear how far the term sycophant was meant to apply merely to false accusers and to imply dishonest activity. Adkins has argued persuasively that under certain conditions the term could even be used to criticize a volunteer prosecutor proceeding in the most honorable and legal manner. See Arthur W.H. Adkins, '*Polupragmosyne* and "Minding One's Own Business": A Study in Greek Social and Political Values,' *CP* 71 (1976) 307–11, 316–19. The extent to which these prosecutors were both encouraged and despised is a measure of the ambiguous tension in Athens between democratic equality and aristocratic privilege and prestige.

38. Ar. *Vesp.* 33, 103. See Douglas M. MacDowell *ad loc.* for many other Aristophanic references.

39. See Isae. 5.43, 7.39, 11.47; Lys. 20.23; Isoc. 7.35, 18.48, 60; Dem. 28.2,7,24; [Dem.] 42.23; Aeschin. 1.101; Din. 1.70 for such charges or defenses against them. The references were collected by Wyse in his note to Isae. 7.39.

40. W. Robert Connor, *The New Politicians of Fifth-century Athens* (Princeton University Press, Princeton, 1971) 67–79.

41. Connor, *New Politicians*, 87–136.

42. Connor, *New Politicians*, 79–84. See Antony Andrewes, in Arnold W. Gomme *et al.*, *A Historical Commentary on Thucydides*, vol. 5, book 8 (Oxford University Press, Oxford, 1981) 257–64 (*ad* Thuc. 8.73.3. Hereafter cited as *HCT* preceded by author responsible for the cited volume or section).

43. Xen. *Hell.* 2.3.39, 2.3.15.

44. Calhoun, *Athenian Clubs*, 17.

45. Calhoun, *Athenian Clubs*, reports and analyzes their activities in detail.

46. Also *enochlein* and *spoude*: Calhoun, *Athenian Clubs*, 75 note 1. See Dem. 21.4; Aeschin. 3.1.

47. Isoc. 18.9–10; Dem. 58.34; Lys. 25.3; Aeschin. 1.107; Xen. *Mem.* 2.9.1.

48. The sentiment occurs with great frequency and is often expressed in legal terms. Soph. *O.T.* 614, 1213ff.; fr. 62P, 301P; Eur. *Hipp.* 1051–2, fr. 60 (with Euripidean irony and complication). There is a clear early statement by Pindar at *Ol.* 10.53ff. and fr. 132. Related are Solon fr. 36 West (24D) and Soph. *Aj.* 646.

49. *Ath.Pol.* 57.2; Antiphon 6.42.

50. Calhoun, *Athenian Clubs*, 40–1, n.5.

51. Ar. *Nub.* 876, *Vesp.* 1007.

52. Thucydides may well want his criticism to apply even more to Cleon than to the Athenians themselves. But even if one can distinguish the exploiter from the exploited in this phenomenon, it is no less real.

53. Dem. 24.7–8; Lys. 13.1, 14.1–2. See *B and Sm* vol. 2, 41–2.

54. Gernet, *Droit et société*, 81.

55. Harrison, *LA*, vol. 1, 161–2. Douglas M. MacDowell, *The Law in Classical Athens* (Cornell University Press, Ithaca, 1978) 95–8, 102–5 (hereafter cited as *LCA*). J.P Gould, 'Law, Custom, and Myth: Aspects of the Social Position of Women in Classical Athens,' *JHS* 100 (1980) 43–5. For the significance of this parallelism, see below p. 84 ff.

56. Harrison, *LA*, vol. 1, 10, 159; Gernet, *Droit et société*, 69–70.

57. Gernet, *Droit et société*, 70–1.

58. Isae. 3.58, 4.25; Dem. 43.4ff., 43.16. Harrison, *LA*, vol. 1, 160–2; MacDowell, *LCA*, p. 103.

59. Louis Gernet, 'Recherches sur le développement de la pensée juridique et morale en Gréce: Étude sémantique' (Ph.D. diss., Ernest Leroux, Paris, 1917) 92–3.

60. For *graphe xenias* see Dem. 59.16; *phasis*, Dem. 58.13; *apographe*, Dem. 53.1–2. See also Dem. 40.20–2, 49.45–7, 59.7; Lys. 17, 19; Hyp. *Eux.* 34.

61. The exact uses of *antigraphe* are difficult to classify partly because the suit usually comes in what is already a legal tangle. There is a very helpful discussion and collection of data in Harrison, *LA*, vol. 2, 131–3.

62. Harrison, *LA*, vol. 2, 192–5.

63. Ibid. 197–9.

64. Lys. 9; Harrison, *LA*, vol. 2, 5–6, 211ff.

65. Harrison, *LA*, vol. 2, 208ff.

66. For this analysis it does not matter whether the author of the *Ath.Pol.*'s limitation to the sixth prytany or Gilbert's extension to all prytanies is correct. (Gustave Gilbert, *The Constitutional Antiquities of Sparta and Athens* (Sonnenschein and Co., London, 1895) 303 note 3.) The process was a competitive election rather than a qualitative evaluation or judgement.

67. Calhoun, *Athenian Clubs*, 49ff.

68. Geoffrey E.R. Lloyd, *Science, Folklore and Ideology* (Cambridge University Press, Cambridge, 1983) 89–90.

69. See Thuc. 4.74.4, 5.74.1, and 8.97.2 with Andrewes' notes to the last two in *HCT* Gomme *et al*.

70. *Il.* 3.363, 13.20, 14.148; Pind. *Ol.* 1.60. The last is much discussed, but perhaps is merely emphatic: 'the worst trials — and even more.' Pind. *Nem.* 7.104; Aesch. *Cho.* 791ff.; Soph. *Aj.* 432–3, *Phil.* 1238; Pl. *Phlb.* 60a. The phrases began to fall into regular idioms such as the group in *Nem.* 7.104, *Phil.* 1238, and *Phlb.* 60a. But the pattern was the same in all. It occurs occasionally in Latin verse: Verg. *Aen.* 1.94, Hor. *Sat.* 2.7.76.

71. Gernet, 'Recherches,' 159–60.

72. For a third fee, *parastasis*, we have no quantitative information. See Harrison, *LA*, vol. 2, 92–4, 179–83.

73. Ibid. 183–5.

74. The information comes from many sources most helpfully collected at Harrison, *LA*, vol. 2, 47 note 2 and Rhodes, *CAAP*, p. 723–30 on *Ath.Pol.* 67.4–68.1.

75. Again, information is scattered. See Harrison, *LA*, vol. 2, 236–8 on *antidosis*. The fullest discussion with bibliography is W.A. Goligher, 'Studies in Attic Law: II,' *Hermathena* 33 (1907) 481–515.

76. Goligher, 'Studies in Attic Law,' 512.

77. Harrison, *LA*, vol. 2, 162 reports this last category without qualification, but the text is disputed. Rhodes, *CAAP*, gives alternative possibilities. In any case, if this paragraph treats only cases for over a thousand drachmas, the lesser cases with their smaller juries will almost certainly have had less time.

78. For the two minutes and all other estimates of time see Rhodes, *CAAP*, p. 717–34 on *Ath.Pol.* 67–9. The more ample proportional allowance is proposed by Douglas M. MacDowell whose emendation of *Ath.Pol.* 69.2 makes this interpretation possible: see 'The Length of the Speeches on the Assessment of the Penalty in

Athenian Courts,' *CQ* 35 (1985) 525–6.

79. Harrison, *LA*, vol. 1, 78, 118. Harpocration *s.v. kakoseos*.

80. See Unger, *Law in Modern Society*, 50–5 on the characteristics of custom versus law which apply precisely here.

81. Harrison, *LA*, vol. 2, 193–5.

82. Perhaps, like some modern readers of Isaeus, fourth-century juries tired of the intricacies of inheritance; sometime after the 370s the reply was eliminated and the main speech was limited to about twenty-five minutes. See *Ath.Pol.* 67.2.

83. Eur. *Sthen*. Prologue 22ff.; *Theseus* fr. 388N²; Pl. *Symp.* 180cff.

84. See John Boardman, *Athenian Black Figure Vases* (Oxford University Press, New York, 1974) 105ff., plates 161–4 and Boardman, *ARF Handbook*, 15ff., plates 2, 8.,

85. See Susan Woodford, 'Ajax and Achilles Playing a Game on an Olpe in Oxford,' *JHS* 102 (1982) especially 174–6.

86. Delphi. Their golden images flanked the omphalos. See Pind. *Pyth.* 4.6; Soph. *O.T.* 480; and Eur. *Or.* 311 with the scholia to all three; Plut. *De def. or.* 1; Strabo 9.419ff.

87. Geoffrey E.R. Lloyd, *Polarity and Analogy: Two Types of Argumentation in Early Greek Thought* (Cambridge University Press, Cambridge, 1966) 90–4 is exceedingly clear and helpful on this subject. However, anyone interested in Wilamowitz's original list of these phrases should go rather to the second edition of *H.F.* (1895) 231–2 than to the first, cited by Lloyd. Chaotic printing errors plague the entry for *H.F.* 1106 in the 1889 edition.

88. Soph. *Ant.* 1109ff. Jebb here and Denniston at Eur. *El.* 564 are respectful of custom, however peculiar it be. At Eur. *H.F.* 1106 Bond and Wilamowitz are more matter-of-fact and cite many similar inappropriate completions. See especially Eur. *Hel.* 229.

89. See Wilamowitz at Eur. *H.F.* 1106 and Gomme *HCT ad loc.*

90. Peter Galison called my attention to the mismanagement at Sphakteria.

91. Diog. Laert. 9.51 claims priority for Protagoras.

92. The treatise *Dissoi Logoi* (DK 90), though inept, collects such arguments.

93. Even rhetoric embodied makes its chastising harangues with charmingly human motivation. See especially Right at lines 961–83.

94. See note 84 above.

95. For willful damage see Dem. 21.42ff. Homicide is discussed below. The universalizing doublet is found in Eur. *Bacch.* 800–1. For the other see Hes. fr. 286 MW; Pind. *Nem.* 4.32; Aesch. *Ag.* 533, 1527ff., *Cho.* 313; Soph. *Ant.* 914, fr. 229P; Pl. *Leg.* 872d–e.

96. Michael Gagarin has suggested that all references to just and unjust homicide result from similar manipulations of the *hekon/akon* division and polar expressions one of whose members is not relevant: 'The Prohibition of Just and Unjust Homicide in Antiphon's *Tetralogies*,' *GRBS* 19 (1978) 291–306.

97. Here and with all these references to Isaeus see Wyse who is always alert to the artificiality of the arguments.

98. *IG* i²115. Michael Gagarin notes the instances in *Drakon and Early Athenian Homicide Law* (Yale University Press, New Haven, 1981), 155.

99. I owe my awareness of the phenomenon to Gagarin's discussion in *Drakon and Early Athenian Homicide Law*, 155–8. However, his negative opinions about the role of artistic effect in the use of this feature have no foundation. How, or even whether, the chiasmus in archaic prose pleased the artistic concerns of Drakon and his fellow citizens we cannot hope to know.

100. Soph. *Aj.* 642ff., *Trach.* 132ff; Eur. *Phoen.* 541ff. Helen F. North discusses the passages from *Ajax* and *Phoenissae* as examples of natural order and regularity in *From Myth to Icon: Reflections of Greek Ethical Doctrine in Literature and Art*

(Cornell University Press, Ithaca, 1979) 26–7.

101. See her whole speech at *Phoen.* 535ff.

102. This is one of the uses of *antigraphe* discussed above pages 69–70.

103. Hyp. *Lyc.* 8–10; Lys. 9.1–3.

104. See the analysis in *On the Crown*, edited by William Watson Goodwin (Cambridge University Press, Cambridge, 1904) 259–60.

105. Aesch. *Eum* 198; Soph. *O.T.* 408–9, 543–4; Xen. *An.* 2.5.16–17.

106. See Frederick A. Paley, *Euripides: The Works*, vol. 2 (Whitaker and Co., London, 1858) xv–xxi.

107. The actual list, based on the Oxford text, is somewhat tedious, but I present it assuming that although few would want to compile it, more might want to look at it.

    a. Nicias and Alcibiades (Book 6), 108 lines each
    b. Hermocrates and Athenagoras (Book 6), 89 lines each
    c. Corcyra and Corinth (Book 1), 103 lines, 109 lines
    d. Cleon and Diodotus (Book 3), 137 lines, 144 lines
    e. Plataea and Thebes (Book 3), 153 lines, 143 lines
    f. Hermocrates and Euphemus (Book 6), 106 lines, 114 lines

The remaining major group of speeches took place in Sparta, not a democratic setting. But the speeches may be grouped as follows: Corinth 111 lines, Athens 125 lines, Sparta (= Archidamus plus Sthenelaidus) 116 lines (= 98 + 18 lines).

108. See discussion above.

109. John H. Finley, Jr. 'Euripides and Thucydides,' *HSCP* 49 (1938) 64–7.

110. More perhaps, could be made of these syndics in this context than has. The tablets seem to indicate widespread frustration at least. See *IG* IIIiii 66, 88, 94, 103, 105, 106, 107, 173.

111. *IG* IIIiii 106, cited by Helen McClees, whose work first drew my attention to these tablets, the *tabellae defixionum:* see *A Study of Women in Attic Inscriptions*, (Columbia University Press, New York, 1920) 28–31.

112. Walter K. Lacey, *The Family in Classical Greece* (Cornell University Press, Ithaca, 1968) 173–4 cites both these passages.

113. Gould, 'Law, Custom, and Myth,' 55. This article is simply the single best starting point for any one interested in women in Greece.

114. The details are somewhat complicated but clearly set forth in most standard sources: see conveniently Gould, 'Law, Custom and Myth,' 43–4; for more detail *LA* (above, note 16) 1.122–62.

115. Harrison, *LA*, vol. 1, 32–6.

116. For details and sources of all these provisions see Harrison, *LA*, vol. 1, 45–57.

117. There is a full collection of evidence for women's activities in Donald, C. Richter, 'The Position of Women in Classical Athens,' *CJ* 67 (1971) 7–8. It is not a *discriminating* collection; some of his citations, in fact, point to the exceptional nature of these excursions outside the home.

118. Isae. 8.9–10, 6.13–16, and especially Dem. 43.29–46.

119. The great consistency with which these rules are followed has been demonstrated with elegance and clarity by David Schaps, 'The Woman Least Mentioned: Etiquette and Women's Names,' *CQ* 71 (1977) 323–30.

120. It has been argued by Philip Slater that the confinement of women *created* the situation in which they had certain profound psychological effects on their children which in turn had far-reaching cultural consequences: *The Glory of Hera: Greek Mythology and the Greek Family* (Beacon Press, Boston, 1968).

121. Lys. 32.11–18; Dem. 36.14, 41.8–21: all cited in this connection by Gould, 'Law, Custom and Myth,' 50.

122. For the importance — actual or expected — of the mother's father see Isae. 8.15; Lys. 32.16, 24, 27; of the mother's brothers — Aeschin. 2.78; Andoc. 3.29; Dem. 48.8, 59.12; Isae. 3.26, 29ff. These references are collected and discussed with many other fascinating related materials by Jan Bremmer, 'The Importance of the Maternal Uncle and Grandfather in Archaic and Classical Greece and Early Byzantium,' *ZPE* 50 (1983) 173–86. Important relationships are not always pleasant. Some legends associated the founding of the Areopagus with the murder of a sister's son who was being educated by his uncle. Also, for a particularly unhelpful mother's brother not cited by Bremmer see Hierocles in Isaeus 9.

123. See Harrison, *LA*, vol. 1, 93–4. The main evidence is Isae. 7.25.

124. Lys. fr. 8, 8a Thalheim are the scraps from which the consideration of abortion law begins, but any substantive discussion depends on second-hand references in Theon and Sopater. All the information is difficult to evaluate. See Harrison, *LA*, vol. 1, 72–3.

125. The connection between the tragic pattern of danger and the legal provision for wills seems to have gone unnoticed even where it would seem most appropriate: it would certainly add, for example, to the discussions in Froma I. Zeitlin, 'The Dynamics of Misogyny: Myth and Mythmaking in the *Oresteia*,' *Arethusa* 11 (1978) 149–84, and R.G.A. Buxton, *Persuasion in Greek Tragedy: A Study of Peitho* (Cambridge University Press, Cambridge, 1982) especially 105–14.

4 Law and Drama

1. Introduction

The legal and dramatic competitive activities of one of the most famous Athenians are fused by the biographical tradition. Using a standard Athenian suit, Sophocles' son charged his aged father with mental incompetence in order to gain control of the estate. To prove his sanity, Sophocles recited part of a chorus from *Oedipus at Colonus*, which he had just written. The victorious old man was escorted from the court, Plutarch reports, as if from the theater amid the admiring applause and shouts of the jurors.[1] The anecdote perfectly illustrates the complexity of the relation between law and drama in Athens. First, *Oedipus at Colonus* itself contains a bitter *agon* or debate between the old Oedipus and his son Polyneices. And not only is the content, a father-son struggle, related to Attic law, but the form as well is that of a court trial with opposing speeches of roughly equivalent length. Such sets of legalistic speeches or confrontations abound in mid- and late fifth-century drama. *Oedipus at Colonus* alone has three such debates.[2] Every Aristophanic comedy features some sort of contest or *agon*,[3] and the description and analysis of the *agones* of tragedy fill a large book.[4]

The second link between law and drama which the Sophoclean story reveals is their broad institutional similarity. The characters opposing each other in the plots of the plays were set in motion by dramatists competing against each other before the citizens at the dramatic festivals. Rival playwrights, like litigants, set forth conflicts in words before their audiences; and the city, in the form of judges or jurors, chose a winner. Since both the form and content of the plays and the nature of dramatic competition linked the theater and courts, the bonds between these two social institutions were stronger than those between the law courts and athletic competitions. Moreover, a host of formal institutional details combined with a concentration on conflicts between individuals made the popular courts even more closely related to Athenian tragedy and comedy than they were to the political assembly. We have no date or author for the story of Sophocles' dramatic court reading. But

95

extant court speeches and passages from the plays discussed below
show that the Athenians saw the two types of competition as
equivalent in many ways. This may be partly because the popular
courts and dramatic competition developed and gained importance
as civic institutions at much the same time.

2. Historical Development

Aeschylus brought Greek tragedy to maturity at the City Dionysia,
yet he died too soon after the reforms in the Areopagus to have seen
the subsequent flowering of the popular courts. His plays lack
formal *agones*, the legalistic paired speeches of later drama. Their
absence is especially striking in those plays such as the *Eumenides*
and *Suppliant Women* which are centered around the formal adjudication of a dispute. The scenes of judgement contain elaborate
symmetries but not balanced judicial speeches.[5] Apparently the
trials at the Areopagus with their controlled speeches before small
juries of distinguished Athenians had little influence on the early
tragedians. The dramatic festivals and the form of tragedy had more
in common with the athletic and other literary competitions than
with the traditional homicide procedures of the Attic courts.

However, changes in the administration of law after Aeschylus'
death drew the courts and theater much closer together. Unlike the
Areopagites, the citizens in the large juries of the new popular
courts formed audiences much like those of the dramatic festivals.
Moreover, the shift was not only qualitiative. As Pericles instituted
pay for the jurors and the growing city and its empire generated
more and more legal activity, the number of citizens involved in
these more theatrical trials greatly increased. At the same time,
Athenians began to attend more plays. Around 442 the city-state
provided support for comedy at the festival of the Lenaia, and about
ten years later, tragedy was added as well.[6] Such conditions help
explain the rapid spread of the formal legalistic debate from the
court to the stage. The *agon* already figures in Sophocles' plays from
the 440s and becomes a fixed feature of Euripidean drama, and
Aristophanes used litigious confrontations for both the content and
the form of his comic tilts at Athens and her citizens.

The striking and pervasive effect which the popular courts had on
tragedy seems a further reflection of the sharp division between the
homicide courts and the popular courts described in Chapter 2. That

is, the early plays, even ones directly concerned with an Athenian homicide court as is the *Eumenides*, seem little concerned with or related to Athenian law and its adjudication. But the popular courts, being new and partly as a result of their youth being quite different, have an impact on society which is indicated in part simply by the fact that they *have* an effect on tragedy. The particular ways in which that effect is manifested in the tragedies of the second half of the fifth century is further evidence both of the extent to which the popular courts were felt to be different and of how the difference was perceived.

3. Dramatic Festival and Court: Institutional Similarities

These legal and dramatic verbal contests shared various details of procedure and administration which suggested their equivalence to democratic audiences. Some of the resemblances were elaborately specific. Each year three tragic poets were chosen to compete at the City Dionysia, an honor which constituted a sort of victory in itself.[7] Around the mid-fifth century, three protagonists were selected as well, probably beginning in 449 when prizes for actors were introduced.[8] The festival itself was the arena for the second and more important contest among both groups of three. The legal counterpart was the annual choice of three citizens and three metics to be tried as sycophants, although there the initial nomination was itself a distinct annoyance, and conviction in the actual trial was as ruinous as victory in the Dionysia was prestigious.[9] The parallels in the procedure demonstrate how completely the Athenians could conceive and treat the workings of justice as simply another city-wide competition.

The intense Athenian desire to win, or at least to see one's enemies lose, made bribery a potential problem in any competition. So the city devised an elaborate system to choose judges for plays and choruses through a series of stages designed to hinder tampering. First a list of potential judges was drawn up for each tribe. Each of the ten sets of names was then sealed in a *hydria*, or water-pot. Just before the competition, ten judges were chosen by drawing one name from each urn.[10] Similarly, when bribery became a greater problem in the courts late in the fifth century, the Athenians discontinued long-term assignments of jurors to a particular court and began reassigning them daily.[11] The type of urn used for the new pre-trial drawings was precisely that used in the theater — the *hydria* (*Ath. Pol.* 63.2; Isoc. 17.33). Moreover, although Athenian government, religion and daily life involved the use of urns in various votes and lotteries, as far as we know only these procedures, which were specifically devised to hinder tampering by introducing a last-minute random factor, used water-pots. That is, when an innovation was required in legal administration, theatrical competition provided a model not only for the procedure but even for the exact equipment. We have already seen that the voting urn (a different type of vessel) was a powerful symbol for the conclusion of trails.[12] Theatrical competition too ended with the judges putting their ballots into an urn from which half were drawn back out to determine the outcome of the contest. However, although this last selection was a further effort to reduce the efficacy of outside influence, such procedures did not prevent bribery in the theater any more than they did in the courts. Aristophanes disavows involvement in such activity (*Ach.* 657–9), but other Athenians certainly tried to manipulate the results covertly and even openly if they wielded sufficient power: Pythodorus, friend of the well-known Athenian banker Pasion, apparently tried to tamper with the selection of judges for the festival of Dionysus in 395 or 394 (Isoc. 17.33–4); and in the related Dionysian competition of lyric choruses around 350 BC Demosthenes' old enemy Meidias combined private bribery with public intimidation of the judges — apparently with success (Dem. 21.17–18).

If there was little hope of insuring impartial competition by limiting the aggressive attempts of interested Athenian citizens, another approach remained. The ten tribal judges took an oath of impartiality which more than one comedian made it a point to mention, even though the judges listening could not conceivably have had time to forget it.[13] But even though the dramatic festivals had more connection to religion and ritual than the popular courts did, the oath was no more serious than the jurors' oath which litigants also recalled to their audience in frustration if not in hope. The theater simply provides another example of the pattern of Athenian competition which informed legal behavior as well. So far from being regularly cast on objective grounds, a judge's vote for first place could be cited in court as proof of friendship between the judge and a man whose tribe's chorus received the vote (Lys.4.3–4).

Even without the testimony of Plato and others, common sense would tell us that the theater audience could influence the judges with noisy demonstrations in support of or in opposition to a given play.[14] The jurors in the popular courts conducted themselves in the same noisy way, creating unwelcome disturbances which are constantly mentioned by writers in the fifth and fourth centuries. We may doubt Philocleon's assertion that the feared outbursts were as loud as Zeus' thunder (Ar. *Vesp.* 619–30), but they no doubt could affect other jurors just as audience reaction affected the theater judges. And whatever impression the jurors' shouts of disapproval produced themselves, they hindered the litigant from presenting his arguments.[15] A skeptic might defend doubts about further connecting legal and dramatic institutions in Athens through the similar behavior of their audiences if the observation were merely modern. But the Athenian of Plato's *Laws* describes the popular courts as filled with noisy shouts of praise and blame for each speaker *just like the theaters* (*kathaper theatra*: 876b).

So far the discussion has included only points of congruity between the administration or institutional procedure of theater and of law. Generally the evidence indicates that these resemblances were perceived and sometimes even intentionally instituted by the Athenians. The extent and variety of the connections suggests a basic kinship between the forms of competition.

Another anecdote — this time about Euripides — suggests that the Athenians were well aware of this situation. Apparently during a trial for *antidosis* Euripides' opponent Hygiaenon accused him of impiety for having encouraged perjury in the *Hippolytos* (line 612). Euripides' protest that the judgements should not be transferred from that contest to this is itself an indication of the close relation between the two types of contest. Perhaps more important is the fact that Aristotle uses the anecdote to illustrate the judicial principle that a verdict once given closes the case (*Rh.* 3.15.8). Aristotle also shows the tendency to approximate the two competitions in his discussion of delivery: in current theatrical competition, he claims, the actor's delivery is more important in determining the prize than the actual content of the poetry, just as delivery is more important than the actual argument in the courts and assembly (*Rh.* 3.1.4–5).

4. Complications and Comedy

There are other straightforward indications of the ties between drama and law: court speeches of Antiphon and Andocides underline the simple similarity in subject matter by drawing on well-known crimes and criminals from Athenian tragedies in references to Clytemnestra, Oedipus and Aegisthus (Antiphon 1.77, Andoc. 1.129). But in a culture whose elements were richly interrelated and isomorphic, the combination of related structures and shared subject matter to be treated in formally paired speeches produced complicated and elegant types of contact and reflection between these young developing inventions of the democracy.

One might expect a clever and closely observant Athenian to find and express such complex relationships in these civic activities. Fortunately, a near perfect witness left a number of his own plays. Aristophanes made Athenian law and tragedy the subject of several works. If our ignorance condemns us to be less appreciative than their original audiences of all the entertainment they provided, it makes us all the more grateful for the information they preserve. Aristophanes' comparisons and comments subtly blend legal and dramatic conventions of form and content.

When Philocleon describes the pleasures of jury duty, the initial implied comparison to theater attendance is quite simple. An actor appearing as defendant is made to recite his finest speech; the jurors are entertained just as audiences are (*Vesp.* 579–80). But the next example immediately extends and complicates the implications. A flute player having won his case plays an exit-tune (*exodos*) as payment to the jurors (581–2). Now the jurors, who in the previous two lines were an entertained audience, are also the dramatic judges who have selected the winner. A successful court appearance is crowned with victory like a successful dramatic presentation. And like a play, the trial ends with a dramatic decision and musical exodus. But in withdrawing from the court to the strains of the exodus, the jurors have clearly become the chorus as well as the audience and judges. And this brings out a comparison between trials and drama which depends on the internal structure of Greek tragedy and comedy rather than on any procedural or institutional feature of dramatic competition. The Greek chorus usually had an interested and involved relation to the protagonist on stage, just as the Athenian jurors often did to their fellow citizens appearing as litigants in court, especially in public suits.

The implications of Philocleon's comments all follow from the language condensed into four lines which incredibly retain an effortless and casual tone. Elsewhere Aristophanes creates his effect by suddenly crystalizing an image which has been developing throughout the play. The *Birds* opens with Euelpides and Peisthetairus seeking refuge from the laws and courts of Athens. The usual references to tragedy begin with an early joke on Sophocles (100). There is further fun with Athenian litigiousness, and Sophocles' praise of man's civic accomplishments is challenged by criticism and the plan for an alternative order among the very tribes of birds that Sophoclean man had so cleverly overcome (*Ant.* 343ff.). Eventually a herald reports that the Athenians have turned to the birds' life among the fields, marsh papyrus and shore pebbles (1286–9). But the puns in the description suggest that the Athenian citizens are as busy as ever with their laws, legal documents and voting disks (*nómos-nomós*; *biblia*; *psephismata*). Then comes an Athenian with a speech taken directly from Sophocles. Although it is only three lines long, it draws on and draws together all that has been said and implied about tragedy and law.[16] 'I wish I were a soaring eagle,' he says, 'so that I could fly over the sea.' In tragedy this is the conventional wish in an unbearable situation: Hermione, Creousa, and many tragic choruses long for wings in vain.[17] Although Aristophanes' humor makes wings available on request, the escape is deceptive. In the end this suppliant does not escape the Athenian law against father-beating even though he has come specifically because the birds had promised to allow it (757–79, 1347–69). Once we have realized that the wish is Sophoclean or even simply that it is tragic, that is exactly what we must expect. No matter how deeply the longing of Euelpides, Peisthetairus, and the suppliant, Athenians could not escape the laws of Athens any more than the actors and choruses of tragedy could grow wings and escape the unpleasant events taking shape around them. Even though the laws were in some ways a symbol of Athens' freedom, as conservative an Athenian as Aristophanes could also see them as inescapable external limitations which bound the citizens, often against their will, like the fates of tragedy. This is a lot, but it is not more than Aristophanes' craft implies.

5. Law in the Content and Tone of Tragedy

If an Athenian could not leave the laws behind him by going to Cloud-cuckoo land, he could certainly not expect to have his tragedy without them. The action of the plays often advanced through the elements of legal procedure, as, for example, in *Hippolytus*, where the *agon* between Theseus and Hippolytus explicitly takes the court form of accusation and defense with all the appropriate vocabulary and commonplaces of argumentation.[18] It is true that the legalism of the *Hippolytus* 'trial' is limited, since father and son can only appeal to witnesses dead, divine and geographical. Nevertheless, this common Euripidean device elsewhere even more closely resembles normal courtroom usage. So, for example, Medea (*Med.* 476), Helen (*Tro.* 955), and Iolaos (*Heracl.* 219) all call on human witnesses when arguing their cases.[19] Similarly, the procedure of *apagoge*, the immediate seizure of certain criminals caught in the act, provided the model for Antigone's arrest and arraignment.[20]

In addition to including elements of fifth-century procedure, stage versions of the myths often refer to or develop in accordance with specific Athenian laws. So, to continue with the plays just cited, the reason Antigone is arrested is that she has broken a Theban law very like one the audience would know well, the Athenian law prohibiting the burial of a traitor on local soil.[21] And once the dispute between father and son has reached its sad end, Hippolytus absolves Theseus of further consequences, as any victim could under the provisions of Attic homicide law (1449).[22] The pronouncement saves Theseus from a trial for homicide committed under compulsion (*phonos akousios*), which, as the forensically knowledgeable Artemis has made clear, would have been the applicable point of law.[23]

In *Hippolytus* the last-minute reconciliation lends a certain importance to these details, but elsewhere the tragedians often make legal points more in passing. So, for example, Agamemnon's closing sneer at Teucer refers to the exclusive speaking rights of free men in Athens' courts (Soph. *Aj.* 1259ff.), and Admetus' equally unfriendly parting shot at Pheres concerns the legal impossibility of disinheriting one's parents as opposed to one's children (Eur. *Alc.* 737–8). Sometimes, indeed, the most subtle use of legal language can convey essential information about a character. For example, the preposition *en* is regularly used with the dative plural to indicate a tribunal or group of jurors who judge someone, and in the *Oedipus Tyrannos* Creon so uses it when he asserts the chorus' recognition of his innocence despite Oedipus' accusations (676–7). Now in *Antigone*, if we forget this and read Antigone's *en theoisi ten diken dosein* (459–60) as 'render justice among the gods' or even 'pay the penalty among the gods', we will miss what Sophocles is showing of Antigone's character. She refers to a court or tribunal of the gods (this is the point of *en*); but, as Chapter 2 made clear, there was no such tribunal. The usage reveals how idiosyncratic Antigone's imagination is, and this, in turn, helps to make more comprehensible the behavior which isolates her from society. She envisions and describes an afterlife much more vivid, specific and significant than the dreary, unimportant, shadow existence of traditional belief. Because of her beliefs she feels certain obligations and commitments on which she acts (69ff., 451–2). Her fleeting reference to a private picture of a heavenly tribunal is a sure clue to this side of her character, but it is one that we are liable to miss.

As important as these legal references are to the plays in which they appear, legal statute and trial procedure play an even more extended and obvious role in *Oedipus Tyrannos*. Here the *agones* have an even more legalistic setting than usual since Oedipus' declaration and efforts closely parallel the complicated stages in Athenian homicide investigations and suits.[24] The question of which court would have had the jurisdiction over Oedipus had he been tried at Athens has provoked various comments from modern critics, some irrelevant, some simply wrong; but despite the interest in the legal aspects of the play, some of the most important points have remained untreated.[25] If Oedipus' encounter with Laius could have passed either for self-defense, at the Delphinion, or for unintentional homicide, at the Palladion, he might have received the most lenient treatment Athenian law allowed, but for one obvious problem: the man he killed was his father. Plato's exclusion of patricides and matricides from the plea of self-defense may not necessarily reflect Athenian law (*Leg.* 869b–c), but Pollux (8.117) records another provision directed solely at one who had killed his parents. According to it, although any other defendant in a homicide trial could choose exile after the first speech, those accused of killing their parents were not allowed to leave voluntarily in mid-trial, but rather were required to remain for the jurors' verdict.[26] Lack of evidence outside Pollux for this exception has prompted some skepticism, but in fact it both explains and is made more likely by the end of *Oedipus Tyrannos*.[27] There Oedipus is not allowed to leave the city as he wishes, but is forced to wait for the final pronouncement of Delphi, and this would seem to be because the murderer of Laius has been found to be his son. Oedipus falls between paradoxical oppositions even in legal technicality, since his deed, seen in one way, as *akousios* or *dikaios phonos*, deserves the greatest available lenience under Attic law, while seen in the other, as patricide, it must be treated with unique strictness. Only our lack of familiarity with the categories of Attic law makes the detainment of Oedipus seem puzzling.

Just as legal procedure influenced the events of tragedy, so also did the style of legal rhetoric influence the tone of tragedy. As an example of the sources of such influence, we can take Antiphon's *Tetralogies*. In terms of later rhetorical standards, they have little ethos or characterization, and it is often pointed out that they are mere exercises.[28] Nevertheless, the arguments of the finished speeches are hardly less mechanical or more personalized, and we know that the style must have been acceptable if, in an age of magnificent speakers, Antiphon could earn the title *kratistos* from as practical a writer and experienced a listener as Thucydides (8.68.1). The *Tetralogies* thus prove that fifth-century taste accepted and even craved a style of public debate which seems to us coldly artificial and impersonal, and this fact can help us to understand the tone of tragic debate.[29]

When, in tragedy, logic becomes forced, generalizations grow questionable or strained in relevance and substance surrenders to word-play, the cry is that characterization has been abandoned or at least 'hampered.'[30] Of course everyone knows that pitfalls fill the path which approaches tragedy through the examination of characterization. If Tycho von Wilamowitz failed to convince classicists of this, his followers have had more success. But even assuming that the tragedians were most concerned to keep their characters realistic and true-to-life, the objection to the tragic use of impersonal commonplaces in situations of personal importance is senseless because it forgets the social context of Attic tragedy. The settings of some of these 'non-characterized' speeches may be more judicial than those of others, but all of the speeches fall within the conventions of fifth-century rhetoric with its tolerance for specious logic and artificial argument.[31] What's more, they display the type of argumentation used in homicide trials and critical assembly meetings, and consequently they can only have seemed natural on the fifth-century stage.

Antigone's final iambic speech provides an excellent example of the misreadings encouraged by a failure to recognize perfectly regular court behavior. Creon has just reaffirmed her death sentence after her 'arrest' and 'trial.' She responds with a last justification of her actions which is often rejected as an interpolation.[32] Jebb, admittedly a sensitive reader of Greek, found the passage 'crude and blunt sophistry.'[33] Certainly the explanation comes ready-made either from Herodotus or from a source used by him as well (3.119), but, as we have seen, Athenians did not consider the use of stock arguments unworthy of law, and they will not have thought less of Antigone for a bit of nice logic. Successful speaking did not depend on original inspiration. Moreover, there is even a personal touch, for although the application to the dead of a speech originally made for the living has been thought absurd, it is totally in keeping with Antigone's character.[34] We have already seen one legal example of her idiosyncratic projection of this world onto the next. If, in the end, the lines are rejected, it must not be because they contain specious generalizations or are lacking in or thought to be out of character.

6. Tragedy and the Development of Attitudes towards Law and Justice: Preliminary Considerations

Because the tragedies so frequently contain or turn on legal materials or analogies and because the disputes in them often resemble formal litigation, attitudes about laws and their administration often emerge in the course of a play. Moreover, since the popular courts largely arose and developed within the second half of the fifth century, ideas and opinions about their activities were developing and changing precisely during the period when Sophocles' and Euripides' extant plays were written and produced. Therefore, a roughly chronological examination of the plays could reasonably be expected to expose general trends in developing or changing attitudes. However, certain difficulties complicate such an undertaking. Among other things the Athenian legal process and Athenian dramaturgy shared a tendency to fluidity and experimentation. As a result, any shifting in attitudes *toward* law must be sorted out from a background in which both legal and dramatic strategies are themselves evolving.

A few examples may help clarify how complex the products of these developing strategies were. During the second half of the fifth century, the Athenians found new uses for old procedures such as *diamartyria*, a formal witness assertion, and introduced and adapted new ones such as *graphe paranomon*, the prosecution for illegalities in procedure or legislation.[35] By manipulating these and other legal actions, complicated strings of suits could be and were made to interrupt and blend into each other. Antiphon's speech for the chorister gives a good sense of the tangle which could develop: upon hearing that a clerk and three other citizens were embezzling public money, the chorister impeached them; when his opponents learned that one of the chorus boys in his charge had died, they tried to delay or dissolve their case by having the boy's brother charge the chorister with murder; their attempt having failed, the chorister successfully prosecuted yet more people — including the boy's brother — with embezzlement; and finally the chorister was brought into homicide court.[36]

Similarly, whether partly because of the abandonment of the unified trilogy or simply as a result of a natural urge to innovate, the tragedies of the period use increasingly complex juxtapositions of the traditional elements of dramatic action. By the time of Euripides' *Orestes*, multiple actions of suppliancy, rescue and vengeance dissolve disastrously one into the next in a baroque battle of vain efforts.[37] Then, two years later, in 406, the Athenians played out a terribly similar, complicated plot on the political stage, as various legal actions were undertaken, threatened and interrupted in the trial of the Arginousae generals. In that case, however, there was no divine machinery to avert the final catastrophe. Ultimately this parallel growth in sophisticated manipulation and combination of both legal suits and dramatic actions provides evidence for the ways in which attitudes towards laws and concepts of law and justice were developing. But if we use tragedy as one polished stone giving reflections of another which is law, we must remember that as the facets of both simultaneously increase, the images are likely to be somewhat kaleidoscopic and ornate.

Another problem arises with artistic archaizing. We have noted that the terminology of litigation comes from a description of pursuit and flight in the fight for vengeance envisioned as a hunt (*diokein, pheugein, agon, dike*). Amid the carnage of the *Oresteia* the phrase 'to go after vengeance' (*meteimi diken*) literally describes the successive pursuit and entrapment of various murderers (*Eum.* 231).[38] Although the same phrase occurs a half-century later in Euripides' *Bacchae* (345–6, 516–17), this does not mean that ideas of justice have not changed. Here images of the hunt and destruction of animals culminate in the capture and rending of the theriomorphic Pentheus. It is a brutal justice or vengeance, but it is completely in keeping with the archaic formal construction, diction and style of the tragedy.[39] The Sophoclean use of this idiom some time between the *Eumenides* and the *Bacchae* introduces a final *caveat* which is related to our now familiar distinction between the homicide courts and the popular courts.

In the Sophoclean *Electra* it is vengeance itself which comes in pursuit (*Dike, meteisi*: 475–6), and it is a violent vengeance of bloodguilt which the chorus carefully equates with the Fury (*Erinys*).[40] For the same reasons that the Areopagus and the other homicide courts were sharply distinguished from the popular courts, the tragedies concerned with murder must be treated differently from those which do not. Even though justice may be unclear and troubled in these plays, religion and tradition dictate certain actions and control values and attitudes much more strictly than they do in disputes which do not involve killing. As we have seen, Glotz examined Athenian criminal law in relation to family solidarity; and Gernet found homicide and crimes against the family the best models for legal process in Athens. Their approach is in fact related to Aristotle's opinion that the best tragedy was that which treated actual or attempted murder or other such acts among family members (*Poet.* 1453b19ff.),[41] for all three men were influenced by the prominence in tragedy of the unhappy internal struggles of a few mythological families.[42] And although our remnants of Attic tragedy include many scenes and even whole plays in which the discussions of laws or claims are not limited to or even involved with homicide, murder still pleases the modern reader as much as it did Aristotle and has attracted more than its share of attention from the critics.

The importance of separating homicide from other crimes can be demonstrated by a consideration of a recent book on tragedy.[43] In an extensive historical examination of the plays, Suzanne Saïd asks whether the responsibility for the wrongdoing or errors in tragedy lies with gods or with men, whether man's responsibility for wrongdoing is collective or individual, and whether the wrong-doing offends gods or men. In answer to the first question she finds that whereas in Aeschylus divine influence and personal decision are integrated, they become more separate in Sophocles, where deliberate actions are differentiated and men commit great errors in which the gods play no part. Finally, divine responsibility diminishes even further in Euripides, where the emphasis falls on the psychological, while supernatural explanations are rejected.

Similarly, she sees collective and individual responsibility as inseparable in Aeschylus but claims that Euripides and the late Sophocles show a much greater interest in motivation and intent and therefore are more concerned with individual responsibility. Finally, in seeking to establish who is offended by wrong-doing in tragedy, she ascribes a consistent religious dimension to Aeschylus which unites piety and justice and integrates religious, legal and moral values. Again, she outlines gradual change both in Sophocles, who, in contrast to Aeschylus, depicts offenses more exclusively against men and therefore more secular, and in Euripides, who, she claims, presents most crimes as illegal rather than impious.

In all this analysis, Saïd fails to distinguish homicide from other types of wrong-doing even though the Athenian courts radically separated them. As a result, her analysis is troubled in several ways. At the level of individual action, Saïd puts more legal weight on Ismene's awareness of Antigone's plans than it will bear since 'planning' (*bouleusis*) was a charge only if the contemplated crime either was or resulted in homicide.[44] More generally, her analysis of human responsibility and intentionality in Sophocles depends almost entirely on cases of homicide, and thus largely ignores *Ajax* and *Philoctetes*.[45] But in Athens, the categories 'voluntary' (*hekon*) and 'involuntary' (*akon*) had special legal relevance in homicide suits. Moreover, these different categories of responsibility were set by homicide laws which had established different administrative procedures and punishments for well over a century. Similarly, *Philoctetes* enters Saïd's discussion only to demonstrate the religious approach and emphasis of Aeschylus as opposed to Sophocles' more worldly and human treatment of problems.[46] But the real distinctive feature, leaving aside the eventful half-century which separates *Philoctetes* from any work of Aeschylus, is that *Philoctetes* does not deal with murder. It is no accident that Saïd does not try to use *Oedipus Tyrannos* or *Antigone* to contrast Sophocles with the author of the *Oresteia*. Similar difficulties trouble her treatment of Euripides. In order to present a worldly Euripides who has little concern with religion, Saïd reverses the direction of Gernet's generalization. Rather than claim that the intense religious feelings of the family were transferred to civic matters, she makes even offenses against and within the family a secular affair.[47] She does not recognize that in struggles over murder and supplication, *nomos* and related words stand not merely for 'law', but laws bound to centuries of *nomoi*, traditions and customs from which religion and piety cannot be excluded. The following analysis separates these types of wrong-doing in order better to isolate developments connected with the popular courts and the conflicts dealt with there.

7. A Chronological Study

By fortunate coincidence, a play which almost certainly falls near the beginning of the great growth of the popular courts, around 440, contains explicit statements about laws and also conveys attitudes toward legal administration through references to and scenes of adjudication.[48] When, in the *Ajax*, Menelaos insists that fear is required to make laws function well in the city and to keep men in line, he is not expressing an idea new to tragedy (1073–86). Both the Eumenides and Athena had been equally insistent on this point some years before (Aesch. *Eum.* 516–25, 699), and the occurrence of the same sentiment in Herodotus (7.104.4) and Thucydides (2.37.3) indicates that it was the standard attitude in the mid-fifth century. But by the time Isocrates wrote his *Areopagiticus* a century later, fear is no longer indispensable for maintaining lawful cities. Isocrates knows the possibility of an independent and abstract ideal of justice followed by choice rather than imposed through fear: for him, *dikaiosyne* is an *arete* (7.41, 46ff.).

The beginnings of this alternative vision will be found in later plays, but already in the *Ajax*, the picture of legalistic adjudication suggests that the popular courts were making a vivid impression as a new civic institution. The play opens after Ajax has been driven to despair by a tribunal judgement in which the votes or jurors were tampered with, and it closes with wrangling speeches in which arguments take no precedence over character accusation or even family insults.[49] Against the ever-present background of Ajax's duel with Hector, this form of settling disputes seems petty and base, yet it has a relentless power which drives Ajax from the world and outlasts him. In the tribunal, swords have given way to words, and manipulation has replaced muscle, but the consequences of debate are as decisive as those of combat.

Of course the *Ajax* nominally depicts a distant past, despite its reference to the voting of jurors (*dikastai*), but this same vision of powerful popular courts appears in a description of Athens which also dates from the third quarter of the fifth century.[50] The oligarchic author of the *Constitution of Athens* emphasizes the

pervasiveness (3.6–7) and power (1.18) of the popular courts and
the stupidity (1.5) and greed (1.13) of the citizens who manned
them, and whatever his bias or exaggeration, his description
explicitly supports the implications of the *Ajax*.

The *Antigone* appears in most if not all discussions of the concern
with laws and claims at this time. Although many of the play's legal
concerns have already been discussed, two more deserve notice.
First, Creon's sensitivity to the mention of gain and his outbursts
against bribery suggest the contemporary civic problem of financial
corruption and are further evidence for the type of cases with which
the courts may have been busy at this time. Certainly in the fifth
century there were frequent trials of generals; large boards of public
officials and their private accomplices were convicted of embezzlement; and all but one of the ten Hellenotamiae were convicted and
put to death (Antiphon 5.69–71). The almost casual, off-handed
nature of the last reference suggests that there may well have been
other such incidents which have left no trace in history.[51] Second,
Creon's and Haimon's conflict, described with the terminology of
formal legal dispute, is the first of a series of such father-son
quarrels or struggles which occur in almost all of the extant plays of
Sophocles and Euripides for the next fifteen years. Besides the
incidents in *Alcestis* and *Hippolytos* mentioned above, the
Trachiniae closes with an argument between Heracles and Hyllus.
Otherwise the plays of this period contain almost nothing of
relevance to the administration of justice in the popular courts. The
charges made in terms of *dike* and *nomoi* revolve around claims and
customs of family obligation. Even the *agones* of the plays of the
430s, *Alcestis* and *Medea*, do not take the forensic form; and the
debate in the *Trachiniae* over Deianira's responsibility for the
unwilling murder of her husband Heracles simply consists of the
usual voluntary/involuntary distinction always applied in such
matters.[52]

In 430 the plague came to Athens and brought with it a
lawlessness which extended to a disregard for even the most sacred
customs. Men who expected to die before any case could come
before the courts simply had no interest in laws (Thuc. 2.53); but
after the epidemic had run its course, the courts remained. The
plays of this period after the plague in the first years of the Peloponnesian War touch both more frequently and more variously on the
administration of justice and matters of innocence and guilt. With
the calls to witnesses noted above, the *agones* now take a more

formal forensic turn in the *Hippolytos*, and Phaedra expresses a concern with inner innocence of intent, a rather new, subjective standard, the unfamiliarity of which Euripides emphasizes by placing it fairly noticeably outside the nurse's comprehension.[53]

Even a suppliant drama such as the *Heracleidae*, in which the basic claims (*dikai*) have the full backing of religious custom and tradition, suggests an increasing preoccupation with the assumptions and implications of adjudication. The uses of the words *dike* and *dikaios* probably exceed the silent Heraclids in sheer number and certainly surpass them in variety. *Dike* is now brutal penalty and harsh vengeance, now the sacred custom or right which protects suppliants.[54] The right to traditional funeral honors is *dikaion* (567ff., 588ff.). Applied to persons, *dikaios* must be translated sometimes as 'empowered, entitled' and sometimes as 'obligated' or 'deserving' (142, 773). In the opening lines, it means something like 'law-abiding' in a way which limits self-interested efforts at gain (1–5). A Greek does not take on such restrictions simply as a matter of course, and consequently even though it is clearly *dikaion* to help allies and suppliants, the Athenians argue bitterly about undertaking an action which may be folly (415). At one point, however, a discussion of *dikaion* touches not simply on its consequences or desirability but on its actual nature (252ff.). The herald raises the possibility that the protection of *dike* might depend on some level of ethical excellence or innocence in the suppliant rather than being an absolute customary right. Although the herald and his commander are not sincere seekers in moral matters, this is the first hint of an approach and a problem which later plays treat more fully.[55]

Suppliants appear in the opening scenes of both *Oedipus Tyrannos* and *Andromache*, the other two plays which probably belong to these early war years. What remains to be said of the *Oedipus Tyrannos* comes in a general discussion below. The *Andromache* has little to say about civic justice. As usual in suppliant drama, violence and force threaten sacred custom, and here the two spheres stand particularly in opposition to each other. Andromache and Neoptolemos move in a grand old world of altars and temples with whose gods they have direct and personal connections, but like Dostoevskian characters they have come into contact with creatures who are virtually of a different world. Hermione, Menelaus, and Orestes show no concern for altars, oaths, or gods. Their lies and murders serve petty jealousies that the heroic characters cannot even understand, and this play has no popular institutions, autonomous legal standards, or ideals of justice to mediate between, or even to relate, its two dissimilar elements.

Like the *Andromache*, the *Hecuba* contains both a heroic world and base characters, but it includes the problems and mechanics of popular adjudication as well. Just as in the *Ajax*, the consequences of Achilles' death give rise to a series of judgements and actions. The vote to sacrifice Polyxena to Achilles' ghost is followed by her death. Then after Hecuba's vengeance on Polymnestor for the murder of her son, there is a final dispute and judgement.

Between the sacrifice and the vengeance, Hecuba makes a speech about the gods, *nomoi* and *dikaia* (799ff.), but she is not defending legality and justice in any abstract sense. Murderous violations of the customs (*nomoi*) of supplication and hospitality have robbed her of two children, and she has a strong traditional claim (*dikaia*) to exact a penalty (*dike*) from a sacrilegious killer. Even so, Agamemnon hesitates to help her. The force which restrains him figures in every debate and judgement in the play, and it has nothing to do with any abstract merit or objective standard: it is the opinion and desire of the army, the voting body of Greek men (852ff.). Hecuba has no illusions about the men whose democratic vote condemned her daughter. One need not have done any despicable deed to be despised by this lawless crowd (606–8). This is why she does not rely on the force of *nomos* to move them from their original decision even though 'homicide law' should have protected Polyxena. Instead, she asks Odysseus to use the influence of his own persuasive speech (*logos*) which will count for more (291ff.). And although in order to motivate Odysseus she first explains the propriety of her claim (*to dikaion*) — Polyxena's innocence — she counts more on his indebtedness to her past hospitality (271ff.). Since she knows that either the people or the laws can keep a man from acting on his opinions (864–9), Agamemnon's fear does not surprise her. Even Agamemnon's ultimate condemnation of Polymnestor reflects his concern with public approval (1249).

Thus although the play recounts and presents a series of trials or judgements, legality and justice have no superior authority and little independent force. The institution of popular legal administration is the people's vote, exerting steady pressure on the courts and decisions: autonomous legal values are conspicuously absent. The fighting is done; but war is continued by ballot and judgement.

When the battle between Athens and Thebes is over in Euripides' *Suppliant Women*, the victory announcement opens with the words *aktis heliou* (beam of the sun), which Sophocles had borrowed twenty years earlier from Pindar for the beginning of the parodos in *Antigone*.[56] But whereas Pindar and Sophocles had hailed the ray of the sun as a sign of Thebes' salvation, Euripides uses their phrase to declare that city's defeat. Once the words have been used both for Theban victory and defeat, they no longer naturally suggest either. The legalistic discussions and debates in this play work the same mischief with the arguments, successively applying, fracturing, and revising them until they begin to rob both themselves and the propositions they support of any stable value. Almost in one breath Theseus finds fault with Adrastus both for following divine oracles and for going against them (219ff.). His mother Aithra has similar habits of mind. She concludes her encouraging approval of her son with a prediction of victory, but her logic, typical of much of the argumentation and many of the implications of this play, extends hope for immediate comfort while it simultaneously rules out any possibility for long-term success: the gods reverse everything (328–31). War and peace are treated with a certain amount of comprehensible but nevertheless noticeable inconsistency. The same herald who eloquently explains the virtues of peace immediately threatens battle (486ff., 572ff.). And after Adrastus has twice spoken convincingly about the folly of military violence, Athena cheerfully foretells a new and glorious war of which the gods will approve (745–9, 949–54, 1214–26).

In the same play, political problems produce a most puzzling series of statements. It is logical but still odd when Theseus explains that because he freed the city from the rule of one man it will do virtually anything he wants (350ff.). Later he hotly attacks tyranny (403–8). Yet the herald's defense of one-man rule and criticism of democracy (410ff.) use a description of humanity very close to the one Theseus has given in an earlier conversation with Adrastus (238–42). If these arguments, especially Theseus', are presented with Euripidean irony or disapproval, it is much more than usually hidden. Rather, the resulting impression is that, except perhaps in the case of the very sacred custom such as the burial of the war-dead, arguments and discussions, like old tags from lyric poetry, can be equally well put to opposite uses. Thus although Theseus asserts a certain legal ideal in claiming that with written laws the lesser man can defeat the great as long as he has a proper claim (433–8), the nature of debate throughout the play assumes a more Protagorean and arbitrary fluidity. In other words, it corroborates the picture of sophistic and legal debate in Aristophanes' *Clouds* and *Wasps*, which had probably been produced quite recently.

By 416 BC, when Alcibiades and Nicias were disagreeing over whether or not to divide Athens' resources with an expedition to Sicily, legalistic debate, accusation and defense were being used even more in tragedy. Melanippe evidently made elaborate if unsuccessful arguments in her two Euripidean appearances. We can only speculate about the extent to which the numerous lost twin plays of this period took advantage of geminate brothers to present arguments or debates like those between Amphion and Zethus in *Antiope*, but the play and fragments that we do have from 415 show an obsession with litigation and a conviction that in various ways it has failed as an institution.[57]

Each of the tragedies of Euripides' 'Trojan Trilogy' contains a formal trial. The exiguous remains of the *Alexander* discourage detailed interpretation of the adjudication there, but no ambiguity clouds the *Palamedes*. Despite the assertion that one man can defeat many if he is in the right (fr. 584N²), Odysseus secures the execution of the innocent Palamedes through lies and false evidence. Odysseus never suffered for his actions, and the case became a famous example of the conviction of a man for something he did not do.[58] In the third play, the *Troades*, Helen's trial is preceded by Cassandra's and Andromache's specious defenses of several paradoxical propositions. First, Cassandra demonstrates that Troy and the Trojans are more fortunate than the Greek victors (365–99). Next, since the devastation of war is of such extent and variety that a case for having suffered the greatest loss can be made for anyone living or dead, Andromache can make the claim that Polyxena met the better fate by being slaughtered for Achilles (630ff.). In the course of explaining that her life is worse than death, she shows additionally that noble conduct and a good reputation are directly responsible for her present misery. Later, the order for Astyanax's execution prompts a related reflection: although a father's nobility normally saves a child, Hector's destroys Astyanax (741–4).[59]

Hecuba is the third and final Trojan woman to set forth her logical arguments. They come after Helen's defense and match it persuasively point for point. But the most important aspect of the trial is that Hecuba's refutation of Helen is completely irrelevant, thus preparing for the fact that Menelaos' judgement involves no principles of justice or objective standards of guilt or innocence.

Despite all the argumentation, rational and irrational, it is simply his personal desire which puts Helen aboard and which will eventually save her when they reach Sparta.

As a group, the Trojan plays suggest a new concern or realization about the nature of formal adjudication. The insistent repetition of disastrously disconnected events, arguments and decisions indicates that malfunction in trial procedure is perceived as a regular and characteristic pattern. As yet there is no explicit diagnosis nor any specific blame; but dissatisfaction leads to articulation, and one of the immediately following plays goes further and begins to suggest an abstract ideal of legality.[60]

The year after *Troades*, Aristophanes' Peisthetairus and Euelpides went to live among the birds in order to escape Athens' laws. About the same time, perhaps a year later, Euripides gave the Athenians a charming variation.[61] His Ion lives blissfully, high among the birds at Delphi, talks to and scolds them, is even saved by one of them, and is determined not to live in Athens. He sings while he sweeps, and his voice is a new one. In the course of the play this boy, about to become a man, blends notes of traditional piety and restless rationalism to quite a new effect. A devoted servant of Apollo, he explains in detail that it is impossible to force the gods into unflattering confessions and unintelligent even to try (369–80). Yet when faced with a visitor who claims to have been wronged by the Delphic god, Ion is troubled, and the reasons for his feelings are quite complicated. It is not only authority and custom which have kept Ion in a right relation with his god, but also his own nature (643–4). And although no authority can coerce Apollo and the other immortals, Ion feels their behaviour should conform with the laws and standards of the men who admire them (436–51). Since earth and heaven meet at Delphi, there are new strangers for Ion to greet every day (640–1), and the variety and extent of his experience have helped lead him to the articulation of a desire for common standards or ideals. His own deep piety and inner consistency make him impatient even with some sacred custom: he would have supplication at altars limited to the innocent (1312–19). If he will not exempt gods from his requirements, men should certainly not expect formal loopholes or technicalities to protect them. Unlike his future British incarnation, he does not need to wait until the tokens with which he was abandoned finally reveal his identity in order to learn the vital importance of being earnest.

Thus Ion's attitude differs substantially from the typical Athenian one toward laws and litigation. True to his city, Xuthus lightly uses a technical legal term when claiming Ion (*ou rhysiazo*: 523). The same uncommon term reappears when Creousa claims Ion, but this time he who is the object of the claim uses it, and his disgust and impatience distance him from Athenian litigiousness. 'I am being distrained on like property by a verbal pretext,' he says (*rhysiazomai logoi*: 1406).[62] The usage here has been dismissed as a 'rather precious legal joke,'[63] but the intent is much more serious than such a judgement recognizes. The pointed repetition of the term underlines a contrast of great importance in the play: Ion will have none of the verbal tricks of the city's courts or the behaviour they seek to camouflage.

To the very end Ion is concerned to establish the ultimate truth or falseness of Apollo's prophecies, even though the practical outcome of the action seems entirely successful (1537, 1546–8). Those who write about Ion join him in making an issue of Apollo's behavior. Certainly, he is not the active, partisan god of *Iliad* 24 who chides the other gods for their heartlessness. Rather he is the fifth-century Apollo from the western pediment of the temple of Zeus at Olympia: he is aware of the struggle about him, but calm, extending his hand without actually touching anything. His acts are not subject to men's laws and he does not provide a legal ideal, but he is not needed for that. Instead, his temple makes a setting for the original revealing 'weekend in the country' where both he and the Athenians provide specific examples in contrast to which Ion can express the longing for some positive alternative, a consistent legal ideal rather than mere clever litigation. Longing and expression are less concrete than existence; but they are a beginning.

By 412 the Sicilian expedition had ended in complete disaster and the painful, damaging revolts of Athens' allies had begun. Yet amid the deepening ugliness of war, Athenians witnessed ever more exquisite artistic creation. Kallimachos, said the ancients, so elaborated his scenes in marble that they threatened, in their fineness, to float away or melt into nothing, and the art of the Euripidean *Helen* was of the same sort.[64] Like Kallimachos' *saltantes Lacaenae*, Helen and Menelaos dance a precise choreography of action clothed in conventions of character drawn to an aery fineness. The resulting transparency of the garments allows Euripides to make hilarious revelations even as it demonstrates his mastery, while all about the frivolous frieze of the narrative every column of the stagecraft culminates in flowery Corinthian capitals of Kallimachean invention.[65] But in the heart of this ornate temple stands the solemn Pheidian statue of Theonoe. She is said to save the story from silliness, and it is claimed that she does this by giving voice to a moral conscience and by administering a justice which belongs to a higher order of permanent absolutes.[66] We must carefully examine the trial at which she presides in order to judge whether or not this is the case.

Theonoe's entrance amid sulphurous fumes and torchlight and her reference to her *nomos* (ritual service) which is rendered to the gods indicate that religion will be her law. Helen accordingly includes in her speech the argument that god (*ho theos*) hates both force and the seizure (*harpage*) of possessions (904–6). At first this statement may seem new and startling, but in fact, Helen is simply conveying her first-hand knowledge of the gods' reaction to her case. After all, they sent her to Egypt to spare her from the seizure (*anarpage*) Menelaos nevertheless fought to avenge (50). And the reference to possessions is quite natural since Athenian law treated women and property as virtually identical. When Theonoe gives her verdict she makes it absolutely clear that she is acting on grounds of piety and self-interest. Not to honor Helen, who was her father's guest and friend and is now a suppliant, would greatly harm both his fame and Theonoe's (998–1001). Although much has been made of her mention of the altar of *dike* in her nature, it signifies no new values or conscience, for her decision to help a friend and suppliant is strictly dictated by sacred custom and tradition. As Helen has said, albeit somewhat idiosyncratically, suggesting her familiarity with immortals, it is a god to recognize friends (560). Moreover, Theonoe's choice to honor her dead father simultaneously helps her brother by saving him from impiety (1020–9). Her choice is infinitely easier than Antigone's had been, and with her ability to see into the future, Theonoe must know that she will ultimately be saved.

A number of details indicate that the trial at which Theonoe presides is not to be taken too seriously. The proceedings resemble those in the *Eumenides*, with Theonoe casting the final vote like Athena (1005), but this Euripidean play has no bloodstains, madness, or goddesses of vengeance.[67] In fact, both litigants in this trial plead the same case, a unique circumstance, which makes it possible for Theonoe actually to comply with the chorus' unusual instruction to give a decision which will please everyone (996–7). In other words, in its formal structure, the hearing has only one possible outcome — the pleasant one. And this is entirely in the spirit of a play where everyone is continually rescued and outbursts of anger are regularly followed by polite apology.[68] Someone in Euripides' *Andromeda*, produced the same year, said, 'They say that Dike is the child of Zeus and dwells near man's error' (fr. 151N[2]). Perhaps she did, especially if Dike is revenge or punishment. But in *Helen* disagreements always dissolve before error and revenge can even take shape. By the close, the brilliant sun has evaporated the Trojan Helen and winds are hurrying the Egyptian Helen across the waves to Sparta. Presumably the barbarian king, still ignorant of Greek custom, will continue to run his dogs across the dry sands, and the priestess will go in and out of the high-walled, hellish palace purifying the arid Egyptian air with fire and brimstone. The Olympian gods who had originally upset the Mediterranean world for their own entertainment finally have restored what is left of it to its previous state after almost two decades of death. And the weary Athenians, who would have to wait even longer for peace, had, however briefly, been beguiled into laughter at the elegant, irrelevant and lovely marvel that is *Helen*.

The following year, the instability which haunted appearances in *Helen* repeatedly shook the Athenian government. When order began to be restored, there was a whole new set of suits for the courts: charges were brought against those who could be linked either with the planning or the implementation of the oligarchic revolution. There remain from such trials the fragments of one speech and the whole of another. Antiphon's fatal day in court came during the intermediate government before the restoration of the full democracy. The text of the major fragment from his defense gives a vivid and convincing impression of the pervasiveness and importance of litigation before the revolution.[69] In fact, it even includes as reasons for desiring a new government both dissatisfaction with the results of several types of lawsuits and fear of impending ones. And this leads to the clever if specious point that a professional writer of forensic speeches like Antiphon would be unlikely to try and put himself out of a job by undoing democracy, a form of government which provided him with such an abundance of work.

Antiphon's speech glances at past administration of law, but another, delivered a little later under the restored democracy, points to the future. The city had survived the first great crime against it, its constitution, and its laws, but the oligarchs had seriously threatened the rights of most of the citizens and even endangered the autonomy of the city itself. The events made government by laws and behavior in accordance with laws and legal claim much more generally attractive and created a new, strong and more immediate defense for legality, since the dangers and disadvantages of lawlessness were now clear. Within a few years, the takeover of the Thirty Tyrants would unleash much worse chaos and tragic violence. The nature of the reaction to that revolution is foreshadowed in the recovery from this first smaller upset. In the speech for Polystratus, his son assumes the opposition of *kalos* (fine or good) to *me dikaios* (not justly) confidently and without further explanation or argument (Lys. 20.5–6). The association of *adikos*-words with the threatened loss of privilege to citizens and jurors and of *dikaios*-words with the constitutional order preserving their rights had a great effect on the status and value attached to legality in general. This effect shows up immediately in the plays of the restored democracy.

One of these is Euripides' *Phoenissae*, which apparently so captured the imagination of the Athenians that soon it was sufficiently well-known to serve as the object of frequent allusion.[70] It was said that before the battle of Arginousae in 406 BC the general Thrasyllus dreamed that he and six of his colleagues, all of whom would eventually be tried and convicted for their part in the victory, were acting this Euripidean play (Diod.Sic. 13.97). Whatever the truth of the anecdote, it shows how closely Athenian thought linked warfare, theater and litigation. The same is true of Aristotle's mention of this play, which comes in a discussion much more relevant to the Athenian political problems of 411 than to those of Antigone's Thebes, where the play is set (*Eth.Nic.* 1167a32–4).

The legal and political issues are concentrated and stand out most clearly in the debate between Polyneices and Eteocles (446–637).[71] Just as Theonoe judged the trial in *Helen* (*brabeuein*: 996), here Jocasta will suggest a settlement (*brabeiai*: 450) of the dispute. For his part, Polyneices stresses that his claims against his brother are justified and lawful, for he aspires *syn dike* — justly, with right — to the power of which Eteocles has deprived him *ater dikes* — without right or unjustly (467–92). Eteocles, on the other hand, simply asserts his intention to continue tyrannical rule, even if that requires trampling on someone else's rights (504–25). After the recent constitutional struggle and political trials, Eteocles' declaration was a painful reminder of the general danger associated with the transgression of rights. For the same reason, Jocasta's defense of *isotes* and *to ison* (535–48), an orderly and regulated equality, was now more attractive than it could have been before.

Similar developments in the uses of the words *dike* and *dikaion* are found in Sophocles' *Philoctetes* which was produced in 409.[72] In some ways this is a play of conflicting claims much like *Antigone*; but whereas Creon refuses to recognize the validity of Antigone's obligations, Philoctetes succeeds in persuading Neoptolemus to act in accordance with certain standards of behavior even though this ultimately requires Neoptolemus to disobey the demands of the people and the decisions of their leaders.[73] Furthermore, while Antigone's alternative to obeying civic authority and the religious matters which it seeks to protect is the fulfilment of another sacred duty to a family member, Neoptolemus is won over to a much more general commitment to fairness and honesty — things *dikaia*.

This value and praise eventually given to *dikaia* is by no means easily won. Even though Neoptolemus hesitates to lie and steal, Odysseus convinces him fairly easily that the capture of Troy requires the deception: the glory of victory is a great prize. But Philoctetes presents Neoptolemus with quite a different set of values. The old man has nothing but contempt for the scheming Odysseus who never does anything *dikaion* (openly, honestly), and in lamenting the Greek heroes who have died he praises them as the world's just (*dikaia*) and finest (*chresta*) things (407–9, 449–50). Although Neoptolemus tries to reassure himself that obedience to the Greek army is just (*endikon*), he finally accepts Philoctetes' order of values (925–96, 1224ff.). As a result, *dike* and *dikaia* are placed above cleverness (*sopha*) and above success which would require lies or theft; and the immense personal advantage which would come with a great military exploit is abandoned (1245–6).[74]

Even so, this lawful *dikaion* so highly praised by Philoctetes and eventually chosen by Neoptolemus still has limited power or appeal. The chorus, for example, uses *dikaion* in the sense of a plea or claim which may certainly be asserted but commands no supreme respect (1140–2). Furthermore, as has been well pointed out, Neoptolemus comes to his final position quite slowly and only after repeated pitiful appeals from Philoctetes.[75] Finally, Neoptolemus is moved by personal obligations of the friendship which develops between him and the old man in the course of the play and which involves appeals to the old ties with his father's great nobility. Nevertheless, with all these limitations, just as in the *Phoenissae*, a more general standard of justice and lawful action is presented as preferable to personal gain and the acquisition of power; and, as in the *Ion*, the idea is expressed by an outsider who eventually agrees, however reluctantly, to leave a life of isolation among the birds and join the larger community.

The last of our extant plays produced during the lifetime of the great tragedians is *Orestes*. Although it contains endless arguments and claims about *dike* and *dikaia*, the subject, as in the Electra plays, is murder which avenged murder; but it is nevertheless relevant to this discussion because Euripides, not content to confine the drama to private vengeance, also included first a defense and then an unflattering description of popular justice.[76] The law, Tyndareus says, protects men and cities from bestial, bloody violence, and Orestes should have taken the case of his father's murder to court (491–525). Yet when Orestes stands trial for murdering his mother, all the speeches address the welfare of the community, indicating that the popular court is much more concerned about the people than about justice (885–952).[77] Of course, this is not an Athenian trial, and criticism of it cannot be applied directly to Athenian government: in terms of simple mechanics, a popular jury would never have heard a homicide case; but even in the solemn homicide courts with their religious traditions, the juries, so far as we know, were not faced with crimes laid to the orders of the gods. Nevertheless, it seems that Euripides was becoming more acutely aware of an abstract justice and concerned that it was not necessarily administered well by the popular vote.

Sophocles' last play deals more with sacred tradition and personal destiny than with the problems of popular justice. Whereas Euripides' *Orestes* is tried in public assembly, Oedipus seeks asylum in a sacred sanctuary; and although Apollo is apparently of little interest to the men of Argos, the Athenians have the greatest respect for the Eumenides at Colonus. The holy grove provides a setting appropriate to the entirely traditional treatment of customs and rights; the law and justice required of Athens is the protection of the suppliant Oedipus; and when Creon is condemned as unjust (*ekdikos*) and base (*kakos*), it is for violating the suppliant's rights (919ff.).[78] As to his past offense, the murder of Laius, Oedipus provides the two most customary defenses: first, as he emphasizes repeatedly, he was acting *akon* — a combination of 'unwillingly' and 'unintentionally;' and second, he retaliated in self-defense.[79] In fact, retaliation or vengeance is the chief concern both of Oedipus and of the Furies to whom he is so closely linked throughout the play.[80] The Ancient Justice which guides him metes out good to friends and harm to enemies, and it is this program, rather than any detached, objective sense of justice, which determines his attitude to Creon, Theseus and his sons (1381–2).[81] Finally, the religious and traditional tone of the drama's conflicts reflects the fact that 'here . . . benefit and injury, love and hate, arise within the context of the family — a context which imposes duties paramount in the Greek moral scheme.'[82]

Although Euripides' posthumous plays do not lack religious elements, scenes of supplication, or familial obligation, they differ greatly from *Oedipus at Colonus*, deepening the darkness of *Orestes*. The arguments for lawfulness and standards of right action found in the plays around the revolution of 411 have disappeared; now instead of positive proposals there are merely pictures, brilliant and realistically detailed, of various types of chaos. The less finished of the two plays, *Iphigeneia at Aulis*, concentrates more on problems of community and politics. To begin with, the leaders are loathsome. The Atreidae are not simply liars: Menelaos, who has taken advantage of an old oath, is whining and cleverly hypocritical; Agamemnon, who gained his power by various manipulations, is now hesitant, fumbling and fearful. Achilles displays cold and colossal conceit (961–7); and the ambitious Odysseus waits silently to profit from his rivals' grief (524–7). Furthermore, it is not even clear that the Greeks deserve better leaders: Agamemnon fears death at the hands of his men; Clytemnestra assumes they are ready for lawless violence and bold base deeds; and Achilles is almost stoned to death by troops eager for Iphigeneia's slaughter (533–7, 913–14, 1267–75, 1346–55). If the news could have reached Euripides, he would hardly have been surprised at Athens' murder of the Arginousae generals or the threats against those who tried to stop the assembly from abandoning the regular legal procedures. Violence as vicious and much more widespread would terrorize the city before law and justice could be re-established.

Although the *Bacchae* features a ruler who is at odds with the desires of his city, the crisis at the heart of the play is more philosophical than political. Religious belief is at stake, for Pentheus doubts the powers of the very god of Athens' dramatic festivals. In the end Dionysus' power is demonstrated by the destruction of Pentheus; but the questions of law or custom, justice and wisdom, which arose repeatedly in the course of the play, remain unsolved. Instead, a relentless, destructive doubling, unlike the playful process in the *Helen*, has undermined even the possibility of solutions. Not only do Pentheus and Dionysus each have a dual nature, but they actually mirror each other; the Asiatic maenad chorus has for its twin the Theban women on the mountainside; and eventually Pentheus will even see two suns and two Thebes (917–18). Pentheus, Dionysus and both the choruses alternate between passive tranquility and violent brutality. Theirs is a whole world of sophistic speech and reasoning in which every idea or entity contains its opposite and can display either aspect: pain is sweet and labor easy; grace is raw and bloody; what has always been custom is newly introduced; what is wise is not wisdom, and what something wise might be is asked but not envied (68–71; 183–9, 395, 877; 1005). Accordingly, the finest and wisest possession of man is respect for the gods, for only the god is wise enough to thread his way through the shifting appearances of complex reality (1150–1). Again, in the court of men, the finest gift from the gods is the power of vengeance over one's enemies (877–80). Yet only Dionysus exacts revenge from his enemies; men destroy themselves and each other because they cannot sort out their own and each others' double natures and disguises. Dionysus' vengeance is just but excessive (1249–50, 1346). In a world so complex, justice is too abstract to understand and too brutal to bear. In going to see the theater of Dionysus on the mountain, Pentheus died. By the time the play was produced, both Euripides and Sophocles were dead and unable to give the Athenians any other vision of morality and justice. Aristophanes' Dionysus would have brought back Aeschylus to do the job; but the defeat at Aegospotami ushered in a civic catastrophe, a tragedy which was played out throughout Athens. Sometimes great calamities simplify the search for justice. This one did; but before turning to it, we must take a final look at some general similarities between tragedy and the courts.

8. The Final Outcome

No matter how ideas of justice and legality changed and developed, the action of the plays almost always centered on a day of decision. Both tragedy and trial come as the culmination of earlier events, often complex or extended; but all previous history had to be narrated in the course of the day to which trials always, and tragic actions usually, were confined.[83] In plays such as *Ion*, *Phaethon*, *Antigone* and *Iphigeneia at Aulis*, dawn and/or dusk explicitly mark the beginning and/or end of the drama just as they did the city's court proceedings. During this crucial period actors or litigants secured vengeance or salvation through the machinations and persuasion of accusation and defense. The urgent concentration of the issue made this day different from all other days, as speakers emphasized both on stage and in court. Andocides reminds the jurors that for generations his family has helped Athens without ever asking any favor in return and begs them now on this day — just once — to remember all those deeds and not to condemn him to death (1.146–8). At an equally critical moment. Orestes reminds Menelaos of all the help his father Agamemnon had provided and urges Menelaos to cooperate with him this one day (Eur. *Or.* 646–57). His request closely echoes both the tone and content of Odysseus' to Neoptolemus to give himself up for one day to achieve victory in the struggle against Philoctetes (81–5). An actor may even exhort himself to recognize different standards or requirements of behavior for one day in order to resolve a tragic crisis, as does Medea (1244–50). At the end of the typically eventful tragic day, the chorus exits having witnessed a resolution as final and decisive as the verdict a jury left behind it at the end of each trial. The messenger in *Oedipus Tyrannos* recites an impressive list of the events which have crowded the day, and Lykos makes a similar speech at the end of *Antiope*.[84] The five-line formula which closes so many of Euripides' plays well describes the nature of these days: in the end there is some sort of settlement, but many times the results are unexpected.[85]

That the outcome was always uncertain and that the better man might not necessarily win were sources of articulated anxiety in tragedy and in court. After Ajax had both lost in the peaceful judgement of Achilles' arms and failed to work a violent revenge, he could make the clear if anguished declaration that even an inferior man can escape a stronger one if a god interferes (455–6). The Greek camp at Troy had seen not only the escape of the guilty, but the execution of the innocent Palamedes as well. Both Euxitheus (Antiphon 5.3,6) and Simon's rival for the love of Theodotus (Lys. 3.2) express dread at the unpredictable outcome of litigation and the ability of false words to save the guilty and destroy the innocent.[86] This was more than mere rhetoric in a city which had once wrongly executed nine of its ten Hellenotamiae (Antiphon

5.69–71). Such incidents gave some credibility to the warning against mistaken and hasty judgements, an admonition which was regularly made by tragic characters and defendants in the course of drama and litigation.[87] But despite all pleas, the plot and proceedings pushed swiftly to inevitable if uncertain ends.

Faced with uncontrollable events and fate in tragedy or unpredictable verdicts in court, dramatic characters and Athenian citizens might respond with humble passivity, resolute action, or some combination of the two. Pericles, the engineer of the popular courts, while recognizing that events can turn out more stupidly than the plans of men and that chance or fate must simply be borne, nevertheless urged planning and actions which assumed human responsibility (Thuc. 1.140.1, 2.60–4). These two attitudes and views frequently form the basis for modern discussions of responsibility and blame in tragic action. Such analyses broadly contrast the willful behavior and choices of character (*ethos*) with external forces or fate (*daimon*) over which the actors have no control.[88] The extent to which each of the two elements is emphasized in any given play varies greatly. Sophocles often presents characters whose stubborn personal choices so facilitate oracles or family curses that *ethos* and *daimon* (character and fate) seem almost perfectly blended even though they remain distinct entities. In the end, however, the emphasis falls on humility, for human effort and desire always fail when they conflict with fate: the ode of joy or confident hope followed by a scene of disappointment or disaster is a Sophoclean device.[89] Euripides can present an equally sobering picture of human helplessness, but often in his plays men's and women's plotting and planning lead to more successful actions, and the efficacy of *ethos* gives the plays a lighter and more optimistic tone, even when a god appears for a little last-minute tidying and prediction. Responsibility and the possibility of positive action stand out most completely in Aristophanic comedy where scheming sophists and sycophants are met and defeated by better citizens; but Sophoclean tragedy comes closer to the forces which could crush individuals in Athenian civic life. At the turn of the century, fate and character combined to make the first great defender of law and justice a victim of the courts. The same political and intellectual crises which led to the trial and conviction of Socrates eventually made his ideas and personal example more acceptable in the fourth century than they could ever have been in the fifth. This transition and contrast are the subjects of the next and final chapter.

126　*Law and Drama*

Notes

1. Cic. *Sen*. 7.22 is the earliest source for the story. Plutarch's version is *Moralia* 785a–b. See also Lucian *Macr*. 24; Apuleius *De Magia* 298, Val. Max. 1.7.12, and the anon. life of Soph. The account is discussed by Jebb in his introduction to *O.C.* pages xl–xli and by Bernard Knox, *Word and Action: Essays on the Ancient Theater* (The Johns Hopkins University Press, Baltimore and London, 1979), 22.

2. Creon and Oedipus at 728–60, 761–99; Creon and Theseus at 905–36, 939–59.

3. Paul Mazon, *Essai sur la composition des comédies d'Aristophane* (Librairie Hachette et Companie, Paris, 1904), 173.

4. Jacqueline Duchemin, *L'AGON dans la tragédie grecque* (Les Belles Lettres, Paris, 1945).

5. Ibid. 109–11.

6. Sir Arthur Pickard-Cambridge, *The Dramatic Festivals of Athens* (Oxford University Press, Oxford, 1953) pp. 73, 114–17. *IG* ii²2325.

7. The *Suda s.v. choron didomi*.

8. Pickard-Cambridge, *Dramatic Festivals*, 94.

9. See Chapter 4, p. 70, *Ath. Pol.* 43.5

10. For this and the following details of dramatic competition see Pickard-Cambridge, *Dramatic Festivals*, 96–100. The main Athenian sources are Lys. 4.3, Isoc. 17.33–4, and Dem. 21.17–18.

11. See Alick R.W. Harrison, *The Law of Athens*, vol. 2 (Oxford University Press, Oxford, 1971) 239–41 (hereafter cited as *LA* followed by volume and page).

12. Chapter 2, pp. 46–7.

13. Ar. *Eccl.* 1160 and Pherecrates *Crapataloi* fr. 96K.

14. Pickard-Cambridge, *Dramatic Festivals*, 98–9. See especially Pl. *Leg.* 659a, 700c–701b.

15. There are references to the phenomenon in over half the orators as well as in Aristophanes, Xenophon and Plato. Some will be found at Harrison, *LA*, vol. 2, 163. There is a fuller collection and discussion in James F. Croinin, 'The Athenian Juror and His Oath' (Ph.D. diss., University of Chicago, 1936) 38–41.

16. Lines 1337–9. These lines themselves are taken from Sophocles' *Oinomaos* fr. 476P.

17. Eur. *Andr*. 862, *Ion* 796ff., *Hel*. 1478ff., *Hipp*. 732–4, *I.T.* 1138ff.; Soph. *O.C.* 1081ff. Closely related is the wish simply to be elsewhere: Eur. *Bacch*. 402–16; Soph. *O.C.* 1044, *Ant*. 245, 1217, *Trach*. 953ff., and probably P.Oxy. 2452 = Soph. *Theseus* (?) fr. 730d Radt = fr. 1 Richard Carden, *The Papyrus Fragments of Sophocles: An Edition with Prolegomena and Commentary with a Contribution by W.S. Barrett* (Walter de Gruyter, Berlin, 1974) 112–13.

18. W.S. Barrett on Eur. *Hipp*. 936–1035, especially 985–82 = pp. 345–8.

19. See Page on Eur. *Med*. 476 and Bond on Eur. *H.F.* 177, 181, 185, 368ff.

20. Soph. *Ant*. 385, 39506, 406, 496. See Suzanne Saïd, *La Faute tragique* (François Maspero, Paris, 1978), 202. Harrison, *LA*, vol. 2, 222–9.

21. Thuc. 1.126.12, 1.138.6; Lycurg. *Leoc*. 113; Xen. *Hell*. 1.7.22; Paus. 4.22.7; Victor Ehrenberg, *Sophocles and Pericles* (Basil Blackwell, Oxford, 1954), 29. Saïd, *La Faute tragique*, 121–2.

22. See Barrett *ad loc*. Saïd, *La Faute tragique*, 249–50.

23. This translation for *akon* is defended by Douglas M. MacDowell, 'Unintentional Homicide in the *Hippolytos*,' *Rheinisches Museum für Philologie* NS 111 (1968) 156–8.

24. For the *agones* see Duchemin, *L'AGON*, 59–60. There is a full analysis of legal parallels for the action of the play by Gottfried Greiffenhagen, 'Der Prozess des Oedipus,' *Hermes* 94 (1966) 147–76.

25. See Michael Gagarin, 'Self-defense in Athenian Homicide Law,' *GRBS* 19

(1978), 118 for Oedipus. This article is thoughtful and perhaps correct about Athenian law but without consequence for Sophocles. Saïd's assertion that Oedipus should have been tried and acquitted at the Palladion, *La Faute tragique*, 29 for *phonos dikaios* is incorrect. However, hers is a long book, and by page 151 she has learned that such cases were tried at the Delphinion.

26. For the choice of exile, see Antiphon 5.13, 4.4.1; Dem. 23.69.

27. Douglas M. MacDowell, *Athenian Homicide Law in the Age of the Orators* (Manchester University Press, Manchester, 1963) 114; Harrison, *LA*, vol. 2, 87. Robert J. Bonner and Gertrude Smith, *The Administration of Justice from Homer to Aristotle*, vol. 2 (The University of Chicago Press, Chicago, 1938), 202 are particularly hesitant to accept the testimony of Pollux.

28. For criticism of their failure to characterize see Richard C. Jebb, *The Attic Orators from Antiphon to Isaeus*, vol. 1 (Macmillan and Co., London, 1976) 31.

29. J.H. Finley, Jr., 'The Origins of Thucydides' Style,' *HSCP* 50 (1939) 43–4. As Finley has pointed out, if this was not the regular manner of speaking, then both the style and the content of Cleon's and Diodotus' speeches on the fate of Mytilene are fabricated anachronisms. And this seems quite unlikely.

30. C. Garton, 'Characterization in Greek Tragedy,' *JHS* 77 (1957) 253.

31. See, for example, the proof of Heracles' cowardice at *H.F.* 151–64 and Bond's helpful note there. There is a series of defenses of unlikely propositions in the *Trojan Women* (notably by Cassandra and Andromache) culminating with Helen's personal defense at her 'trial' (see below pp. 114–15). In *The Suppliant Women* Theseus and the herald make speeches which undercut both each other's and their own. See below pp. 112–14.

32. The speech runs from 891–928. Lines 904–20 are commonly deleted.

33. Appendix, p. 261. His whole discussion, pp. 258–65, is characteristically fair and illuminating.

34. For the supposed absurdity, see Jebb, Appendix, p. 260. Furthermore, the whole commos episode is a series of 'misapplications.' Antigone has just supplied herself with a consolation speech since the chorus would not — a sort of inversion of the genre. And Antigone's questioned lines are almost immediately followed by the fourth stasimon, the chorus' *own* unusual version of a consolation — in some ways as odd as Antigone's 'brother-speech.'

35. For the history of *diamartyria* see Louis Gernet, *Droit et société dans la Grèce ancienne* (University of Paris, Paris, 1955) 83–102.

36. For procedures which can undergo metamorphoses in the course of action see P.J. Rhodes, '*EISAGGELIA* in Athens,' *JHS* 99 (1979) 113–14.

37. For this type of plot analysis see Anne P. Burnett, *Catastrophe Survived: Euripides' Plays of Mixed Reversal* (Oxford University Press, Oxford, 1971).

38. See also *Cho.* 273, *Ag.* 1666.

39. See Dodds, xxxvi–viii.

40. Cf. 489–91. Reginald W.B. Burton, *The Chorus in Sophocles' Tragedies* (Oxford University Press, Oxford, 1980), 224 correctly emphasizes that vengeance and justice are here identified.

41. The text at 1453b19ff. could be taken to mean 'friends;' but the examples are all of relatives.

42. Arist. *Poet.* 1453a17ff. For Glotz and Gernet see Chapter 2 pp. 32–5. Knox, *Word and Action*, 9 tallies the 300 plays whose titles we know; his results strongly support Aristotle's generalization.

43. Saïd, *La Faute tragique*, 1.

44. Ibid. 122, 203–4.

45. Ibid. 199–221.

46. Ibid. 378–408.

47. Ibid. 410ff., especially 424–5, 438–9.

48. Although the precise date of the *Ajax* is not determinable, it is almost certainly among the earliest of Sophocles' extant plays and is so accepted. Most recently, Burton, *The Chorus in Sophocles' Tragedies*, p. 1 places it first chronologically. Similarly, Reginald P. Winnington-Ingram, *Sophocles: An Interpretation* (Cambridge University Press, Cambridge, 1980) accepts an early date and begins his book with a discussion of the *Ajax*. See his Appendix G on the chronology, p. 341.

49. Lines 1135–6 especially emphasize the conception of the original decision as a courtroom trial.

50. Glen Bowersock suggests 443 BC for the date of the *Constitution of Athens* (wrongly attributed by tradition to Xenophon) in his edition of the pamphlet included in volume seven of the Loeb Xenophon (Harvard University Press, Cambridge, Mass., 1971), 465. Perhaps more commonly used is Busolt's placement between 431–424 BC: Georg Busolt, *Griechische Geschichte bis zur Schlacht bei Chaeroneia*, vol. 3.2 (Perthes, Gotha, 1904) 609–12, followed, for example by P.J. Rhodes, *A Commentary on the Aristotelian 'Athenaion Politeia'* (Oxford University Press, Oxford, 1981), 343.

51. For the generals, see W. Kendrick Pritchett, *The Greek State at War: Part II* (University of California Press, Berkeley and Los Angeles, 1974) 5–7, a convenient table with references to primary sources. Antiphon 5.69–71 is the sole source for the tantalizing story of the conviction and execution of the Hellenotamiae.

52. On *Alcestis* and *Medea* see Friedrich Solmsen, *Intellectual Experiments of the Greek Enlightenment* (Princeton University Press, Princeton, 1975), 28.

53. See Barrett on Eur. *Hipp.* 317.

54. Eur. *Heracl.* 59–60. 879–82, 104. If *dike* is the word Euripides wrote for line 460, it would signify something like 'non-hybristic treatment' which one might hope for from a victorious enemy. Like Paley, I find the line very odd. (Murray's text and apparatus give no hint of a problem here.) It was an old idea that the strong might wisely restrict their violence (Hes. *Op.* 212ff.). But a Greek expected vengeance (*dike*) from a true enemy. And that is certainly what Alcmene wants and gets through the execution of Eurystheus (879ff., 1049–50).

55. See the discussion of *Ion* below. The speaker in Eur. fr. 1049N^2 asserts that a suppliant must have a proper claim in order to be protected by the gods. Unfortunately, no date can be assigned to the fragment.

56. Eur. *Supp.* 650; Soph. *Ant.* 100; Pindar *Paean* 9. Sophocles and Pindar, of course, have the lyric form *aeliou*.

57. It seems likely that Sophocles' *Tyro* and Euripides' *Melanippe Desmotis*, *Melanippe Sophe*, *Hypsipyle* and *Antiope* all appeared within less than ten years. See Sir Arthur Pickard-Cambridge, 'Tragedy' in John U. Powell (ed.), *New Chapters in the History of Greek Literature*, Third Series (Oxford University Press, Oxford, 1933) 103–23.

58. By the time Plato made Socrates refer to this mis-trial in the *Apology* 41b, there had been a number of tragedies named for Palamedes, and speeches for his trial were composed as rhetorical exercises. Many of the sources are discussed by Ruth Scodel, *The Trojan Trilogy of Euripides* (Vandenhoeck and Ruprecht, Göttingen, 1980) 43–6, 90–1.

59. As Scodel notes, *Trojan Trilogy*, p. 74, this echoes a paradox from *Alexander* fr. 58N^2 about intelligence which promises to prove fatal rather than useful.

60. In fact, *I.T.* may have been produced in 414. But it is a play of mutual cooperation among family and friends sealed with divine aid, and it has little to do with serious conflict. The two *Electras*, which fit somewhere in this period, are irrelevant for the opposite reason. They deal with no nice points of law. *Dike* is everywhere, but it is a dark vengeance for kindred murder.

61. James Diggle, in the new Oxford text, sets the *Ion* around 413.

62. *Logoi* is better here than Jacob's *doloi* which Diggle prints in his new text.

63. Oliver Taplin, *Greek Tragedy in Action* (University of California Press, Berkeley and Los Angeles, 1978), 138.

64. So Kallimachos' epithet was *katatexitechnos*, one whose technique melts down his own art. Paus. 1.26.7; Vitruvius 4.1.10; Pliny *HN* 34.92.

65. The way in which Euripides achieves all this is fully explained by Burnett, *Catastrophe Survived*, 76–100.

66. Burnett, *Catastrophe Survived*, p. 100, and Gilberte Ronnet, 'Le Cas de conscience de Théonoé ou Euripide et la sophistique face à l'idée de justice,' *Revue de Philologie* 53 (1979) 251–9 especially 256–9.

67. Burnett, *Catastrophe Survived*, 89.

68. See Teucer at lines 75–80 and the Portress at lines 481–2.

69. Fr. la Thalheim (*Peri tes metastaseos*). Since Antiphon's life was at stake, it is fair to assume that he included nothing which would arouse doubt in the jurors. Moreover, Thucydides, who apparently had a written copy to consider carefully, found it a remarkably fine defense. See Thuc. 8.68.2 and Antony Andrewes in Arnold W. Gomme *et al.*, *A Historical Commentary on Thucydides*, vol. 5, book 8 (Oxford University Press, Oxford, 1981) *ad loc.*

70. References from comedy and other sources are collected by John U. Powell in the introduction to his edition (Constable and Co., London, 1911) 1–6.

71. There are additional matters elsewhere. For example, Polyneices emphasizes more than once that he is attacking Thebes *akon* (involuntarily) rather than *hekon* (voluntarily) (lines 432, 629–30). The legal distinction technically applied only in homicide matters. But the emphasis on motivation indicates a concern with the spirit of action and intent more to the taste of Ion and his standards.

72. Many interpretations of the *Philoctetes* which have tied the characters and actions of the play to specific figures and events in recent Athenian politics are reviewed in M.H. Jameson's 'Politics and the *Philoctetes*,' *CP* 51 (1956) 217–27. There is not room here for a detailed criticism of such readings, but in general I find that the characterizations, affiliations and tactics of Neoptolemus, Odysseus, and Philoctetes do not suggest enlightening analogies to the conflicts between oligarchs and democrats.

73. Charles Segal mentions the division between 'the larger and the private justice' in this play in *Tragedy and Civilization: An Interpretation of Sophocles* (Harvard University Press, Cambridge Mass. and London, 1981) 356–7, but the interest lies not so much in the conflict between private and public as in the values which motivate Neoptolemus.

74. See Arthur W.H. Adkins, *Merit and Responsibility: A Study in Greek Values* (Oxford University Press, Oxford, 1960), 183, 189.

75. See David Grene, *Reality and the Heroic Pattern* (University of Chicago Press, Chicago and London, 1967) 145–6 and Peter W. Rose, 'Sophocles' *Philoctetes* and the Teachings of the Sophists,' *HSCP* 80 (1976) 71–2.

76. Burnett has convincingly demonstrated that Euripides used the public trial of Orestes to criticize 'the secular optimism of the *Eumenides*': *Catastrophe Survived*, 205–9.

77. Burnett, *Catastrophe Survived*, 208.

78. See Adkins, *Merit and Responsibility*, 173, 175.

79. For *akon* see 521–2, 962–4, 976–7, 985–7. Cf. Antigone at 239–40. For self-defense, 991ff.

80. The importance of the theme of retaliation and Oedipus' association with the Erinys is discussed fully by Winnington-Ingram, *Sophocles*, 261–7.

81. Oedipus' narrow fixation on satisfying this desire is acutely brought out by Grene, *Reality and the Heroic Pattern*, 162–4.

82. Winnington-Ingram, *Sophocles*, p. 278.

83. For the limits of trials see Harrison, *LA*, vol. 2, p. 161.

84. *O.T.* 1282–5; *Antiope* 98–102, in D.L. Page, *Select Papyri*, vol. 3 (Heinemann, London, 1970), 70.

85. These lines close the *Alc.*, *Andr.*, *Hel.*, and *Bacch.* and are only slightly modified at the end of *Med.*

86. Actually Simon's opponent expresses confidence in the Areopagites, but he contrasts their court with all others.

87. In tragedy there are Hippolytos (1055–6), Andromache (549–50, 567–8), and Hypsipyle (fr. 60.6, 47 Bond) — all cited by Saïd, *La Faute tragique*, 417–18. From the court speeches see Antiphon 5.87–9, 6.3–4.

88. See Reginald P. Winnington-Ingram, 'Tragedy and Greek Archaic Thought' in M.J. Anderson (ed.), *Classical Drama and Its Influence* (Methuen and Co., London, 1965); Jean- P. Vernant and Pierre Vidal-Naquet, *Mythe et tragédie en Grèce ancienne* (François Maspero, Paris, 1981), 24, 30, 70, 72.

89. Burton, *The Chorus in Sophocles' Tragedies*, 30–1 discusses this type of ode. See *Aj.* 692, *Trach.* 633, *Ant.* 1115, *O.T..* 1086 and *Phil.* 719.

5 The Fourth Century

1. Introduction

Restorations or revivals, however they succeed at reproducing originals, are generally distanced from their models by self-consciousness. This process, whereby the very desire to imitate may create a significant difference between the past and the present is one of the most important features of fourth-century Athenian law. The task of this chapter is to bring out a deep shift in the place of law in Athenian society, a change which is partially obscured by superficial continuities. On the one hand, the Athenians in the fourth century were extremely concerned to preserve the laws and legal system of the preceding century. Yet, on the other hand, this desire reflects a new veneration which the laws had acquired. They now represented the past, the city-state in the days of the Empire; and they thus were invested with that very legitimacy of tradition which had been so obviously lacking in the fifth century. The awkward adolescent which had grown so fast and been so out of place had somehow become the ancient ancestor.

The most urgent and immediate motivation for preserving the laws was the political chaos which followed the end of the Peloponnesian War. The Thirty Tyrants who seized power soon after peace terms had been imposed on Athens brought in a reign of terror: their power suspended laws and courts, their desires became actions, and robbery, exile and murder became entirely commonplace. When the Athenians regained their democracy, they were determined to put oligarchy behind them. The local judges who handled small disputes had traditionally numbered thirty; but such an inauspicious figure could not be tolerated, so they were increased by ten to become the Forty (*Ath.Pol.* 26.3, 53.1–3). The laws not only for homicide but for other matters as well were collected, revised, reinscribed in stone and housed or displayed at the august Stoa Basileios.[1] As we shall see, those legal changes which the Athenians subsequently made and the speeches they delivered in the reopened courts showed the profound effects of the political turmoil at the turn of the century.

Once order was restored, however, the new democratic city-state was not merely a continuation of the old one. The present was radically and sharply cut off from the past. It is true that the Greeks, like other peoples before and since, were used to seeing the past as much different from the present. The old Nestor had survived into a newer and paler time, and singers of the *Iliad* must have felt more removed from the world of Achilles than did Nestor from that of his youth; Theognis railed against social changes in Megara (57ff., 189ff.); and certainly the extended debates between Right and Wrong, Strepsiades and Pheidippides, and Aeschylus and Euripides in Aristophanes' *Clouds* and *Frogs* indicate that in fifth-century Athens many of the older citizens felt that, like Nestor, they had known a much different and grander life, even if it was difficult precisely to pinpoint the differences.

Yet in the fourth century there were a number of obvious changes which would give rise to the perception that things had been bigger and better in the old days, even though it has been objected that 'degeneracy' is not a proper word for fourth-century Greece.[2] Despite remarkable individual achievements in philosophy, science and art, civic activity, especially in Athens, declined. The loss of the Empire and the fleet meant an immediate and drastic reduction in income; and the population, greatly reduced by war and plague, remained low and may even have declined, with consequences for the democratic government.[3] It seems that no one wrote great tragedies for the city's festivals; and it is certain that all large-scale architectural projects ceased completely. Actors and theaters spread in all directions from Athens; the building of temples, like Alexander, moved east to Asia Minor; and an Athens of perpetually growing power, wealth and domination became for some a memory and for others simply a tale of the past. Unlike the fifth-century Athenians who were suddenly confronted with a huge new legal system, the fourth-century citizens considered the laws and courts integral to the greatness of Periclean Athens; the legal system now took a place alongside other governmental institutions and religious rituals as part of the society's inheritance from the past. The three sections below deal first with the expression of these new attitudes and their use as arguments in court speeches, second with changes in law and in court procedure which reflect these same attitudes and finally with a glimpse of the place law gained in the theater and literature of the fourth century.

2. The New Arguments

When the courts were reopened after the overthrow of the Thirty Tyrants, among the first matters to be taken care of were the crimes of the tyrants themselves. But their deeds had left such a mark on Athenian life that they remained an important topic of litigation for the next two decades. Over a dozen of the extant speeches from this period deal with the actions of these men and the alleged support or opposition of others.[4] Together they convey the atmosphere which encouraged some Athenians to tyrannical imitation on a small scale. Dicaeogenes may have needed the instigation of an Egyptian villain to begin his illegal acquisitions (Isae. 5.8), but other citizens apparently seized their opportunities with characteristic Athenian quickness. Such, at least, is the state of affairs described by Isocrates: debtors would fearlessly defraud creditors even when there had been witnesses to the original transaction (Isoc. 21.7). Before long the currency and urgency of this theme in the restored democracy helped give rise to a new rhetorical *topos* of considerable importance for the development of legal thought and argumentation.

The argument of this new theme was a simple and essentially negative one: laws should not be broken because lawlessness under the Thirty had been so horrible. Isocrates described this reaction as part of a recurrent human pattern — men acting in excess always create their own opposition. The madness of the Thirty, he said, had made us all more democratic than the democrats who overthrew the tyrants (8.107–8). Such a reaction was certainly understandable; it was reported in antiquity that upon the death of a king the Persians always observed five days of lawlessness. By means of these regular interludes of chaotic horror, the people were made to appreciate their laws and leaders (Sext. Emp. *Against the Prof.* 2.33–4).

Almost half a century before analyzing the genesis of this rhetorical *topos*, Isocrates had used it in his speech against Lochites (20). Here the crimes of the Thirty and their contempt for the laws are already seen in general terms. Thus Isocrates makes the lawlessness of a citizen more serious by comparing his illegality with that of the Thirty, even though the citizen had no connection with them or their rule. My opponent Lochites, says the plaintiff, has contempt for the laws; and it was such men who betrayed us to our enemies, razed our city's walls, and put fifteen hundred citizens to death without a trial. Such men must be hated as enemies of mankind and punished before they unite and destroy the city (20.10–14) — and all this for someone who had delivered a blow which apparently resulted in no serious wound.

If this historical, political argument occurred only here, we might be uncertain of its popularity, for Isocrates had more abstract reasons, as did Socrates and Plato, to consider justice (*dikaiosyne*) an excellence (*arete*). Fortunately, however, two speeches in the Lysian corpus use the same approach. In one the defendant first reminds the jury of the harm done to individuals and the city as a whole by the Thirty and their illegal prosecutions of Athenians, and then likens his own accusers to the tyrants (25.25–7, 31). That is, he holds up past harms which had resulted from irregular convictions as a threat, a typical example of lawlessness and its consequences. Similarly, in a speech against Ergocles, the speaker attacks illegal conduct in office as a dangerous abuse equivalent to the actions of the Thirty (28.7, 11, 13–14). There now was a general argument against breaking the law which carried what seems likely to have been a terribly effective, immediate emotional charge.

Moreover, even as the events of the oligarchic revolution slipped further and further into the past, this rhetorical use of references to the Thirty was retained. Even at the end of the fourth century Aristotle can cite as an illustration of a standard rhetorical topic, 'He says he loves you, but he conspired with the Thirty.' (*Rh.* 2.23.23.) And although our only surviving court speeches from the 370s and 360s do not mention the Thirty, our sample is probably not representative. Certainly the tyrants reappear as a negative example in the next three decades in speeches of Demosthenes, Aeschines and Lycurgus.[5] Now, however, there is an additional development. The arguments against illegality are increasingly combined with a *positive* argument for laws and legal tradition, an argument also based on history. Here, as we shall see, the reference exactly complements that to the Thirty, for it holds up the shining tradition of democratic legality in the golden days before the Thirty reduced Athens to terror and chaos.

Immediately after the restoration of the democracy in 403, the Athenians began to refer in their speeches to the former greatness of their city. They praised Athens' past prosperity, its military achievements and even its lawgivers and their laws (Isoc. 18.30–1; Andoc. 1.106–9; Lys. 30.28). As the fourth century progressed, allusions to the past continued, but accuracy of detail rapidly diminished. A mere decade into the fourth century, Andocides could present a wildly inaccurate sketch of fifth-century history to the Athenian assembly (3.3–12). He confuses the circumstances of a truce of five years with those of a thirty years' peace and speaks of a fifty years' peace instead; he speaks of Miltiades when he means Cimon as a negotiator returned from exile; and he hopelessly scrambles the chronology of events surrounding the revolt of Euboea. Apparently such an account was quite acceptable: Aeschines reused it years later in his speech on the Embassy (2.172–6). Others' mistakes were not always so glaring; but as memory faded, opportunity for distortion broadened.[6] When Isocrates describes the very early days of democracy, he praises a number of facets of civic life which he has idealized completely unrealistically, including the laws and the citizens' attitude toward them (4.75ff.). This is very much the sort of description which begins frequently to be applied to Periclean Athens in the extant court speeches about thirty years later; but before examining these speeches, it will be helpful briefly to consider some further Isocratean passages which demonstrate a very different view of Periclean Athens and justice. Like Plato, Isocrates was devoted to the ideal of just behavior and considered justice (*dikaiosyne*) a great excellence (*arete*) for philosophical reasons (Isoc. 1.15, 3.29–30, 43, 15.67). His pamphlets are harshly critical of the unjust wealth of the Periclean Empire, of its mighty walls, its huge population — of the superlatives in which Pericles has taken so much pride (Isoc. 8.83–6, 96, 104; 7.13). Isocrates had too vivid a sense of Periclean Athens to idealize it; he simply pushed his golden age further into the past. For purposes of his legal thought this did not matter. Because his conceptions were theoretical, he had no need of a historical justification for the laws as part of tradition, and, in fact, he considered the written laws themselves only indirectly relevant to lawful behavior (7.39–41). Such was the reasoning of the contemplative, intellectual students of Socrates.

A far different defense of law was developed for use before the assembly and popular juries. Here the emphasis was all historical, appealing to pride in the tradition of the past. Along with the architectural and financial achievements of Periclean Athens, the speeches praise the law-abiding and constitutional spirit of the fifth-century citizens. It was a time, Demosthenes assures us, when the people so respected the constitution that they fiercely prosecuted everyone who threatened it, even the greatest citizens. Moreover, even these greatest citizens were unselfish and indifferent to private magnificence. For skeptics he offers as proof a detail he seems to have been particularly fond of citing: the humble dwellings which housed these men, the equivalent of the American log cabin of Lincoln (3.24–7, 23.204–7). We will be less quick to see Miltiades and Xanthippus or Pericles and Cimon guarding the city selflessly from each other; and unlike Demosthenes we will remember that Miltiades, *not* Cimon, was fined fifty talents (23.205).

The same great respect and veneration is also accorded to the laws of the Empire, and the distortion of history played a significant role here as well. Once the laws were reinscribed at the turn of the century, they were constantly referred to as the laws of Solon, even though many of them dated from the mid- and late fifth century and some even from the fourth.[7] As a result, the laws used in the fourth-century courts were not only honored as having been a part of the magnificent Athens of Pericles but also, from the hazy perspective of the fourth century, were given a fictional origin in the golden age of the democracy. The appeals for adherence to laws because of their Solonian associations, some short and simple, others quite elaborate, occur in the most polished speeches of Demosthenes and Aeschines as well as in speeches delivered and written by other Athenians. In fact Aeschines closed his speech against Ctesiphon by invoking as the opponent of lawlessness the philosopher and lawgiver Solon; and Demosthenes immediately countered in the opening of his speech with a plea to the jurors to follow the laws and thus maintain the power assured them by Solon, the friend of democracy.[8] The frequency and variety of these appeals suggest the possibility of new respect for the law; certainly, at least, they were made on grounds which would not have been available in the fifth century.[9] While it is true that we can seldom gauge the effectiveness of argumentation in the speeches, we shall see further signs that the sentiments described above enjoyed a certain popularity. Here the ground becomes more solid, for the following evidence involves specific changes in the laws and court procedures of the fourth century.

3. Legal Change

By recognizing law and government as an objective set of rules which required careful collection and accurate preservation, the restored democracy of 403 virtually defined itself in terms of writing. This new devotion to a basic legal code was a radical, sudden change. In the course of the fourth century there followed a number of related innovations in legislation and in lawsuits concerning constitutionality which are discussed below. These, along with certain procedural developments, eventually provided a basis for more sophisticated attitudes towards law. More immediately and simply they reflect a gradual dissipation of the traditional distrust in writing and, as one might expect, a simultaneous increasing reliance on documents.

The beginning of Greek literature itself is inextricably bound up with the secondary or even marginal position of writing in early society. The riddle of the exact relation of our Homeric texts to their oral origins seems unlikely ever to be solved. But whoever set our *Iliad* down in ink included an inauspicious first mention of writing in the tale of Bellerophon, the first of those messengers in Western literature who bear the orders for their own death (*Il.* 6.168–9). Centuries later, Thucydides implied that Pausanias regularly sent his messengers to the East with just such fatal instructions (1.132) — and that these devious writings eventually contributed to his own end. Finally, dangerous documents figure on the fifth-century tragic stage: a forged note destroyed Palamedes and a false one doomed Hippolytus, both in clearly marked legalistic proceedings.

Such incidents from Athenian history and drama help prepare us for the place of writing in the courts of classical Athens. There, written agreements were apparently rare until the mid-fourth century and are simply not referred to in early speeches, even when the cases turn on points of fact in matters of finance, marriage and adoption.[10] As a result, the indispensable proof for contracts and agreements was not written evidence but rather witnesses.[11] In accordance with this state of affairs there are two complementary *topoi*. The first assumes the absolute need for witnesses in all circumstances. As Isaeus explains, one secures witnesses ahead of time if at all possible; but if anything important arises unexpectedly, witnesses are simply gathered on the spot as chance allows (3.18–19). This is why Demosthenes can claim complete incredulity that anyone would undertake a transaction of any moment without witnesses: Athenians *always* provided them (30.20–1). The corresponding commonplace asserts the negligible value of written documents. Since they are easily forged and therefore suspect, they are routinely dismissed in the speeches of Isaeus as weak and unimpressive forms of asserting a claim (1.41–2, 2.44, 7.2). As he explains, then, when one is forced to resort to a written document, one has it made in the presence of as many *witnesses* as possible (3.20–1).

Nevertheless, by the institution of the mercantile laws in the mid-fourth century, business had become so complicated that written contracts were required.[12] And even before then, the use of documents was gradually becoming a more regular feature of court procedure. It was probably soon after 380 BC that litigants in Athenian courts had to submit written complaints; and they were certainly required both for public and private suits by the time of Demosthenes.[13] Similarly, by the mid-fourth century, law required that testimony be submitted in writing — a change which seems to have occurred at about the same time as that for the manner of lodging complaints.[14]

Finally, the most recent evidence for the extent to which documentation came to be used in fourth-century legal procedure is the inscription on the lid for a vessel (some sort of *chytra*) in which relevant materials were sealed for use in court.[15] While it has long been known that testimony, laws and challenges from arbitration proceedings were sealed in such pots, this inscription makes it clear that testimony from pre-trial hearings was also taken down in writing for use in court. All these gradual changes seem to indicate that laws and legal system were gaining increasingly fixed and independent institutional status. Their significance in this process appears more certain when they are considered together with contemporary changes in the legislative apparatus and the lawsuits used to enforce its operation.

With the reinscription of the laws in 403–399 and the additional measures such as those limiting legal validity to written laws and establishing the superiority of laws over decrees, the democracy took what has recently been described as 'the most important step ever taken in developing Athenian law.'[16] Certainly these reforms were the prerequisite for the legislative procedures and safeguards which were set up at the same time or soon after. The details of the various laws concerning legislation (*nomothesia*), including exactly how many provisions there were and how they were modified in the course of the century, cannot be established with certainty.[17] Their general outlines, however, are reasonably clear: they provided for the proposal, examination and adoption of new laws, the periodic review of the laws as a whole to eliminate inconsistencies and defects and the repeal of laws found unsatisfactory. Thus, the fourth century set up an entire secondary apparatus to preserve and protect the rule of law in the city. The requirement that no law be repealed without the simultaneous proposal of a satisfactory replacement reflects this careful, conservative spirit.

Suits for the prosecution of those who proposed laws or decrees which contravened the existing code (*graphe paranomon*) or even simply for making 'an unsuitable law' (*nomon me epitedeion theinai*) complemented the legislative apparatus. Although the *graphe paranomon* dated from the fifth century (Andoc 1.17), it seems to have become important only with the new fourth-century urgency over constitutionality. The frequency with which the charge was brought is indicated both by the fact that there was a special penalty, partial disfranchisement (*atimia*), upon a third conviction (Hyper. 4.11), and that Aristophon could claim to have been acquitted of the charge seventy-five times (Aisch. 3.194). The closely related procedure, prosecution for making an unsuitable law, appears to be an exclusively fourth-century process. Conviction brought harsh fines and sometimes even death (Dem. 24.138). It is true that these suits were sometimes used by litigants for personal and political motives rather than in unbiased concern for the laws, as the case of Demosthenes' crown shows. Moreover, the outcome of Ctesiphon's trial indicates that the juries could be as uninterested in the law as the litigants were; for although Aeschines lost his case by a disastrous margin, at least some of his charges of illegality appear to have been quite justified.[18] Nevertheless, like the new arguments for laws and a legal tradition and the other legal changes mentioned above, the use of these suits and their serious consequences which made them potentially powerful weapons further reveal the increasing recognition of the laws as an established and valuable part of Athens.

One last phenomenon helps clarify how these legislative provisions and suits were bound up with the trend towards legitimation of the legal system. Incredible as it seems, by the mid- and late fourth century, the provisions for legislation and the suits against unsuitable laws, both of which had been created by the restored democracy, were already being attributed to or associated with Solon. This is apparently what Aeschines means when he ascribes the annual review of the laws to the lawgiver who established the democracy (3.38). Demosthenes leaves no doubt whatsoever: not only does he make Solon the author of the constitutional controls to maintain a consistent legal code; he even relates an anecdote in which Solon makes use of the procedure for prosecuting the legislator of an unsuitable law (20.90,93; 24.212–14). These historical inaccuracies have been labeled as some of the 'grossest anachronisms' tolerated by the Athenians about constitutional matters.[19] Yet they are not simply undetected errors. Rather, they have a very specific legitimating function: just as the legal code had been dressed up in a fantastic costume which gave it the respectability of age, so the even younger secondary apparatus for protecting that code took the same disguise. The largely new and unestablished court system of the fifth century was inadvertently strengthened and stabilized by the tyrants who sought to destroy it — and in a way that it might never have been without them. Inspired by the bad memories of the oligarchic revolution, the restored democracy put its legal system on a firmer foundation than it had ever had before. Then a different sort of bad memory — the misremembering which supplants history with myth — cemented the place of law in society by making many elements of the administration of justice much older than they were, a process made possible by the actual passage of time. Thus what had been new or even nonexistent in the fifth century was believed in the fourth century to have been already old and accepted in Pericles' time. It is an outstanding and clearly documented example of how bad memory makes good tradition. Interestingly, a very similar process had apparently taken place in Athens' great rival city-state, only much earlier. Major reforms in Sparta in the early sixth century seem soon to have become regularly attributed to Lycurgus. Thus the so-called Lycurgan system had no more to do with Lycurgus than many of the so-called laws of Solon had to do with Solon. The Spartan rewriting of history has been called 'one of the most successful frauds in history.'[20] The parallel Athenian one seems to have been one of the most beneficial.

4. Fourth-century Literature[21]

The increased use of writing in the courts of the restored democracy was hardly an isolated phenomenon. There was simply more writing of most sorts in the fourth century than in the fifth, and some of the men who wrote court speeches wrote other things as well. Although Isocrates gave up writing speeches for forensic use, he continued to express his ideas in that form. For example, his *Antidosis* is a defense of his career and teachings and a philosophical and cultural criticism of his rivals, yet it minutely follows all the conventions of a speech in a suit for property exchange. Similarly, Polycrates, a slightly older contemporary of Isocrates (Isoc. 11.50) who also wrote legal speeches (Dion. of Hal. *Isaeus* 20), composed a fictitious accusation of Socrates (Isoc. 11.4). Creating such speeches of accusation or defense for Athenians who had actually been on trial seems to have become a popular undertaking, although the purpose for such writing probably ranged from philosophy and politics to mere entertainment or display. In addition to Plato's and Xenophon's well-known speeches for Socrates, there was definitely one by the orator Theodectes (Arist. *Rhet.* 2.23.13) and almost certainly one by Lysias (D.L. 2.40, Quintill. *Inst.* 2.15.30, 11.1.11, Cic. *De Orat.* 1.54). The equally artificial defense of Theramenes (P. Mich. 5982) was put together partially with the help of other written legal sources such as Lysias 12 and 13.

Besides these speeches based on recent events, forensic writers and others wrote as rhetorical exercises or display pieces trial speeches for mythical figures. Polycrates composed defenses for Busiris (Isoc. 11.4) and Clytemnestra (Quintill. *Inst.* 2.17–4). Antisthenes has left us a pair of speeches for Odysseus and Ajax delivered before their juries, and there was once a defense of Orestes as well (D.L. 6.15). We also have 'Odysseus' accusation of Palamedes' from either Alcidamas or a contemporary.[22] It is true that such writings grew out of fifth-century works: Antiphon composed schematic arguments for trials, and Gorgias had developed elaborate artificial defenses. But these fifth-century compositions are not meant to read exactly as court speeches in the way the fourth-century works often are. Moreover, the variety of purposes for which the genre of the lawcourt speech is used dramatically increased in the fourth century. Apparently, as the law and the courts were increasingly accepted as a natural and traditional part of the society, the institutions and conventions of the legal system became available for comfortable use in other areas of life. The cultural isolation of the popular courts was rapidly disintegrating.

It remains to consider how drama, the fifth-century Athenian institution most obviously attuned to the courts, developed in relation to law in the fourth century. Here, any conclusions must be quite tentative since the originally great volume of fourth-century tragedy has disappeared almost without a trace. Perhaps one indication of the direction of change is Aristotle's statement that the speeches of fourth-century tragedy are more rhetorical than those of the fifth century (*Poet.* 1450b7). Since rhetoric was developed and learned for use in court and the assembly, one might guess that the speeches had a somewhat precise, legal flavor. Such language should have come naturally to tragedians such as Astydamas, Aphareus and Theodectes who were pupils of Isocrates. Furthermore, we know that Theodectes wrote on technical contemporary legal problems (Arist. *Rhet.* 2.23.11,17). His tragedies seem to have been characterized by technical legal language and arguments set forth in trial scenes and rhetorical contests. At any rate, this is what stands out in Aristotle's discussion of *Alcmaeon, Orestes* and *Ajax* (*Rhet.* 2.23–4, cf. fr. 805N[2]). Again, with hesitancy, we can say that Carcinus seems also to have featured technical, legalistic argumentation and trial scenes in his plays. The debates in his *Medea* were apparently more like Antiphon's *Tetralogies* than like Euripides (Arist. *Rhet.* 2.23), and his *Ajax, Orestes* and *Oedipus* all probably involved trials. The efforts of these two tragedians certainly pleased their audiences, for Theodectes managed eight victories in eleven competitions, and Carcinus, a more productive playwright, won first place eleven times. Thus, although in itself it remains inconclusive, the general picture of fourth-century tragedy points in the same direction as the other literary and institutional evidence considered in this chapter.

The laws, the courts and even a fairly abstract idea of legality had found both an acceptance and widespread cultural associations in fourth-century Athenian society which contrasted greatly with the novel and uncomfortable place they had held in the previous century. They now had not only much more of a real history but a complex and laudatory fictional one as well. The disappointment of military defeat and the chaos of bloody revolution had provided vivid and persuasive lines of defense for legal justice and inspired the Athenians to institute constitutional and legal measures to protect their laws. There were, of course, philosophical developments in the problems of just behavior and the importance of justice to the individual and the community. I have not dealt with those here, in part because others have already done that job so well, but more because this study is aimed at clarifying the place of law in society rather than in the history of ideas.[23] Moreover, in the end, even Plato was quite hard pressed to defend justice purely for its own sake in the soul of man. Yet even though Socrates' greatest pupil could still not absolutely prove the worth of the ideas his teacher died for, time and social change were working in his direction. A century after Socrates' efforts to examine ethics, Aristotle could begin his treatise on the subject simply by assuming that his students accepted and somehow believed in the excellence of justice.[24]

Notes

1. See P.J. Rhodes, *A Commentary on the Aristotelian 'Athenaion Politeia'* (Oxford University Press, Oxford, 1981) p. 134–6; T. Leslie Shear, 'The Athenian Agora: Excavations of 1970,' *Hesperia* 40 (1971) 243ff.; and Homer A. Thompson and Richard E. Wycherly, *The Agora of Athens: The History, Shape and Uses of an Ancient City Center*. vol. 14. *The Athenian Agora* (The American School of Classical Studies at Athens, Princeton, 1972) 87–8.
2. Arnold W. Gomme, 'The End of the City-state,' in *Essays in Greek History and Literature* (Basil Blackwell Oxford, 1937), 234.
3. The population figures for the late fourth century are still being debated. See P.J. Rhodes, 'Ephebi, Bouleutai and the Population of Athens,' *ZPE* 38 (1980) 191–201, and M.H. Hansen, 'Demographic Reflections on the Number of Athenian Citizens 451–309 BC,' *AJAH* 7 (1982) 172–89.
4. These are, in rough chronological order, Lys. 12 and 34; Isoc. 21 and 18; Lys. 31 and 25; Andoc. 1; Lys. 30, 13, 18, 16, 10 and 26.
5. Dem. 22, 24; Aeschin. 1, 2, 3; Lycurg. *Leoc.*
6. There is an excellent discussion of fourth-century ideas about the fifth century in Moses I. Finley's essay 'Myth, Memory, and History,' in *The Use and Abuse of History* (The Viking Press, New York, 1975) 11–33. For specific analyses, Lionel Pearson's 'Historical Allusions in the Attic Orators,' *CP* 36 (1941) 209–29 is quite useful. There are also some helpful collections of references in S. Perlman's 'The Historical Example, Its Use and Importance as Political Propaganda in the Attic Orators,' *Scripta Hierosolymitana* 7 (1961) 150–66.
7. This convention is discussed fully by Joseph C.S. Schreiner, 'De Corpore Iuris Atheniensium' (Ph.D. diss., University of Friedrich Wilhelm on the Rhine, Bonn, 1913) 21–60. See also C. Hignett, *A History of the Athenian Constitution to the End of the Fifth Century BC* (Oxford University Press, Oxford, 1952) 18–21.
8. Aeschin. 3.257, Dem. 18.6. See also Dem. 36.26–7, [Dem.] 42.1.
9. It is true that the attribution of post-Solonian laws to Solon had apparently begun even in the fifth century, as in the reference to the inheritance law in Ar. *Av.* 1660ff. However, almost no other examples survive, and the fifth-century Athenians were very much aware of the explosion in new legislation, as the same play makes abundantly clear.
10. This is implied by Moses I. Finley in *Studies in Land and Credit in Ancient Athens 500–200 BC: The Horos Inscriptions* (Rutgers University Press, New Brunswick, 1952), 21.
11. This is clearly demonstrated by Fritz Pringsheim, *The Greek Law of Sale* (Hermann Boehlaus Nachfolger, Weimar, 1950) 18–28. For the importance of witnesses in general in legal proceedings see André Soubie, 'Les preuves dans les plaidoyers des orateurs attiques (II),' *Revue Internationale des Droits de l'Antiquité* 21 (1974) 125–6.
12. Douglas M. MacDowell, *The Law in Classical Athens* (Cornell University Press, Ithaca, 1978) 231–3.
13. This subject is treated carefully by George M. Calhoun, 'Oral and Written

Pleading in Athenian Courts,' *TAPA* 50 (1919) 177–93. He settles on 379/8 as the most likely date for instituting the requirement that complaints be written.

14. Calhoun, 'Oral and Written Pleading,' 190–1.

15. Alan L. Boegehold, 'A Lid with Dipinto,' *Studies in Attic Epigraphy, History and Topography, Hesperia: Supplement* 19 (1982) 1–6.

16. Raphael Sealey, 'On the Athenian Concept of Law,' *CJ* 77 (1982) p. 295.

17. The most important sources are Dem. 20.88–101, 137, 164; Dem. 24.20–3, 33; Aeschin. 3.38–40. Their implications have been recently re-examined and debated by Douglas M. MacDowell 'Law-making at Athens in the Fourth Century BC,' *JHS* 95 (1975) 62–74, and Mogens H. Hansen, 'Athenian *Nomothesia* in the Fourth Century BC and Demosthenes' Speech against Leptines,' *Classica et Mediaevalia* 32 (1980) 87–104.

18. See MacDowell, *The Law in Classical Athens*, 51–2.

19. Hansen, 'Athenian *Nomothesia*,' 90–1.

20. Antony Andrewes, 'Eunomia,' *CQ* 32 (1938) 102. See also pages 100–101.

21. For many of the references in this section I am indebted to the following series of articles by Edward M. Cope: 'The Sophists,' *The Journal of Classical and Sacred Philology* 1 (1854) 145–88; 'On the Sophistical Rhetoric: I,' *The Journal of Classical and Sacred Philology* 2 (1855) 129–69; 'On the Sophistical Rhetoric: II,' *The Journal of Classical and Sacred Philology* 3 (1856) 34–80; 'On the Sophistical Rhetoric: III,' *The Journal of Classical and Sacred Philology* 3 (1856) 253–88.

22. See Robert Renehan, 'The Michigan Alcidamas-Papyrus: A Problem in Methodology,' *HSCP* 75 (1971) p. 91.

23. For excellent examinations of the philosophical approaches to law and justice see Jacqueline de Romilly, *La Loi dans la pensée grecque des origines à Aristote* (Les Belles Lettres, Paris, 1971), especially chapters 8–11, and Arthur W.H. Adkins, *Merit and Responsibility: A Study in Greek Values* (The University of Chicago Press, Chicago, 1975) especially chapters 13–16.

24. See Adkins, *Merit and Responsibility*, 316–51.

Bibliography

Editions of classical works appear in the Bibliography under the name of the ancient author rather than that of the editor.

Adkins, Arthur William Hope. '*Arete, Techne*, Democracy and Sophists: *Protagoras* 316b–328d.' *Journal of Hellenic Studies* 93 (1973) 3–12.

——— 'Basic Greek Values in Euripides' *Hecuba* and *Hercules Furens*.' *The Classical Quarterly* NS 16 (1966) 192–219.

——— 'Law versus Claims in Early Greek Religious Ethics.' *History of Religion* 21 (1982) 222–39.

——— *Merit and Responsibility: A Study in Greek Values*. Oxford, Oxford University Press, 1960. Reprint: Chicago, The University of Chicago Press, 1975.

——— *Moral Values and Political Behavior in Ancient Greece: From Homer to the End of the Fifth Century*. New York, W.W. Norton and Co., 1972.

——— '*Polupragmosune* and "Minding One's Own Business": A Study in Greek Social and Political Values.' *Classical Philology* 71 (1976) 301–27.

Aeschylus. *Agamemnon*. Edited by Eduard Fraenkel. 3 vols. Oxford, Oxford University Press, 1962.

——— *The Oresteia: Edited with Introduction, Translation, and a Commentary in which is included the work of the late Walter G. Headlam*. Edited and translated by George Thomson. 2 vols. Cambridge, Cambridge University Press, 1938.

Andrewes, Antony. 'Eunomia.' *The Classical Quarterly* 32 (1938) 89–102.

Aristophanes. *Wasps*. Edited by Douglas M. MacDowell. Oxford, Oxford University Press, 1971.

Aristotle. *Constitution of Athens: A Revised Text with an Introduction, Critical and Explanatory Notes, Testimonia, and Indices*. Edited by Sir John Edwin Sandys. 2nd edn. London, Macmillan, 1912.

Beazley, John Davidson. *Attic Red-figure Vase-painters*. 3 vols. 2nd edn. Oxford, Oxford University Press, 1963.

Bieber, Marguerete. *The History of the Greek and Roman Theater*. 2nd edn. Princeton, Princeton University Press, 1961.

Boardman, John. *Athenian Black Figure Vases*. New York, Oxford University Press, 1974.

——— *Athenian Red Figure Vases: The Archaic Period: A Handbook*. New York and Toronto, Oxford University Press, 1975.

Boegehold, Alan L. 'A Lid with Dipinto.' *Studies in Attic Epigraphy, History and Topography, Hesperia: Supplement* 19 (1982) 1–6.

——— 'Philokleon's Court.' *Hesperia* 36 (1967) 111–20.

Boer, W. den. 'Aspects of Religion in Classical Greece.' *Harvard Studies in Classical Philology* 77 (1973) 1–21.

Bonner, Robert J. *Aspects of Athenian Democracy*. Berkeley, University of California Press, 1933.

——— 'The Legal Setting of Isocrates' Antidosis.' *Classical Philology* 15 (1920) 193–7.

——— 'Note on Aristotle *Constitution of Athens* xxxix.5.' *Classical Philology* 19 (1924) 175–6.

——— and Smith, Gertrude. *The Administration of Justice from Homer to Aristotle*. 2 vols. Chicago: The University of Chicago Press, 1930/1938.

Bremmer, Jan. 'The Importance of the Maternal Uncle and Grandfather in Archaic and Classical Greece and Early Byzantium.' *Zeitschrift für Papyrologie und*

Epigraphik 50 (1983) 173–86.

Burnett, Anne Pippin. *Catastrophe Survived: Euripides' Plays of Mixed Reversal.* Oxford: Oxford University Press, 1971.

—— *Three Archaic Poets: Archilochus, Alcaeus, and Sappho.* Cambridge, Mass., Harvard University Press, 1983.

Burton, Reginald William Boteler. *The Chorus in Sophocles' Tragedies.* Oxford, Oxford University Press, 1980.

Bury, John Bagnell, Cook, Stanley Arthur and Adcock, Frank Ezra (eds.) *The Cambridge Ancient History: Volume V: Athens 478–401 BC* Cambridge, Cambridge University Press, 1935.

Busolt, Georg. *Griechische Geschichte bis zur Schlacht bei Chaeroneia.* Vol. 3.2. Gotha, Perthes, 1904.

Buxton, R.G.A. *Persuasion in Greek Tragedy: A Study of Peitho.* Cambridge, Cambridge University Press, 1982.

Calhoun, George Miller. *Athenian Clubs in Politics and Litigation.* Vol. 14. Humanistic Series. Austin, University of Texas Bulletin, 1913.

—— 'Oral and Written Pleading in Athenian Courts.' *Transactions of the American Philological Association* 50 (1919) 177–93.

Carden, Richard. *The Papyrus Fragments of Sophocles: An Edition with Prolegomena and Commentary with a Contribution by W.S. Barrett.* Berlin, Walter de Gruyter, 1974.

Claus, D.B. 'Defining Moral Terms in *Works and Days*,' *Transactions of the American Philological Association* 107 (1977) 73–84.

Connor, W. Robert. *The New Politicians of Fifth-century Athens.* Princeton, Princeton University Press, 1971.

Cope, Edward Meredith. 'On the Sophistical Rhetoric: I.' *The Journal of Classical and Sacred Philology* 2 (1855) 129–69.

—— 'On the Sophistical Rhetoric: II.' *The Journal of Classical and Sacred Philology* 3 (1856) 34–80.

—— 'On the Sophistical Rhetoric: III.' *The Journal of Classical and Sacred Philology* 3 (1856) 253–88.

—— 'The Sophists.' *The Journal of Classical and Sacred Philology* 1 (1854) 145–88.

Cronin, James Farley. 'The Athenian Juror and His Oath.' Ph.D. dissertation. Chicago, University of Chicago, 1936.

Davies, John Kenyon. *Athenian Propertied Families: 600–300 BC* Oxford, Oxford University Press, 1971.

—— 'Demosthenes on Liturgies: A Note.' *Journal of Hellenic Studies* 87 (1967) 33–40.

—— Review of W. Robert Connor's *The New Politicians of Fifth-century Athens.* *Gnomon* 47 (1975) 374–8.

Demosthenes. *On the Crown.* Edited by William Watson Goodwin. Cambridge, Cambridge University Press, 1904.

——*The Speech of Demosthenes against the Law of Leptines.* Edited by John Edwin Sandys. Cambridge, Cambridge University Press, 1890.

de Sainte Croix, G.E.M. 'Notes on Jurisdiction in the Athenian Empire.' *Classical Quarterly* 11 (1961) 94–112.

—— 'Notes on Jurisdiction in the Athenian Empire: II.' *Classical Quarterly* 11 (1961) 268–80.

Diamond, A.S. *Primitive Law.* London, Longmans, Green and Co., 1935.

Dickie, Matthew W. '*Dike* as a Moral Term in Homer and Hesiod.' *Classical Philology* 73 (1978) 91–101.

Dover, Kenneth James. *Greek Popular Morality in the Time of Plato and Aristotle.* Berkeley and Los Angeles, University of California Press, 1974.

—— *Lysias and the 'Corpus Lysiacum.'* Berkeley and Los Angeles, University of

California Press, 1968.

Duchemin, Jacqueline. *L'AGON dans la tragédie grecque*. Paris, Les Belles Lettres, 1945.

Ehrenberg, Victor. *Sophocles and Pericles*. Oxford, Basil Blackwell, 1954.

Euripides. *The Works*. 3 vols. with an English commentary by Frederick Apthorp Paley. London, Whitaker and Co., 1857/1858/1860.

—— *Andromache*. Edited by Philip Theodore Stevens. Oxford, Oxford University Press, 1971.

—— *Electra*. Edited by John Dewar Denniston. Oxford, Oxford University Press, 1939.

—— *Euripides Fabulae*. 3 vols. Edited by Gilbert Murray. Oxford, Oxford University Press, 1902/1904/1909.

—— *Euripides Fabulae*. Vol. 2. Edited by J. Diggle, Oxford, Oxford University Press, 1981.

—— *Heracles*. Edited by Godfrey W. Bond. Oxford, Oxford University Press, 1981.

—— *Herakles*. Edited by Ulrich von Wilamowitz-Moellendorff. 2nd edn. Vol. 2. Berlin, Weidmann, 1895.

—— *Hyppolytos*. Edited by W.S. Barrett. Oxford, Oxford University Press, 1964.

—— *Medea*. Edited by Denys Page. Oxford, Oxford University Press, 1938.

—— *The Phoenissae of Euripides*. Edited by J.U. Powell. London, Constable and Co., 1911.

Farnell, Lewis Richard. *The Cults of the Greek States*. 5 vols. Oxford, Oxford University Press, 1896/1896/1907/1907/1909.

Finley, John Huston Jr. 'Euripides and Thucydides.' *Harvard Studies in Classical Philology* 49 (1938) 23–68.

—— 'The Origins of Thucydides' Style.' *Harvard Studies in Classical Philology* 50 (1939) 35–84.

Finley, Moses I. *The Ancient Economy*. Berkeley and Los Angeles, The University of California Press, 1973.

—— *Studies in Land and Credit in Ancient Athens 500–200 BC: The Horos Inscriptions*. New Brunswick, Rutgers University Press, 1952.

—— *The Use and Abuse of History*. New York, The Viking Press, 1975.

Fritzsche, Franz Volkmar. *De sortitione judicum apud Athenienses: Commentatio*. Leipzig, August Lehnhold, 1835.

Fustel de Coulanges. *The Ancient City: A Study on the Religion, Laws and Institutions of Greece and Rome*. Translated by Willard Small. Boston, Lee and Shepard, 1874.

Gargarin, Michael. '*Dike* in Archaic Greek Thought.' *Classical Philology* 69 (1974) 186–97.

—— '*Dike* in *Works and Days*,' *Classical Philology* 68 (1973) 81–94.

—— *Drakon and Early Athenian Homicide Law*. New Haven, Yale University Press, 1981.

—— 'The Prohibition of Just and Unjust Homicide in Antiphon's *Tetralogies*.' *Greek, Roman, and Byzantine Studies* 19 (1978) 291–306.

—— 'Self-defense in Athenian Homicide Law.' *Greek, Roman, and Byzantine Studies* 19 (1978) 111–20.

Gardiner, Edward Norman. *Athletics of the Ancient World*. Oxford, Oxford University Press, 1930.

—— *Greek Athletic Sports and Festivals*. London, Macmillan and Co. 1910.

Garton, C. 'Characterization in Greek Tragedy.' *Journal of Hellenic Studies* 77 (1957) 247–54.

Gernet, Louis. *Anthropologie de la Grèce antique*. Paris, François Maspero, 1968.

—— *Droit et société dans la Grèce ancienne*. Paris, University of Paris, 1955.

—— 'Recherches sur le développement de la pensée juridique et morale en Grèce:

Étude sémantique.' Ph.D. dissertation. Paris, Ernest Leroux, 1917.
—— and Boulanger, André. *Le Génie grec dans la religion*. Paris, La Renaissance du Livre, 1932.
Gilbert, Gustave. *The Constitutional Antiquities of Sparta and Athens*. Translated by E.J. Brooks and T. Nicklin. London, S. Sonnenschein and Co., 1895.
Glotz, Gustave. *The Greek City and Its Institutions*. Translated by N. Mallinson. New York, Alfred A. Knopf, 1930.
—— *La Solidarité de la famille dans le droit criminel en Grèce*. 1904. Reprint: New York, Arno Press, 1973.
Goligher, W.A. 'Studies in Attic Law: II.' *Hermathena* 33 (1907) 481–515.
Gomme, Arnold Wycombe. *Essays in Greek History and Literature*. Oxford, Basil Blackwell, 1937.
—— Dover, Kenneth J. and Andrewes, Antony. *A Historical Commentary on Thucydides*. 5 vols. Oxford, Oxford University Press, 1956/1956/1962/1970/1981.
Gould, J.P. 'Law, Custom, and Myth: Aspects of the Social Position of Women in Classical Athens.' *Journal of Hellenic Studies* 100 (1980) 38–59.
Greiffenhagen, Gottfried. 'Der Prozess des Oedipus.' *Hermes* 94 (1966) 147–76.
Grene, David. *Reality and the Heroic Pattern*. Chicago and London, University of Chicago Press, 1967.
Guthrie, William Keith Chambers. *A History of Greek Philosophy*. Vol. 3. Cambridge, Cambridge University Press, 1969.
Hamburger, Max. *Morals and Law: The Growth of Aristotle's Legal Theory*. New York, Bible and Tanner, 1965.
Hansen, Mogens Herman. 'Athenian *Nomothesia* in the Fourth Century BC and Demosthenes' Speech against Leptines.' *Classica et Mediaevalia* 32 (1980) 87–104.
—— 'Demographic Reflections on the Number of Athenian Citizens 451–309 BC.' *American Journal of Ancient History* 7 (1982) 172–89.
—— '*Demos, Ecclesia*, and *Dikasterion* in Classical Athens.' *Greek, Roman, and Byzantine Studies* 19 (1978) 127–46.
—— *Eisangelia*. Odense, Odense University Press, 1975.
—— 'The Prosecution of Homicide in Athens: A Reply.' *Greek, Roman and Byzantine Studies* 22 (1981) 11–30.
Harrison, Alick Robin Walsham. *The Law of Athens*. 2 vols. Oxford, Oxford University Press, 1968/1971.
Havelock, Eric A. '*Dikaiosyne*: An Essay in Greek Intellectual History.' *Phoenix* 23 (1969) 49–70.
—— *The Greek Concept of Justice: From Its Shadow in Homer to Its Substance in Plato*. Cambridge, Harvard University Press, 1978.
Herodotus. *The Fourth, Fifth, and Sixth Books*. Edited by Reginald Walter Macan. 2 vols. London, Macmillan, 1895.
—— *The Seventh, Eight, and Ninth Books*. Edited by Reginald Walter Macan. 2 vols. London, Macmillan, 1908.
Hesiod. *Works and Days*. Edited by Martin Litchfield West. Oxford, Oxford University Press, 1978.
Hignett, Charles. *A History of the Athenian Constitution to the End of the Fifth Century BC*. Oxford: Oxford University Press, 1952.
Homer. *The Odyssey of Homer*. Edited by William Bedell Stanford. 2 vols. 2nd ed. London: Macmillan, 1965.
Humphreys, S.C. 'The Work of Louis Gernet.' *History and Theory* 10 (1971) 172–96.
—— 'Politics and Private Interest in Classical Athens, *CJ* 73 (1977/8) 103–4.
Jameson, M.H. 'Politics and the *Philoctetes*.' *Classical Philology* 51 (1956) 217–27.
Jebb, Richard Claverhouse. *The Attic Orators from Antiphon to Isaeos*. 2 vols. London, Macmillan and Co., 1876.

Jolowicz, H.J. *Historical Introduction to the Study of Roman Law*. Cambridge, Cambridge University Press, 1954.

Jones, Arnold Hugh Martin. *Athenian Democracy*. Oxford, Basil Blackwell, 1957.

Kitto, Humphrey Davy Findley. 'The *Rhesus* and Related Matters.' *Yale Classical Studies: Greek Tragedy*. Vol. 25, 317–50. Cambridge, Cambridge University Press, 1977.

Knox, Bernard. *Word and Action: Essays on the Ancient Theater*. Baltimore and London, The Johns Hopkins University Press, 1979.

Lacey, Walter Kirkpatrick. *The Family in Classical Greece*. Ithaca, Cornell University Press, 1968.

Lloyd, Geoffrey Ernest Richard. *Polarity and Analogy: Two Types of Argumentation in Early Greek Thought*. Cambridge, Cambridge University Press, 1966.

—— *Science, Folklore and Ideology*. Cambridge, Cambridge University Press, 1983.

Lloyd-Jones, Hugh. *The Justice of Zeus*. Berkeley, Los Angeles, London, University of California Press, 1983.

Lukes, Steven. *Émile Durkheim: His Life and Work: A Historical and Critical Study*. New York, Penguin Books, 1975.

MacDowell, Douglas M. '*Arete* and Generosity.' *Mnemosyne* NS 16 (1963) 127–34.

—— *Athenian Homicide Law in the Age of the Orators*. Manchester, Manchester University Press, 1963.

—— 'Athenian Laws about Bribery.' *Revue Internationale des Droits de l'Antiquité* 30 (1983) 57–78.

—— *The Law in Classical Athens*. Ithaca, Cornell University Press, 1978.

—— 'Law-making at Athens in the Fourth Century BC.' *Journal of Hellenic Studies* 95 (1975) 62–74.

—— 'The Length of the Speeches on the Assessment of The Penalty in Athenian Courts.' *Classical Quarterly* 35 (1985) 525–6.

—— 'Unintentional Homicide in the *Hippolytos*.' *Rheinisches Museum für Philologie* NS 111 (1968) 156–8.

Maine, Sir Henry. *Ancient Law*. 1862. Reprint: New York, Dutton, 1972.

Malinowski, Bronislaw. *Crime and Custom in Savage Society*. 1926. Reprint: Totowa, Littlefield, Adams and Co., 1976.

Mazon, Paul. *Essai sur la composition des comédies d'Aristophane*. Paris, Librairie Hachette et Companie, 1904.

McClees, Helen. *A Study of Women in Attic Inscriptions*. New York, Columbia University Press, 1920.

Nilsson, Martin Persson. *Greek Piety*. Translated by Herbert Jennings Rose. 1947. Reprint: New York, W.W. Norton and Co., 1964.

—— *A History of Greek Religion*. New York, W.W. Norton and Co., 1964.

North, Helen F. *From Myth to Icon: Reflections of Greek Ethical Doctrine in Literature and Art*. Ithaca, Cornell University Press, 1979.

Ostwald, Martin. 'Ancient Greek Ideas of Law.' *Dictionary of the History of Ideas: Studies in Selected Pivotal Ideas*. Oxford, Oxford University Press, 1969.

Parker, Robert. *Miasma: Pollution and Purification in Early Greek Religion*. Oxford, Oxford University Press, 1983.

Pausanias. *Pausanias' Description of Greece*. Translated with a commentary by J.G. Frazer. 6 vols. London, Macmillan, 1913.

Pearson, Lionel. 'Historical Allusions in the Attic Orators.' *Classical Philology* 36 (1941) 209–29.

—— *Popular Ethics in Ancient Greece*. Stanford, Stanford University Press, 1962.

Perlman, S. 'The Historical Example, Its Use and Importance as Political Propaganda in the Attic Orators.' *Scripta Hierosolymitana* 7 (1961) 150–66.

Pickard-Cambridge, Sir Arthur. *The Dramatic Festivals of Athens*. Oxford, Oxford University Press, 1953.

—— 'Tragedy,' in J.U. Powell (ed.) *New Chapters in the History of Greek Literature.* Third series. Oxford, Oxford University Press, 1933.

Plato. *Gorgias: A Revised Text with Introduction and Commentary.* Edited by E.R. Dodds. Oxford, Oxford University Press, 1959.

Poliakoff, Michael. 'The Third Fall in the *Oresteia*.' *American Journal of Philology* 101 (1980) 251–9.

Powell, John Undershell (ed.) *Collectanea Alexandrina: Reliquiae minores Poetarum Graecorum Aetatis Ptolemaicae 323–146 AC: Epicorum, Elegiacorum, Lyricorum, Ethicorum: Cum Epimetris et Indice Nominum.* 1925. Reprint: Chicago, Ares Publ., 1950.

Pringsheim, Fritz. *The Greek Law of Sale.* Weimar, Hermann Boehlaus Nachfolger, 1950.

Pritchett, W. Kenrick. *The Greek State at War: Part II.* Berkeley and Los Angeles, University of California Press, 1974.

Redfield, James. 'Plato and the Art of Politics.' Ph.D. dissertation. Chicago, University of Chicago, 1961.

Renehan, Robert. 'The Greek Anthropocentric View of Man.' *Harvard Studies in Classical Philology* 85 (1981) 239–59.

—— 'The Michigan Alcidamas-Papyrus: A Problem in Methodology.' *Harvard Studies in Classical Philology* 75 (1971) 85–105.

Rhodes, P.J. *The Athenian Boule.* Oxford, Oxford University Press, 1972.

—— *A Commentary on the Aristotelian 'Athenaion Politeia'.* Oxford, Oxford University Press, 1981.

—— '*EISANGELIA* in Athens.' *Journal of Hellenic Studies* 99 (1979) 103–14.

—— 'Ephebi, Bouleutai and the Population of Athens.' *Zeitschrift für Papyrologie und Epigraphik* 38 (1980) 191–201.

Richter, Donald C. 'The Position of Women in Classical Athens.' *Classical Journal* 67 (1971) 1–8.

Romilly, Jacqueline de. *La Loi dans la pensée grecque des origines à Aristote.* Paris, Les Belles Lettres, 1971.

Ronnet, Gilberte. 'Le Cas de conscience de Théonoé ou Euripide et la sophistique face à l'idée de justice.' *Revue de Philologie* 53 (1979) 251–9.

Rose, Peter W. 'Sophocles' *Philoctetes* and the Teachings of the Sophists.' *Harvard Studies in Classical Philology* 80 (1976) 49–105.

Rudhardt, Jean. 'La définition du délit d'impiété d'après la législation attique.' *Museum Helveticum* 17 (1960) 87–105.

Saïd, Suzanne. *La Faute tragique.* Paris, François Maspero, 1978.

Schaps, David. 'The Woman Least Mentioned: Etiquette and Women's Names.' *Classical Quarterly* 71 (1977) 323–60.

Schoemann, Georg Friedrich. *Opuscula Academica.* Vol. 1. Berlin, Weidmann, 1856.

Schreiner, Joseph C.S. 'De Corpore Iuris Atheniensium.' Ph.D. dissertation. Bonn, University of Friedrich Wilhelm on the Rhein, 1913.

Schultz, Fritz. *Principles of Roman Law.* Oxford, Oxford University Press, 1936.

Scodel, Ruth. *The Trojan Trilogy of Euripides.* Göttingen, Vandenhoeck and Ruprecht, 1980.

Sealey, Raphael. *A History of the Greek City States ca. 700–388 BC.* Berkeley and Los Angeles, University of California Press, 1976.

—— 'On the Athenian Concept of Law.' *The Classical Journal* 77 (1982) 289–302.

—— 'The *Tetralogies* Ascribed to Antiphon.' *Transactions of the American Philological Association* 114 (1984) 71–85.

Segal, Charles. *Dionysiac Poetics and Euripides' 'Bacchae'.* Princeton, Princeton University Press, 1982.

—— *Tragedy and Civilization: An Interpretation of Sophocles.* Cambridge, Mass.

and London, Harvard University Press, 1981.

Shear, Theodore Leslie. 'The Athenian Agora: Excavations of 1970.' *Hesperia* 40 (1971) 241–79.

—— 'The Athenian Agora: Excavations of 1973–1974.' *Hesperia* 44 (1975) 331–74.

Shorey, Paul. 'On the Implicit Ethics and Psychology of Thucydides.' *Transactions of the American Philological Association* 24 (1893) 66–88.

Slater, Philip. *The Glory of Hera: Greek Mythology and the Greek Family.* Boston, Beacon Press, 1968.

Solmsen, Friedrich. *Intellectual Experiments of the Greek Enlightenment.* Princeton, Princeton University Press, 1975.

Sophocles. *The Antigone.* Edited by R.C. Jebb. 2nd edn. Cambridge, Cambridge University Press, 1891.

—— *The Electra.* Edited by Sir Richard C. Jebb. Cambridge, Cambridge University Press, 1907.

—— *Electra.* Edited by J.H. Kells. Cambridge, Cambridge University Press, 1973.

—— *Electra.* Translated and edited by William Sale. Englewood Cliffs, Prentice-Hall Inc., 1973.

Soubie, André. 'Les preuves dans les plaidoyers des orateurs attiques (II).' *Revue Internationale des Droits de l'Antiquité* 21 (1974) 77–134.

Szegedy-Maszak, Andrew. 'Legends of the Greek Lawgivers.' *Greek, Roman, and Byzantine Studies* 19 (1978) 199–209.

Taplin, Oliver. *Greek Tragedy in Action.* Berkeley and Los Angeles, University of California Press, 1978.

Thompson, Homer A. 'Athens Faces Adversity.' *Hesperia* 50 (1981) 343–55.

—— 'Excavations in the Athenian Agora: 1953.' *Hesperia* 23 (1954) 31–67.

—— Wycherly, Richard Ernest. *The Agora of Athens: The History, Shape and Uses of an Ancient City Center.* Vol. 14. *The Agora of Athens.* Princeton, The American School of Classical Studies at Athens (Glückstadt: J.J. Augustin), 1972.

Thomson, George. *The Oresteia.* Vol. 1. Cambridge, Cambridge University Press, 1938.

Travlos, John. 'The Lawcourt ΕΠΙ ΠΑΛΛΑΔΙΩΙ.' *Hesperia* 43 (1974) 500–11.

—— *Pictorial Dictionary of Ancient Athens.* New York and Washington, Praeger Publishers, 1971.

Unger, Roberto Mangaberia. *Law in Modern Society: Toward a Criticism of Social Theory.* New York, The Free Press, 1976.

Vernant, Jean-Pierre. *Mythe et société en Grèce ancienne.* Paris, François Maspero, 1974.

—— and Vidal-Naquet, Pierre. *Mythe et tragédie en Grèce ancienne.* Paris, François Maspero, 1981.

Wilamowitz-Moellendorff, Tycho. *Die dramatische Technik des Sophokles.* Berlin, Weidmann, 1917.

Winnington-Ingram, Reginald Pepys. *Sophocles: An Interpretation.* Cambridge, Cambridge University Press, 1980.

—— 'Tragedy and Greek Archaic Thought,' in M.J. Anderson (ed.) *Classical Drama and Its Influence.* London, Methuen and Co. 1965.

Woodford, Susan. 'Ajax and Achilles Playing a Game on an Olpe in Oxford.' *Journal of Hellenic Studies* 102 (1982) 173–85.

Zeitlin, Froma I. 'The Dynamics of Misogyny: Myth and Mythmaking in the *Oresteia*.' *Arethusa* 11 (1978) 149–84.

Index of Passages Cited

Please note that this is only a partial index. However, all relevant passages from the body of the text and the more important ones from the endnotes have been included. Extended discussions of works with multiple references are listed in the general index in sub-entries under the author's name. *See especially* Euripides and Sophocles. Where a passage is cited in an endnote without further discussion, in order to facilitate the easy location of the relevant part of the text the number of the note and *the page of the text to which the note refers are indicated*: e.g. Soph. *O.T.* 1014: page 7n.12 — the note actually occurs on page 27.

General Index

abortion 86
Aeschylus 7, 96–7, 107–8, 117
agon 61
  athletic 61
  dramatic 95–6
    forensic 102, 111
    non-forensic 110
  legal 61
Andocides painter 76, 78
antidosis 63, 68, 73
Antiphon 24, 79, 104, 106, 118
apagoge 107
Apollo 10, 44
  court at Delphinion 37–8
  in *Ion* 116
  lawgiver 39–40
  legal significance 45–6
archons 50
Areopagus 35–7, 42, 96
Aristophanes 71–2, 96, 100–1
Aristotle 1, 20, 143
  competition in law 2
  tragedy 12, 107
athletics 59, 61–3
  metaphor for legal struggle 61–2

bribery 110
  courtroom 65, 97–8
  dramatic festival 97–8

Carcinus 142
choral responsion 7, 27 n.14, 76
class conflict 64–6
Cleon 26, 42, 66
competition 11
  legal vs. other types 2–3, 61–4,
    95–6, 99–100
  limits 8, 14, 18
  political 66–7
countersuit (*antigraphe*) 69, 81
Critias 66
  origin of laws 48
  see also Thirty Tyrants

Demosthenes 82
dikaiosyne 6, 134–5
dike 3, 4–10
  early usage 4–6

  and gods 9–10
  tragedy 6–8, 111–12, 119–20
dike (lawsuit)
  kakotechnion 70
  proikos 85
  pseudomartyrion 61
  sitou 85
  see also graphe (lawsuit)
disenfranchisement (*atimia*) 61, 64,
  84, 139
distrain 116
divorce 14
dowry 14, 39, 85
Drakon 39
  Athenian lawgiver 39
  homicide code 80
Durkheim, Émile 32

Ephialtes 42, 67
eunomia 26
Euphronius 59
Euripides 107–8, 125
  Andr. 111–12
  Bacch. 122–3
  Hec. 112
  Helen 116–18
  Heracl. 111
  Hipp. 102, 110–11
  I.A. 122
  Ion 115–16
  Or. 121
  Phoen. 119–20
  Supp. 22–3, 25, 112–14
  Tro. 114–15
Euthymides 59
evidence 70, 74, 137–8
  see also witnesses
Exekias 76

Farnell, L. 45
fees 72–3

Gernet, L. 1, 32–5, 43, 68, 72, 107
Glotz, G. 34–5, 107
graphe (lawsuit)
  apographe 69–70
  hybreos 34
  nomon me epitedeion theinai 139